L Cunningham

CHRISTUS MEDIATOR

AR

American Academy of Religion
Academy Series

edited by
Carl Raschke

Number 41

CHRISTUS MEDIATOR
Platonic Mediation in the Thought of Simone Weil

by
Eric O. Springsted

Eric O. Springsted

CHRISTUS MEDIATOR
Platonic Mediation in the Thought of Simone Weil

Scholars Press
Chico, California

CHRISTUS MEDIATOR
Platonic Mediation in the Thought of Simone Weil

by
Eric O. Springsted
PhD, 1980, Princeton Theological Seminary,
Princeton, New Jersey

Library of Congress Cataloging in Publication Data
Springsted, Eric O.
   Christus mediator.

   (American Academy of Religion academy series ;
no. 41)
   Bibliography: p.
   1. Weil, Simone, 1909–1943. I. Title. II. Series.
B2430.W474S67 1983   194   82–16972
ISBN 0–89130–596–3

Printed in the United States of America

TABLE OF CONTENTS

TO

Brenda

PREFACE

I first read Simone Weil because of her love for Plato and I was immediately struck by the degree to which she could make him come alive. Further reading, however, produced a realization that Weil is perhaps one of the great thinkers of the twentieth century in her own right. But she is enigmatic and difficult to pin down. That is often a feature common to first rate thinkers when faced by their contemporaries; in Weil's case, the fact is confirmed by the plethora of contradictory, and often just plain wrongheaded, interpretations of her person and thought. How then to approach her?

Thanks to many conversations with Diogenes Allen of Princeton Theological Seminary I realized the case is not hopeless and came to see the central importance of Weil's essay, "The Love of God and Affliction". In that essay she defines a central problem of human existence, affliction, and then by a penetrating analysis of Christ's Cross as the prime case of affliction, argues that it is from the Crucifixion that all genuine life and love come. Simply understanding the central parts played by affliction and the Cross in Weil's thought illumines a great deal of her project. Yet, even with this step taken we are hard pressed to see *how* exactly she moves from the insights of that essay to many of her other concerns. Upon repeated readings of her difficult essay, "The Pythagorean Doctrine, I became convinced that the key to the metaphysical structure of her thought lay in her appropriation of Platonic and Pythagorean mediation.

In what follows I have argued that Weil's thought is a coherent whole and that the key to discovering this is twofold: her understanding of the Cross and the Platonic scheme of mediation which she uses to describe and apply that understanding. I only hope that at the end of the argument some of the depth of what Weil has to say can become apparent as well as her genuine importance as a religious philosopher. That, I hope, will disabuse us of the notion that Weil had some valuable insights

vii

but that her work as a whole does not bear close theological and philosophical scrutiny.

I can only claim that this book is a beginning for understanding Weil and the issues she raises. Although I have tried to be comprehensive, there is a great deal that is omitted. Of particular importance here is her reading of Eastern religions, although I have indicated how she thought they were important. Despite this omission I do not believe that an analysis of the debt she owes to the East would fundamentally alter what I have claimed are the central and cohering aspects of her thought. It would, though, show the richness and resonance of that thought. It would also, perhaps, show that there is, as Weil herself claimed, a strain in Western philosophy and religion which begins in Plato that is not entirely foreign to some sort of *rapprochement* with Eastern thought. Here I think many of those who have found the East more fascinating than their own intellectual and spiritual heritage may be surprised to find that many ideas that they would like to ascribe to the East are, in fact, also in Plato. This perhaps might also cause us to re-examine the anti-Greek prejudice that has been so fashionable in contemporary theologies.

This book was originally presented as a Ph.D. dissertation at Princeton Theological Seminary in slightly different form. I owe particular thanks to three individuals who were of enormous assistance throughout its writing: Diogenes Allen, especially, who first introduced me to Simone Weil and who, as a matter of my highest praise, was Socrates to me, both as teacher and friend; to George Stroup, whose helpful comments and questions kept this on track; and to R. Catesby Taliaferro, retired from Notre Dame, who provided invaluable assistance in the technical and philosophical aspects of Greek mathematics--I only hope my efforts here will not embarass him. I also owe thanks to Andre-A. Devaux of the Sorbonne and president of *l'Association pour l'etude de la pensee de Simone Weil* who helped me gain access to the unpublished manuscripts of Weil in the Bibliotheque Nationale in Paris, and to Florence deLussy who kindly guided me through them.

A note on what follows. I have used published English
translations of Weil's works for quotations when such exist and
have provided my own translations of the French when an English
translation was not available. References in the footnotes to
Greek texts as being Weil's translation of the Greek are, of
course, the English rendering of Weil's French. I have also
made frequent use of the generic term 'man' throughout the following chapters. Whenever the term occurs, except when it deliberately refers to a particular male, it is in no case intended
to apply exclusively to males. The usage is unavoidable because
of Weil's own use of the generic term which is reproduced in
all translations and because in many contexts, the term 'person'
is not substitutable since Weil has a technical definition of
the corresponding "personne" which is incompatible with the
sense in which it would otherwise be understood.

September, 1982

Illinois College

LIST OF ABBREVIATIONS USED IN THE NOTES FOR WEIL'S WORKS

CO	*La condition ouvrière*
FLN	*First and Last Notebooks*
GG	*Gravity and Grace*
IC	*Intimations of Christianity among the Ancient Greeks*
LP	*Lectures on Philosophy*
LR	*Letter to a Priest*
NB	*The Notebooks of Simone Weil*
NR	*The Need for Roots*
OL	*Oppression and Liberty*
PSO	*Pensées sans ordre concernant l'amour de Dieu*
SE	*Selected Essays, 1934-1943*
SL	*Seventy Letters*
SN	*On Science, Necessity and the Love of God*
SS	*Sur la science*
WG	*Waiting for God*

INTRODUCTION

Simone Weil wrote in her last letter to her friend and con-
fidant, Père Perrin, a Dominican priest:

> If no one consents to take any notice of the thoughts
> that, though I cannot explain why, have settled in so
> inadequate a being as myself, they will be buried with
> me. If, as I believe, they contain some truth, it will
> be a pity . . . The fact that they happen to be in me
> prevents people from paying attention to them . . . It
> is a great sorrow for me to fear that the thoughts that
> have descended into me should be condemned to death
> through the contagion of my inadequacy and wretchedness.[1]

Weil believed that there was a great deal of value in her
thoughts and felt that they should be able to stand on their
own, despite the inadequacy of her person. Yet, she was not
overly optimistic that their value would be recognized because
of the person through whom they came. The near forty years since
her death have tended to prove this suspicion. Her person has
obscured thorough research into her thought, particularly in the
English speaking world, for Weil studies have usually tended to
concentrate on biographical issues; although, ironically, not
always for reasons of personal "inadequacy and wretchedness."
This trend is not without reason; her life was remarkable, if
enigmatic, and a major clue to her thought must be found in her
life. Yet, while a final evaluation of Weil as a whole must be
found in the relationship of her thought to her action, this
evaluation must see a *relationship* which reduces neither to the
other.

The necessity of understanding a relationship between
thought and action is particularly important in Weil's case since
many of her actions were extraordinary and it is easy to misplace
their roots and significance. For example, there is the matter
of her death. Weil died in 1943 because of a self-imposed starvation diet which she believed gave her the equivalent amount
of food as the people in occupied France. Because she was also
suffering from tuberculosis at the time, a condition which requires overeating, the coroner's verdict was that "the deceased

1

did kill and slay herself by refusing to eat whilst the balance
of her mind was disturbed."[2] Without an appropriate examination
of the moral motivations that led Weil to take the course she
did, it is all too easy to concur with that verdict and see
nothing else. If, however, the relationship were understood, it
would be entirely possible to accept Cabaud's judgment[3] that
her limited diet was, in fact, the manifestation of the psychologically disordered condition of *anorexia* without necessarily
weakening all that Weil had to say about solidarity with the
oppressed; or, for that matter, without necessarily weakening
the moral and spiritual values that can be possibly concomitant
with such a condition. It may indeed be important that certain
psychological factors have played a role in a person's life, but
the final evaluation of that life must result from the answer
given to the question, "What use was made of these factors?"
As William James puts it: ". . . not its origins, but the *way
in which it works on the whole is* . . . (the) final test of a
belief."[4] Any assumption to the contrary is what James called
the "genetic fallacy." To hope to derive the sum total of a
person and her thought in biographical facts is, therefore, as
much of a mistake as to accuse Christ of having a 'messiah complex.' It is necessary, then, not to allow strictly biographical
concerns to control the field of research, but to spend at least
as much effort in coming to grips with her thought as well.
This is necessary not only for the reason that without such balanced investigation no thorough evaluation can be made of her
thought and life as a whole, but, what is more important, it is
the only way in which her life and/or thought may bear a witness
to the truth in the world in which we live.

     The publication in 1973 of Simone Pétrement's *La vie de
Simone Weil* marked a major step towards making an overall reasoned and critical judgment of the thought and life of Simone
Weil. This book is a thorough and exhaustive biography which
seems as close as possible as the last word regarding the facts
of Weil's life; it also provides a sympathetic and comprehensive
interpretation of them. Unfortunately, the final step towards
the evaluation is the most difficult one of all; for the philosophical analysis of Weil's thought is still far from complete.[5]

The reasons for this are obvious and numerous. Initially, the
problem arises simply from the state of Weil's own writing. In
her lifetime, Weil wrote only one book, which appeared post-
humously, and only published articles. The greater part of the
corpus consists of fragments, longer finished and unfinished
articles which were unpublished during her life and some of which
are still unpublished, and one thousand pages of notebooks, most
of which were written in the relatively short period between
1939 and 1943.[6]

Weil's notebooks present a problem by themselves; for not
only were they quickly written, without erasure, and on an in-
credibly diverse number of subjects, but also, while they are
workbooks and experiments in thought for later, more polished
pieces, they nevertheless, seem to have a life of their own.
For these reasons one has to take what is written there both as
experimentation, and, yet, at the same time as efforts with their
own merit. It is almost as if the notebooks were an effort to
produce the maximum amount of material in the shortest amount of
time, a fact attested to by Weil's own concern for their safety
during her constant voyages during the years of the war and for
what should happen to them after her death. Thus rather than
simply providing background these highly enigmatic notebooks
must be seen as an additional work.

A second problem arises in Weils' own method and style. On
the one hand, like her teacher Alain, she eschewed the idea of
systematizing her work, and preferred to write *topos*. Although
she could bring an enormous amount of material to bear upon any
topic, she would also rigorously follow the topic through to its
ultimate conclusion, without seemingly being worried about
whether or not it then appeared inconsistent with some other
topic that she had treated with no less rigor. On the other
hand, she was also an highly independent thinker who fits into
no particular schools, or at least not all the way. She insisted
on developing and combining seemingly unrelated themes; this
tends, on the surface, towards being seen as the most deliberate
and blatant form of syncretism. Much of this latter tendency
can be ascribed to her mysticism, of which there can be no doubt.
Like so many of the great mystics before her, Weil in her

writings often pushed language to its limits and used it in its
most symbolic forms, almost all of which appear quite fluid. In
itself this sort of use of language makes analysis difficult
enough, but it also invites broad and general interpretations
which can obscure essential elements in the rest of her thought.
When used for apologetic purposes, this tendency to let what is
genuinely mysterious and holy cover the entire spectrum of a
person's life and thought can be regarded as an attempt to revive
the 'genetic fallacy' once more, but this time in a positive
vein. It, unfortunately, does not assist in bringing her witness
to light any more than abnormal psychology does in darkening it.

The final problems in analysis of Weil's thought are by far
and away the most difficult since they are substantial and not
technical. It was Weil's belief that her thought was both valuable and a consistent whole. In one of her last letters to her
parents, she attested this belief:

> I have a sort of inner certainty that there is within me
> a deposit of pure gold which must be handed out. It is
> indivisible, and whatever is added to it becomes part of
> it. And as it grows it becomes more compact. I cannot
> distribute it piecemeal.[7]

Yet, despite Weil's own belief in the value of her thought and
its indivisibility, it has been difficult to define exactly what
it is that makes her thought a consistent whole. In fact, to
many commentators the evidence of inconsistency has tended to
outweigh that of consistency, and so much so that there has often
been assumed to be 'two Simone Weils.' There is on the one hand,
it is said, the social activist Simone Weil. This is the Simone
Weil who was an active participant in many social causes and
who, in her writings, sought to analyze and solve the problems
of society and the individual and of oppression and the worker
by rational means. This is a Simone Weil whom we see particularly
in the years before 1937, although one who also appears in later
years, which compounds the problem. There is, on the other hand,
the religious mystic Simone Weil. This Simone Weil is one who
believes that all earthly life is governed by an inexorable
necessity which admits no exceptions and who also believes that
all goodness in this life is due to a transcendent Good. She
holds that it is an error of the first order to confuse the

operations of necessity with those of Good. She holds, therefore, that in order for Good to be realized fully one must be
'decreated,' which is a state of being stripped of empirical
personality and waiting for God's own action. Closely related
to these beliefs are her views that the social sphere essentially
belongs to the Prince of this World who she says is equivalent
to Plato's Great Beast and the Beast of the Apocalypse. By themselves, these latter views have invited charges of nihilism,
Manicheanism, acosmism and quietism.[8] When they are compared to
those of the 'other Simone Weil,' a situation obtains which is,
to say the least, paradoxical.

It is here relatively easy to begin to hold the belief that
there were indeed two Simone Weils--the mystical Weil and the
activist social critic Weil. Such a belief would say that these
two aspects of her thought are truly incompatible and, with some
notable exceptions in her later writings, more or less easily
divided into two separate periods of her life. With this belief,
one might very well be obliged to concur with Pére Bruckberger
that if she was saved at all she was "saved by her incoherence."[9]

The situation does not improve when we see what appear to
be inconsistencies even within the two poles of her thought.
The social critic Weil was one who had a great sympathy for the
oppressed and laborers of all classes as well as a strong sense
of solidarity with them. Yet, she herself also had deep intellectual interests and a profound commitment to the life of the
mind. While this need not be considered an incompatibility, the
story of her teaching a young peasant girl proofs from Euclid
and commenting to her on Sanskrit poetry is strange, and all the
more so when we learn that the poor girl was completely bored
and continued to listen solely out of politeness. Religiously,
there are also problems in what some have seen to be Weil's almost Manichaean dualism in the relations she saw between God and
the world and the soul and the body. It is not that such a view
is impossible to hold by itself, but it surely presents difficulties when it is held together with her constant belief in and
verbal affirmation of Catholic Christianity. She herself may
have recognized this and as a result kept herself out of the
Church, but what are those already in the Church then to make of
her ideas, especially as Weil herself believed that there was

something for them to make of the ideas? This leads to yet
another problem in that Weil's own personal goals do not always
seem to be those that she thought others should follow. This
may help in evaluating her person, but it presents a myriad of
difficulties to those who want to find the value of her thought
so that they may make use of it. Finally, in regard to her views
on the soul and society, Weil in various writings makes claims
that grace is solely a relation between God and the soul and that
the social influence on this relation degrades it; yet, at the
same time she also calls for a religious basis of culture. How
then can coherence be found in her thought? Clearly the answer
to this question must be given before any final evaluation of her
thought or life can be made.

It is stated intention of this book to find this coherence.

In order to show coherence in Weil's thought it is necessary
to realize that the demonstration of coherence is not necessarily
the demonstration of a lack of every sort of opposition in that
thought but only certain sorts. In fact, in a thinker such as
Weil some opposition may indeed be necessary. As A. Fontaine
says of Weil: ". . . (without this opposition) we would be
dealing with a being who had escaped the human condition, whereas
she had assumed it."[10] This is to say, that within the conditions of existence for humanity that Weil sought to explicate
there may very well be coincidental contrary conditions. A
simple example from *The Need for Roots* helps to show this. In
the section titled "The Needs of the Soul" Weil pairs such contrary needs of the individual soul as truth-freedom of opinion,
equality-hierarchism, private property-collective property, etc.
Here it must be remembered that these needs as claimed are those
of an individual soul, and not the needs of a collectivity, even
if the contraries are resolved at that level. If, then, it can
be shown that the sould has such needs there is *prima facie* evidence of contrary opposition existing at one time in one being.
Such oppositions may be called *real*, for they are not the con-
flicts of two independently developed lines of thought, but are
implicit in the foundations of reality from which thought needs
to begin. It may be as necessary for somebody like Weil to show
that these oppositions are real and inescapable as it is for a

critic to show that they are not; in any case, it still remains
possible that there are such oppositions and their presence does
not count decisively against coherence in one's thought.

A second type of opposition may be called *historical*. This
also need not count decisively against coherence, for all that
is meant by it is that in the course of time a person's ideas
change, and that it is not to be expected that anybody's thought
arises full grown like Athena from the head of Zeus. The awareness of this sort of opposition is the scholar's light touch on
a developing thought.

The third type of opposition, which may be called *fundamen-*
tal, is fatal to coherence. This sort of opposition can result
either from one statement or line of thought fallaciously in-
ferred from a coherent statement; or, it can result from a correct inference drawn from an incoherent statement. There is,
then, internal opposition or incoherence and external or empirical opposition and incoherence. In the former case, this amounts
to saying that no possible logical bridge exists between two
juxtaposed lines of thought. In the latter case, while two
juxtaposed statements may be consistent with each other no bridge
is possible between them and any sort of commonly received primal fact.

It must be noted what is entailed by these sorts of criteria
for coherence. They do not mean that a coherent set of statements, or a coherent *opera* of a single thinker, is necessarily
true, for "it is one thing to show the coherence of a supposition and another to show its truth."[11] It may be the case, however, insofar as the criteria of coherence need reference to
'primal facts,' which is admittedly an indirect approach, that
"the only evidence we have of coherence is also evidence of
truth."[12] This does not mean, though, that there is only one
coherent set of statements based on factual truths; for, indeed,
there may be more than one. Nor does it mean that a coherent
set of statements be developed systematically from the data.
While a deliberately systematic treatment may seek the maximum
degree of evident coherence, coherence does not depend on this
deliberate intention. Thus, when treating a thinker such as
Weil, it is not necessarily troublesome to find no system; for

the thought may actually cohere in an indivisible whole without systematic presentation. All that is required is that plausible bridges be shown to exist between various aspects of her thought.

It is my intention in this book both to claim and to show that these bridges do exist in Weil's thought in what shall be called her doctrine of mediation. Furthermore, it is my contention that not only do they exist but were also of prime importance to Weil herself in her writings and, as such, received particular attention. Insofar, however, as this would only establish internal coherence, it shall also be necessary to show how Weil's religious philosophy is plausibly grounded in certain commonly received facts, at least commonly received by the Christian faith. This will be established by showing how her thought, rather than syncretistically combining her diverse interests, in fact, ultimately springs from her analysis of Christ's Cross and his role as Mediator. From this basis Weil was able to construct a metaphysical doctrine which allowed her to incorporate into her thought diverse areas such as ancient philosophy and her early social analyses. There are, therefore, I claim, not 'two Simone Weils,' nor a syncretistic, superficial one, but rather a profound one that can be seen to remain constant, although not stationary, even through remarkable changes.

Mediation in the writings of Simone Weil is essentially a means of dealing with incommensurate and contrary realities in such a way that, without destroying their individual integrity, they can be harmoniously united. If, then, mediation is the doctrine that makes Weil's thought cohere and was an area of special investigation for her it is hardly surprising to find that thought embracing so many opposing elements and reflecting duality in human life. In a particularly revealing comment about her own work, she says in commenting on Aristophanes' speech in Plato's *Symposium:* "Our vocation is unity. Our affliction is to be in a state of duality . . ."[13] Weil's thought, therefore, is an attempt both to recognize and analyze the affliction of duality in our lives and to find our proper unity.

The location of opposing elements and the conception of what their ideal mediated unity is, however, very much determines the sense of mediation. Within the writings of Simone Weil

there is a definite change of this location and ideal from the
early years to the later. It is a change, though, that reflects
a considerable *approfondissement* of the sense of mediation, and
one in which, with some alterations, allows many of the earlier
views to be taken up and interwoven with the later ones. For
this reason we will begin with the mediation that is implicit
in the early writings and then in the later chapters show how
mediation is recognized and developed as a conscious doctrine.

CHAPTER I

MEDIATION IN THE EARLY YEARS

Simone Weil was one of those most rare and remarkable
people who from a very early age until her death keenly and
really desired truth above all else. She wrote of herself: "I
preferred to die rather than live without that truth."[1] But in
desiring this truth and the "beauty, virtue and every kind of
goodness"[2] which she included under it, she also felt the significant difference between the desired ideal and the present
situation of herself and her fellow humans. Her desire then
manifested itself in the task she set for herself in life and
thought to understand clearly the ideal and make it actual. In
order to accomplish this task she believed that not only must
the ideal and the present situation be brought forth in the
clearest possible light, but, also, all that separates the two
and exactly what means are required by the ideal to bridge the
gulf.

There is a certain biographical consistency in Weil's life
and thought that is due to this pervading desire for truth. At
the same time, however, there is also an apparent disjunction in
the philosophical forms which this desire took over the course
of her life. This disjunction most evidently centers itself
around two separate periods of her life. There is, on the one
hand, the early years up to 1934 which are marked religiously by
agnosticism and philosophically by an involvement with thinkers
such as Descartes, Kant, Spinoza and Marx. During this period
her chief concerns centered mainly around the problems of social
oppression, labor, and the question of mind and matter. The
major works of this period, *Science et perception dans Descartes*,
the *Lectures on Philosophy*, and the major essays published in
Oppression and Liberty all reflect these concerns, particularly
in the inter-relations of oppression and the mind-matter problem.
Here she saw one of the most distressing problems to be that of
mind subordinated to matter, when, she felt that mind should be

the subject of human action and not its object. On the other
hand, there is the period from 1934 onwards. This period is
marked by an explicit avowal of Christianity and a constant
philosophical involvement with Plato and many of the ancient
Greeks. In this period, her concerns were, in the main, religious, and the continued pursuance of social and labor questions
were undertaken in a religious light, as is easily witnessed in
The Need for Roots. Because of these incongruities, it is necessary first to divide the analysis of Weil's thought into these
two separate periods of her life. In doing so, however, I shall
show how, in fact, there is an overall philosophical coherency
covering both periods which is reflected in Weil's doctrine of
mediation.

Mediation does not appear in Weil's writings by name until
her interests become more explicitly theological. But it is
clearly present in her earliest political and philosophical
works in the form that mind's understanding of matter can be the
means[3] for mind to realize itself and take its proper place in
man's life. In these earliest writings, mediation is not so
much a direct object of contemplation as it is a solution for a
problem. This problem is how man, a being of dual nature of two
incommensurate aspects, mind and body, can harmonize both of
these aspects in an order which best realizes good. This solution, in turn, supplies a method by which man can take his proper
place within an otherwise material world. In the theological
works, this solution of mediation then becomes a particular object of reflection by which Weil comes to understand the action
of transcendent good in the natural world.

Because mediation is in essence a reconciliation of two opposed principles, or incommensurates, two things need to be
shown. On the one hand, it is necessary that both be shown to
exist. On the other hand, it must be demonstrated that they
are, in fact, at war with each other and need to be harmonized
in a fashion which they do not, at present, exhibit. Because
of the fact that for Weil the two are not presently related to
each other in such a way that good and truth are realized, I
shall begin the examination of Weil's early years with her considerations of the problem of oppression which then lead to her
analyses of force and power as being the present dominating

factors in human life, instead of mind. From there I shall examine her philosophical anthropology which shows how man can be
subject to material force and yet a free agent. Finally, it
shall then be shown how the mediation of mind is her solution
for the realization of the ideal wherein mind controls matter in
accordance with reason.

1. *Oppression, Force and Power*

A. *The Critique of Marxism*

    The social situation of post World War I France was one of
great turbulence, particularly for the working class. Wages
were low and earned by piece work; unemployment was high and
whatever work there was, was often undertaken in oppressive conditions. These factors resulted in a situation wherein criticisms of social conditions and solutions to them were constantly
being discussed and then acted upon in movements of the political
parties and nascent labor unions. For those of the political
Left during this time one of the chief inspirations for thought
and action was Marx. Because of Weil's deep sensibilities to
the various forms of oppression and her consequent constant involvement with the Left in France, it was only natural therefore
that she would encounter and deal with the twins of Marxism and
revolution as posing both the problem of oppression and its solution. Far from espousing either of these, however, she saw
revolution as basically hopeless in what it is actually able to
acomplish and what she saw as valuable in Marxism was an untried
method that ultimately ran contrary to Marx's own solutions.

    Amidst the general oppression which is manifested in mean-
inglessness of social life and in a constant despair for the
future, Weil saw one great hope that seemingly all people held.
"Ever since 1789, there has been one magic word which contains
within itself all imaginable futures, and is never so full of
hope as in desperate situations--that word is revolution."[4]
Unfortunately, as Weil also saw, the word 'revolution' is of a
magical nature, having neither precise form nor content. It is
used by peoples of all classes and beliefs, and represents for
each his own personal deliverance, regardless of the way in

which this deliverance could or would be accomplished. "At bottom, one thinks nowadays of the revolution, not as a solution to the problems raised at the present time, but as a miracle dispensing one from solving problems."[5] In the face of this confusion Weil found it necessary to undertake an analysis of that in which a true revolution could consist, if the word has any meaning at all, and consequent upon this examination to analyze the real causes of oppression. It is only upon this analysis that she felt anybody could ever possibly be able clearly to see what the possibilities and means of deliverance from oppression are. Without such an analysis, not only does 'revolution' carry only the force of a magical incantation, but means no more than the common desire to be rid of all opposition to one's dreams.

In order to examine critically whatever meaning 'revolution' might have, Weil first turns to look at Marx, "for all those who have experienced the need to buttress their revolutionary feeling with precise concepts have found, or thought they found, these concepts in Marx."[6] In Marx, Weil found a mass of contradictions and unproven assumptions, but she also felt that she found a method that she considered profoundly helpful and which, with her own emendments, she was able to put to good use. As such her critique of Marxism offers not only an insightful analysis of Marx, but, at the same time, the first introduction into Weil's own considerations of oppression which shall ultimately lead to her notions of necessity, power and force.

Weil believed that Marx's analyses were actually quite first-rate in their ability to demonstrate the mechanism of oppression. Marx clearly showed that "the true reason for the exploitation of the workers is not any desire on the part of the capitalists to enjoy and consume, but the need to expand the undertaking as rapidly as possible so as to make it more powerful than its rivals."[7] Because of this need to expand the undertaking, that is, to expand it so that it becomes large scale production, oppression results since everything is sacrificed to the undertaking and poured into it so that it may indeed expand. In fact, oppression even becomes necessary for large scale production to take place. In this sense, for Marx, oppression becomes an

organ of the system of production which is needed to compete in
the struggle for power. In a true socialist state, Marx claimed,
such oppression would finally cease, but, as he himself clearly
recognized, the only way this is possible is when the revolution
has taken place in all areas of the globe. Until that time, he
thought, there is a sort of oppression required even in places
where the revolution has supposedly already succeeded, "lest it
be found weaker than the other nations."[8] In the hands of the
latter-day Marxists, however, Weil saw this line of reasoning
as the excuse for Stalinism.

The problem is that when the system of large scale production becomes all powerful it begins to determine all relations
within a collectivity, for everything is dedicated to this form
of production, and whatever life there is, is drawn from it.
This is true even in Marxist countries; thus Weil saw the problem of large scale production as general and not a problem confined to capitalist systems. Not even juridical or political
moves can significantly change these relations for they, as
agents within the society, are rooted in the system of production and gain their power and authority from it. This general
sort of oppression in a society dedicated to large scale production becomes more specific as the reasoning that uncovered
its general aspects is applied to particular instances such as
factory work. Here the workers are especially exploited and
oppressed to serve the undertaking. They are, as it were, a
sort of raw material to be used in production; as Marx said,
"there exists a mechanism independent of the workers, which incorporates them as living cogs."[9]

Within a large scale system of production not only is all
living labor subjected to the independent mechanism of the
factory, thus resulting in an alienation of labor, but labor itself also becomes split into the "degrading division of manual
and intellectual labor." As production becomes larger and more
complex its organization and modes of work exceed the skills and
thought of individual workers. As a result, two separate classes
of workers emerge: those who execute the work and those who
manage and coordinate it. But within the factory these two
classes are hardly equal; instead, one plays the role of raw

material in the factory to whom the power of thought is never
credited. Thus skill, and even pride in labor is taken from the
worker. The directors, on the other hand, are all powerful,
and, in fact Weil claims, they have replaced the capitalists in
importance. This new phenomenon of a class of directors she saw
as instituting a thoroughly new and more subtle form of oppres-
sion--"oppression exercised in the name of management."[10] This,
Weil felt, was not a phenomenon totally unperceived by Marx, but
in his day the staff of technical managers was under complete
control of the capitalists, whereas today, "the 'technicians of
management' form a distinct social stratum whose importance tends
to increase and which absorbs in various ways a considerable
proportion of the profits."[11] Although this consideration of
bureaucratic oppression is Weil's own, it is an area in which
she thought the Marxist analysis of large scale productive systems was borne out to an even greater degree than hitherto
thought. In the case of the laborer, this new class of technocrats forces an even further distance between him as a thinking
man and the object and conditions of his labor. Ironically, however, although the technocrats may be the ones wielding the
power, they, too, become further alienated from the conditions
of their own work by virtue of their very specialization. "As
science forms an indivisible whole, one may say that these men
are no longer, strictly speaking, scientists, but only unskilled
hands doing scientific work, cogs in a whole their minds are
quite incapable of embracing."[12]

As specialization in the factory leads to bureaucratic oppression so does it also on the level of the State, even in
socialist countries. In fact, in socialist countries where the
working class movement has supposedly taken over, all that has
really happened is that, through its bureaucracy, the State has
taken upon itself the role of technocrats. Thus:

> At all levels we are brought up against the same obstacle.
> The whole of our civilization is founded on specializa-
> tion, which implies the enslavement of those who execute
> to those who co-ordinate; and on such a basis one can[13]
> only organize and perfect oppression, not lighten it.

While essentially agreeing with the Marxian analysis of
capitalist oppression and adding her own further considerations

of bureaucratic oppression which spring from it, Weil at this
point raises a question. The problem which she saw was that the
analysis seems *so* good, how is it possible that the system of
oppression could ever cease to function? Here her own criticism
of Marxism begins. Clearly, in order to alleviate oppression
that is the result of a system of large scale production it is
first of all necessary to emancipate not men directly but the
productive forces. The great advancement that enabled Marx to
come to this conclusion was that he, unlike Feuerbach, was able
to conceive a materialist doctrine wherein human activity was
not only the product of matter, but also was objectively material
itself, so that, through 'revolutionizing practice,' man could,
as part of the material environment, change that environment,
social and natural, and thus himself as well. While this is all
fine and good, it does not necessarily lead to a final and ultimate absence of oppression. What then led Marx to believe
that oppression would ever cease, particularly since he had no
intention of abolishing large scale production? Weil was at
great pains to show that Marx's belief that a final state of non-
oppression is possible, or even inevitable, is founded on a
rather large unproven and unlikely assumption, which she claimed
was not only unreasonable but which ultimately ran contrary to
Marx's own best ideas.

The great unproven assumption which Weil saw Marx making
was that forces inevitably progress, by themselves and with the
help of revolutionary practice by men, to the point where human
liberation would coincide perfectly with the liberation of the
productive forces.

> In his view, modern technique, once freed from capitalist
> forms of economy, can give men, here and now, sufficient
> leisure to enable them to develop their faculties har-
> moniously, and consequently bring about the disappear-
> ance, to a certain extent, of the degrading specializa-
> tion created by capitalism; and above all the further
> development of technique must lighten more and more, day
> by day, the burden of material necessity, and as an imme-
> diate consequence that of social constraint, until
> humanity reaches at last a truly paradisial state in which
> the most abundant production would be at the cost of a
> trifling expenditure of effort and the ancient curse of
> work lifted.[14]

There are two major difficulties which Weil saw with this
assumption of inevitable progress. On the one hand, Marx, like
Lamarck, tended to see humans or other creatures quite naturally
adapting themselves to the changing environment by developing
in a thoroughly preordained manner the necessary organs to cope
with these changes. In this case, Marx, despite his moral
indignation at the fact of oppression, could, at the same time,
see it as a necessary organ of the capitalist system which is
but a step to the final stages of development. But if one
cared to look more carefully at the situation as Darwin,[15] for
example, did, he should be astute enough to realize that the
assumption that living creatures automatically adapt--that the
function creates the organ--has no basis in reason or fact.
Rather, any evolution that might be the case seems to be far
better ascribed to simple accident and coincidence. On the
other hand, Weil also claimed that Marx was able to assert the
continuing evolution of productive forces only at the cost of
re-introducing a concept which he had already dismissed, that of
mind or spirit. This, she felt, was due to the Hegelian origins
of Marxist thought. "Marx claimed to 'put back on its feet the
Hegelian dialectic, which he accused of being 'upside down', by
substituting matter for mind as the motive power of history; but
by an extraordinary paradox, he conceived history, starting from
this rectification, as though he attributed to matter what is
the very essence of mind--unceasing aspiration towards the
best."[16] Thus Weil felt that the notion of the inevitable progress of matter, if not absurd, is at least bought at the price
of self-contradiction. Ironically, Weil notes, this assumption
which Marx makes is tantamount to a crude belief in Providence
which has the effect of making Marxism a type of religion instituting a sort of primitive oppression. This, she believed,
was exactly what had happened with present-day doctrinaire
Marxists who dogmatically swallowed all the suppositions given
by the Father without ever having thought carefully about them.

Despite this strong critique of the Marxist 'religion,'
Weil, nonetheless, did see something of high importance in
Marx's work. This was not, however, the idea of inevitable
progress, but rather an idea concerning social transformations
that has remained basically untried, even by Marx himself.

> Marx's truly great idea is that in human society, as
> well as in nature, nothing takes place otherwise than
> through material transformations. . . . To desire is
> nothing; we have got to know the material conditions
> which determine our possibilities of action; and in the
> social sphere these conditions are defined by the way
> in which man obeys material necessities in supplying
> his own needs, in other words, by the method of pro-
> duction.[17]

The idea that in "nature and human society nothing takes
place otherwise than through material transformations," while,
at first, seeming to be as much an assumption as a material
history evolving towards the best, is far more solidly based.
If there is any validity in the analysis which demonstrates
modern oppression to be the result of a system of material production, then any change in the form of oppression, even as
regards freedom from it, must take place in accordance with some
change in the system of production. This is to say that as long
as the material conditions of human existence, including man's
social relations, are founded and determined by the system of
production, in a strong sense, then these conditions of existence
cannot be altered except by material means. Thus all change
which is real and not simply imagined must involve material
change. The task is then set as to what areas in which one may
expect or hope to effect change.

Although this idea that real change in the material conditions of existence has to take place in accordance with material
transformation is Marx's own idea, Weil, by her critique of the
assumptions of material evolution, deviates significantly from
Marx. This is because, and here is a major point of Weilian
thought, Weil's critique of Marx does not entail any sort of
thoroughgoing materialism, and this for a number of reasons.
Initially, when Weil speaks about the material conditions of
existence she means quite seriously that they are conditions for
human life but this does not mean that they are the only factors
in human life. Marx, also, was admittedly perspicacious enough
to see that men are not simply the products of matter, since
they are also capable of changing matter. Nevertheless, he
never spoke of mind nor did he ever need to do so as long as he
was able to assume that history was moving in a direction which
mind, in earlier and less materialistic thinkers, had previously

been obliged to take man. Yet, once this notion is dispelled as
reasonably, and even materially, improbable, the remaining points
of his argument would tend to make the human subject nothing
more than the product of natural forces because there would be
nothing to assure anyone that human strivings were for anything
at all. Furthermore, once the belief in an inevitable progress
of productivity is dispelled, it leaves Marxian large scale production just as oppressive as that of its capitalist enemies.
Weil, on the contrary, makes the material conditions of existence
necessary, but not sufficient conditions to explain human action.
Second, although she regarded material transformation as indispensable to any real change, she did not regard such change in
itself as any sort of good, as Marx was obliged to do when the
change moved history forward, but rather simply a condition for
good activity by humans. This shall become clearer in the third
section of this chapter.

The particular value, then, which Weil saw to lie in the
idea that "no change takes place without material transformation"
is that of an analytic tool which can help uncover whatever possibilities might exist for establishing a less oppressive society. If there is any truth in the idea, then in order to understand the nature of oppression at its root and to envisage
to what degree it may be alleviated, it is first necessary to
reach a clear understanding of what the possibilities of material
transformation are. And with this understanding comes a knowledge of whether or not a paradisial state where labor exercised
is at a minimum and its fruits at an optimal maximum is possible,
and to what extent. It also brings a knowledge that indicates
whether a revolution can, in any sense, assist in bringing that
state about. If the paradisial state is not possible and large
scale production inevitably leads to oppression, under no matter
what political system, then clearly we must look elsewhere for
a solution to oppression, and if revolution cannot bring this
state about we must look for another means.

The first use to which Weil puts this tool is to determine
whether unlimited progress in technology is possible. Already
she has criticized Marx and his followers for the assumption
that such progress is natural and inevitable; here, she undertakes to see whether this progress is even conceivably possible.

> The problem is fundamental, and of a kind to determine
> all future prospects; it must be formulated with the utmost
> precision. To this end, the first thing is to know in
> what technical progress consists, what factors play a
> part in it, and to examine each factor separately; for
> we mix up under the name of technical progress entirely
> different procedures that offer different possibilities
> of development.[18]

In order, then to determine the extent to which we might
hope for progress in our technical abilities Weil examines three
critical factors which she sees as playing a role in that progress: 1) the utilization of natural sources of energy; 2) the
development of science to better utilize natural resources;
3) the rationalization of labor. In all these areas she not only
sees a limiting factor, but also at various points claims that
we may already have exceeded the limit beyond which progress
turns into regress. As regards natural sources of energy, she
claims, it may indeed be impossible to assign a precise limit to
them, but, nevertheless, this still does not assure us that there
can be unlimited progress in our utilization of these sources.
This is plain because from the very outset the natural sources
of energy do not leap into our furnaces and machines; instead,
they require our own labor to transform raw material into actual
energy. There is no guarantee, nor any reason to believe, that
this will lessen in the future as presently known deposits of
oil, coal, and ore become depleted. Although, theoretically,
energy may be transformed from all sorts of matter, there still
remains a question of whether it can be done so economically,
and, in this area, science, too cannot guarantee any perpetual
progress, for "we do not realize that if certain scientific results depend entirely on the good use the scientist makes of
his reasoning faculties, others are the result of lucky finds."[19]
Thus while scientific method can progress, it does not do so
inevitably in that it often requires the accidental insights of
one man (the discovery of the molecular structure of benzene is
witness enough to this) and "as soon as chance enters in, the
idea of continuous development is no longer applicable."[20] Weil
further goes on to state that while it may possibly be the case
that someday a technological innovation will make all energy
economically utilizable for human needs, "it is possible, too,
that one fine day some sudden change in the astronomical order

may give to vast expanses of the earth's surface the bewitching
climate that enables, so it is said, certain primitive tribes to
live without working."[21]

Only one other resource is left by which the total sum of
human effort can be reduced, namely, the rationalization or
division and co-ordination of labor. Clearly, this as much as
any other factor in the present system of production, is responsible for the present state of man's deliverance from brute
nature. Even in this case, however, Weil sees a limit to the
ultimate productivity of this method, and one beyond which the
labor saving factors become factors of expenditure. There are
a number of reasons for this. Initially, as the undertaking
increases in size so does it also bring both greater waste "and
no doubt to a certain extent, a parasitic increase in the staff
whose task it is to co-ordinate the various branches of the
undertaking."[22] Insofar as much production is only feasible on
an extremely large scale, the benefits derived from it are only
obtained through a certain amount of waste and "squandering of
precious stores of human energy and raw materials."[23] Here
Marx was certainly correct in asserting that the expansion of
the enterprise is primary and that all else becomes subjugated
to it, but he was at least naive in assuming that oppression
would cease when production was finally liberated from the hands
of the capitalists. Second, because matter does not arrange
itself or provide itself in a form conveniently adapted to human
needs, human effort is always required to make the necessary
modifications. As the complexity of an enterprise increases, so,
too, it would seem that the human effort of organizing would
also. Although automation has replaced many laborious human
functions, human effort is still required for the final organization and to secure many of the required materials. The life of
the factory worker may have been eased considerably this century,
but men are still required to go down into mines. Finally, even
if one could assume a continual technical progress in the area
of automation it would still be necessary to take into account
the hard facts of accident and contingency. In this sense, not
only is continual development contingent upon one person's inno-
vations, but human error must always remain a factor wherein an

entire enterprise can be shut down or blown up by a tired
worker's forgetting to tighten a valve. In the same vein, accident and contingency can be applied to the grander international
scale through the everpresent threat of war. Weil roundly crit-
icizes Marx for having neglected to consider this factor,[24] for
as long as war remains a possible and real threat due to the
military and industrial competition between nations, no doctrine
of continual progress can ever confidently be asserted.

But what are we to conclude from this? In the first place,
Weil contends, we must be disabused of the notion that revolution, particularly one undertaken in terms of the Marxist ideal,
will accomplish anything in terms of material progress, for we
may very well be at the limit, if not already beyond it. Yet,
more positively, this critique sets forth the task to determine
how to abolish social oppression, even if we cannot expect a
providential dispensation wherein matter will ultimately and
freely serve human needs.

> The problem is, therefore, quite clear; it is a question
> of knowing whether it is possible to conceive of an or-
> ganization of production which, though powerless to remove
> the necessities imposed by nature and the social con-
> straint arising therefrom, would enable these at any rate
> to be exercised without grinding down souls and bodies
> under oppression.[25]

B. *The Causes of Oppression--Force and Power*

Weil felt that Marx had made a decided advancement in the
understanding of social oppression when he ceased to consider
it as a simple usurpation and discovered that its mechanism
resides in the material conditions of the social system. What
she felt he never did explain, though, is why the division of
labor necessarily or inevitably turns into oppression. In Marx's
case, there was simply an assumption that oppression is an organ
created by a function in the evolution of matter. As such, he
could calmly assert social oppression simply to be a necessary
concommitant of capitalism which will automatically disappear on
the day that the productive forces have reached a sufficiently
high level of development and have been liberated. Weil, on the
contrary, saw that this assumption is basically unfounded, and
that it is far more reasonable to believe that oppression is

already an organ of the higher systems of production which then finds for itself a function to perform within these systems, capitalist as well as socialist. Because of this 'Darwinian' correction to Marx, wherein "adaptation is henceforth conceived in regard to living beings as an exterior and no longer an interior necessity . . . ," clearly, " . . . the causes of social evolution must no longer be sought elsewhere than in the daily efforts of men considered as individuals."[26] Similarly, it would seem that the roots of oppression must be laid to human efforts as well, whether these efforts are the result of a conscious and far-seeing decision or not.

Weil discerned three material conditions of human existence which help determine us and our relations to the world; namely, the natural environment, the existence, activity and competition of other organisms of the same species, and the organization of the natural environment. While the first two factors are for the most part simply givens which are barely susceptible to change, the third is quite obviously the result of deliberate human activity and is most capable of being modified by human reaction. Yet, at the same time, it is this third factor which is most responsible for oppression. The question that then needs to be raised is why does this organization, which should be a means of alleviating the effect of brute force, turn brute force upon the very beings it is meant to serve? The answer to this question will go a long way towards discovery of the root cause of oppression in society and of what, instead of large scale production, is needed for man to be free.

There are two rather strange factors involved in oppression which lead one to suspect a definite link between it and the division of labor, particularly at higher levels of organization of the natural environment. On the one hand, the few forms of social organization which appear to be free from social oppression[27] all correspond to an extremely low level of production. On the other hand, "what is surprising is not that oppression should make its appearance only after higher forms of economy have been reached, but that it should always accompany them."[28] Ironically, man seems to be freest in respect to other men when he is most narrowly confined by the natural environment since

as he gains some dominion over nature, he becomes most oppressed
by other men. "In reality, at these higher stages, human action
continues, as a whole, to be nothing but pure obedience to the
brutal spur of an immediate necessity; only instead of being
harried by nature, man is henceforth harried by man."[29] Despite
the apparent irony, in the last analysis, this fact should not
be all that surprising, "for oppression is exercised by force,
and in the long run, all force originates in nature."[30]

It is this notion of force which is one of the hallmarks of
Weil's philosophy. It is to a certain extent present in Marx's
thought when he saw all oppression as proceeding from purely
objective or material conditions; what distinguishes Weil, however, is that she saw force as a general problem to be analyzed
in respect to its own nature, and not simply as a part of a
larger social critique. In fact, she claims, that it is "the
notion of force and not that of need which is the key to an understanding of social phenomena."[31]

Weil's beliefs that oppression is exercised by force and
that all force ultimately orginates in nature can be explained
partly by means of a likely progression in the development of
man's relations with his natural environment. Primitive man
finds himself in a world in which the natural elements limit and
condition his existence. As such, he is their object and creation. At the same time, however, as a part of the physical world
he is also a subject, possessing within himself a certain degree
of force, no matter how weak it may be in comparison to other
forces. Through application of the force at his disposal, in
such instances as the building of shelters and the production
of tools for food gathering, man is then able to serve his needs
and not be left totally to the blind whims of the external environment. This force of man used against nature, while weak,
increases in strength as men band together socially and divide
their labor to serve a common goal. Thus social organization is
as much an objective and material force as the various elements
of the natural environment are, and within limits can increase
in geometrical proportion to the addition of further individual
forces. As Adam Smith noted, ten workers can produce a thousand
times as many pins in a day as one man.

Insofar as social organization can be regarded as a force
vis-a-vis nature, by parity of reasoning, the actual organization
of human elemental forces within a society is also a force.
Adam and Eve were perhaps the only humans who ever exercised
their own individual powers fully to create a society; since
then the social contract has not been renegotiated upon the birth
of every new child. For this reason society increases the power
of every individual in respect to the environment, but at the
same time it exercises a certain amount of force in respect to
the individual and becomes a complete condition of existence
for any individual. This is true not only in the more general
sense that every individual is born into a world which has already been created and in which certain relationships are already
established, but also in the quite concrete sense in which a
person's activity is conditioned, directed and limited by the
actual forces within a given society. At the most primitive
level, every individual is limited and is bound by the chief who
reigns in that position by virtue of his strength; in capitalism,
the individual is limited by a few monopolists possessing all
the property. This force exists at various levels of subtlety
and need not be dependent upon actual physical strength of body.
Here the 'technicians of management' wield the greatest force
in present society, for they, like the priests of primitive
tribes, "dispose, albeit through a fiction, of all of nature's
powers, and it is in their name that (they) exercise authority."[32] As societies and division of labor become more complex,
it is perhaps inevitable that such a class would arise and claim
privileges not open to the rest of society. As soon as such a
privileged class does exist, as privileged, equality is destroyed in a society and one class becomes subordinate to another, at least in terms of the obedience required to carry forth
the enterprise. In this way, it can begun to be seen how oppression results from an inequal exercise of force, and how force
offers a key to social phenomena.

It would seem that when inequality obtains in a society
that the best way to keep this inequality from being oppressive
is to set up a balancing power between the two poles such that
the power[33] exercised by the commanders could not go beyond the

limits necessary to direct the social enterprise to a common
goal. Yet, Weil claims, due to the real nature of force and
power this hope is a chimera. Whereas in dealing with inert
matter a stabilizing force can be established, as in the case of
a properly placed rudder keeping a wind blown ship on course,
this is not possible with humans who are not inert, but, rather
active beings. For this reason, humans, unlike matter, can and
do always react to any contraining force and this reaction, in
turn, has the effect of upsetting any so-called balance that
might exist. In this way the only complete power would be one
which had exterminated its object, but in this case it would also
cease being a power.

> Thus there is, in the very essence of power, a fundamen-
> tal contradiction that prevents it from ever existing
> in the true sense of the word; those who are called
> masters, ceaselessly compelled to reinforce their power
> for fear of seeing it snatched away from them, are
> forever seeking a dominion impossible to attain. . . .
> It would be otherwise if one man could possess in himself
> a force superior to that of many men put together, but
> such is never the case; the instruments of power . . .
> always exist independently of him who disposes of them,
> and can be taken up by others. Consequently all power
> is unstable.[34]

Because of the natural instability of power and because it
it impossible ever to have true and full possession of it, in
order for those who wield power to secure their privileged position, they are obliged to become engaged in a race for power.
This race is one which has neither proportions nor limits since
the participants are perpetually driven to exceed the power of
the competition. In this sense, as long as the slave is alive
the master must live in some fear of him and seek continually
to reinforce and re-establish his power over him. The master
thus becomes as much enslaved to power as the slave. Here Marx
again seems quite correct in seeing that the exploitation of
the workers is not pure greed on the part of the capitalist,
but something the capitalists are obliged to do in order to
maintain the undertaking which gives them their power; a power
that is oddly independent of them and which they also serve.
But, again, Marx only saw this as a problem of capitalism which
would be superceded, whereas Weil, on the other hand, took it

to be a truth of the general condition of man in society. The
problem of the distribution of force is as ancient as man himself, and, in fact, Weil was willing to claim that one could
see it even in so venerable a source as Homer's *Iliad*. In her
essay, *The Iliad, or the Poem of Might*, she seeks to demonstrate
this contention. But she does more than demonstrate it; she
also uses this essay to show how force comes to dominate so com-
plegely social relations by virtue of the fact that men, instead
of using power as a means to a goal, seek it as an end in itself
and thereby when seemingly exercising power actually come to be
dominated by it.[35]

To the extent that the *Iliad* deals with war it seems fairly
obvious that power is a major consideration of the poem, at leas-
as far as the victims of the war are concerned. It is strength
and power which causes the black blood of warrior after warrior
to flow unceasingly upon the ground. It is the power of the
Achaean kings and the weakness of Thersites which makes the latter an object of scorn and ridicule. Further, it is Agamemnon's
power as leader that unjustly humiliates Achilles by forcing him
to give up Briseis, and, in turn, Achilles' strength which later
forces Agamemnon to abase himself so as to bring Achilles back
into the fight.

Beyond simple killing and abasement, however, might exercises even greater control over its victims, for "Might is that
which makes a thing of anybody who comes under its sway. When
exercised to the full, it makes a thing of man in the most literal
sense, for it makes him a corpse,"[36] but this while he even still
breathes. The warrior defeated in battle suppliantly hugging
the knees of Achilles is this sort of living corpse. "But soon
he has understood that the weapon will not turn from him, and
though he still breathes, he is only matter, still thinking, he
can think of nothing."[37]

Yet it is not only the victim of one day who is broken by
Might, for Might is blind and the victor of one day becomes the
victim of the next. Patroclus, who valiantly begins to rout the
Trojans, falls prey to Hector, who, in turn, is slaughtered by
Achilles shortly afterwards. The Greeks who at one point are
within a hair's breadth of taking Troy the next day have their

ships burned. Because Might acts so blindly, crushing all who come under its sway and with the greatest equanimity, it would seem that those who wield the greatest power would have the foresight to see that they are not exempt from the caprices of Might. But such is not the case, for "as pitilessly as Might crushes, so pitilessly it maddens whoever possesses, or believes he possesses it. None can truly ever possess it."[38] If Might is frightening in its ability to crush, it is even more so in its ability to blind the so-called powerful to their own destiny. For Weil, this is more than a simple assertion of what appears to be an all-embracing phenomenon, for she attempts to go as deeply into the influence of Might over the victors as she does for the victims. In the case of the powerful, the wielding of might produces an illusion as to their own strength and grip on Might, for:

> . . . they never think of their own strength as a limited quantity, nor of their relations with others as an equilibrium of unequal powers. . . . They conclude that destiny has given all license to them and none to their inferiors. Henceforth they go beyond the measure of their strength, inevitably so, because they do not know its limit. Thus they are delivered up before chance, and things no longer obey them.[39]

This blinding illusion is due to the influence of the prestige which is a natural concommitant of holding power. In fact, prestige is not only a matter of spoils to the victor, but also is a power in itself in the inter-relations of men. This is evidenced clearly enough in the *Iliad* in the case of Thersites, a not very prestigious person who, when he begins to speak in the assembly and in not completely an unreasonable vein, is told by the prestigious:

> Miserable one be still, listen while others speak,
> Your superiors . . .
> You count for nothing in battle, for nothing in the assembly.[40]

It is also plain enough in any legal system where the privileged gain added privilege by virtue of their privileged status. As a power, prestige influences those who are accorded it to the point of obscuring in their minds the true nature of that prestige and the Might in which it is rooted. "For the prestige

which constitutes three-fourths of might is first of all made
up of that superb indifference which the powerful have for the
weak, an indifference so contagious that it is communicated even
to those who are its objects."[41] All believe in Might, victor
and victim alike, and none clearly sees its true nature. It is
small wonder that it is the "gods who are credited with the
mysterious influence which nullifies peace negotiations, continually revives hostilities, and brings together the contending
forces urged by a flash of good sense to abandon the struggle."[42]

Since such a picture may depict very well the situation of
man under the sway of Might, it must be asked what exactly has
happened to make this situation possible, if indeed it is not
simply the natural condition of man? On Weil's part there is a
clear perception that what has happened to allow such situations
to occur is that means and ends have become totally reversed.
Any force that individual men might possess is, in the first
instance, a means by which he is enabled to survive in his con-
frontation with nature and meet the ends of his needs. Ideally,
nothing should change when individual forces are pooled to increase the means of the individuals involved, and, yet, a change
does take place. Rather than pooling their powers to exert a
greater force over hostile nature, men seek power over other
men. Because of the relative instability and elusiveness of
power, however, this search in unending and becomes a passion
which eclipses all other considerations. So "power seeking,
owing to its essential incapacity to seize hold of its object,
rules out all consideration of an end, and finally comes, through
an inevitable reversal, to take the place of all ends."[43] The
most bitterly ironical fact of this reversal is that, instead of
using power to subdue nature to meet human needs, men use power
to suppress human needs in order to acquire further power. This
means on the large scale that the directors of the system of
production cease to use it as a means of directing human force
upon nature to reach common goals, and instead use it upon men
to make them serve the source of power. But, of course, the
directors ultimately sacrifice all their efforts to the undertaking, too.

> Human history is simply the history of the servitude
> which makes man--oppressors and oppressed alike--the

plaything of the instruments of domination they themselves have manufactured, and thus reduces living humanity to being the chattel of inanimate chattels.[44]

When the situation of man serving his tools--of man being
a living extension of his machines--obtains, it is evident "it
is things, not men, that prescribe the limits and laws of this
giddy race for power."[45] It is certainly true that even in a
society which has not fallen prey to this reversal, the limits
of the forces of the natural environment condition and limit the
extent to which man can satisfy his needs, but the situation is
significantly different in a case where the reversal has taken
place. In the former case, moderation in the use of power is
possible insofar as its exercise is directed only to the satisfaction of needs; in the latter case, however, such moderation
becomes well-nigh impossible, for when the goal is to outstrip
the competition, moderation seems a foolish suggestion. Once
this race for power has begun, the participants, like the
characters of the *Iliad*, totally fall under the sway of Might,
and like them, refuse to acknowledge what in fact the actual
situation is; thus by the illusion which Might foists upon the
powerful, they become unknowingly subject to destruction by the
very powers which had hitherto favored them. In times of relative prosperity when natural resources are easily obtainable
and competition slight, it is indeed possible that a great number of needs are met through distribution of the surplus of production, although all are, nevertheless, serving the productive
system rather than vice versa. As natural resources become more
difficult to obtain and competiton stiffens, because power is
the main objective whatever surplus there might be is directed
to keeping the enterprise going. In this sense, the extent of
power clearly depends on the limits of resources. But, again,
in the race for power these limits go unrecognized, and time and
time again, power seeks to exceed the limits. It is at this
point that humans most clearly and objectively feel oppression,
although in some sense it has been present all along. When the
limits imposed by matter threaten to weaken a given power, it
does not simply cease functioning at once, its allotted time of
pre-eminence over, but, rather, it begins to mine the one resource left--the members of the society. If surplus once

provided necessities, in this case individuals are deprived of
necessities, not because they cannot be met, but because the
means of power must be met first.

But even this procedure has its limits. Once a system has
begun to spend its capital it is already weak, and it is only a
question of time before it is overtaken, although it may appear
strongest just before the downfall. As a system, a society or
a person attempts to expand the sphere of its influence beyond
its assigned limits it must correspondingly narrow the bases on
which it rests--a tightening of the belt, so to speak--which
makes the limits narrower and narrower. As a result it can only
become weaker the further it attempts to expand its power and,
at the same time, it must become more oppressive unless new resources are found. This is true not only in the international
sphere, as in the case of war, but also within a given society.
When a system has been sufficiently weakened and become intoler-
ably oppressive it then becomes ripe for takeover by the oppressed, for "the strong man is never absolutely strong, nor the
weak man absolutely weak. . . ."[46] Unfortunately, as Weil
claims, neither war no revolution change the objective situation.
The oppressors do not simply fall to the oppressed, because as
the weak and oppressed they have chosen to rise up 'against in-
justice,' for this "would be a victory of weakness over force,
the equivalent of a balance whose lighter scale were to go
down."[47] In fact, what would have happened in such so-called
revolutions is simply the explicit recognition of a transferral
of power that had already taken place, and this, not by human
thought, but by an ineluctable play of blind forces.

> When it seems that a sanguinary struggle replaces one
> system by another, this struggle is in reality more than
> half accomplished, and brings to power a category of
> men who already more than half possessed that power. . . .
> When violent conflicts break out--and they do not always
> do so--they only play the role of a pair of scales;
> they hand over power to those who possess it already.[48]

If this insight is true, it then becomes evident that the
hope of the revolution is as subject to the illusion of power
as any previous system which it might replace and is as prone
to repeat mistakes as the previous system was to commit them.
In any revolution, then, there has not been any 'liberation of

the forces of production'; they have simply taken on a new servant. The victory of one class over another is only possible
because the one has become stronger and the other weaker; in
neither case has either ceased to be given over to serving matter.

> Whatever may be the patterns taken by social transforma-
> tions, all one finds, if one tries to lay bare the
> mechanism, is a dreary play of blind forces that unite
> or clash, that progress or decline, that replace each
> other, without ever ceasing to grind beneath them the
> unfortunate race of human beings. . . .[49] It would
> seem that man is born a slave, and that servitude is his
> natural condition.[50]

2. *The Philosophical Anthropology*

Beginning with a view that she holds in common with Marx
that man is not only an object shaped by matter, but also a subject which transforms the material environment including himself, the presentation of Weil's analysis of man in society has
led to a rather despairing conclusion of man being given over
to servitude. Yet, Weil did not believe that this necessarily
had to be the case, for "nothing on earth can stop man from
feeling himself born for liberty. Never, whatever may happen,
can he accept servitude, for he is a thinking creature."[51] Even
if she felt that there is no reason to assert an ever-evolving
technical progress which will yield a paradisial state where
productivity and needs perfectly coincide, she, at the same time,
felt that man has the capability of so directing his activity
in a way in which means and ends are held in their proper relations and in which the individual can attain his proper dignity.

Although it is activity which places man within the world,
and in this world "no change takes place without material transformation," it does not mean that human activity is merely of a
kind with material transoformation nor can it be reduced *totaliter*
to material action and reaction. Despite the twin facts that
man is first identified by his objective material activities
and that at higher stages of development he can still be identified thusly, it still remains possible that there is an aspect
of man in which he is not fully described by material activity.
In order then to see what human possibilities are for Weil in a

world otherwise made of blind forces, it is necessary to turn
to her consideration of man and of what constitutes his being
in such a world. This consideration will yield man to be one
unitary being of two incommensurate aspects of matter and mind
which need to be mediated into a proper order for man to gain
liberty. For this purpose, two works, the *Lectures on Philosophy*
and *Science et Perception dans Descartes* are crucial.[52]

In the *Lectures on Philosophy* Weil employs a method of procedure similar to that which has been presented in *Reflections
Concerning the Causes of Liberty and Social Oppression*. In both
cases, before undertaking any discussion of mind or of the liberty
for which man is born, she first carefully begins an examination
of man considered as an active material being. It is this active
being that she analyzes as object in terms of the conditions of
existence external to him which condition and limit him, and
then as a subject who is capable, to a certain extent, of creating and changing his environment and himself, particularly
through social organization. At this beginning point, the issue
at stake is far less a question of how a being capable of thought
might act than it is a question of the ways of thought of an
active being. It is, in her terms, a description of man from
the "materialist point of view."

Two reasons exist for the order of considering matter before
mind. On the one hand, as she claims, "the more honestly we are
materialists in this study we are making, the better we shall be
able to defend ourselves against them later."[53] On the other
hand, and far more importantly, she offers the second reason
"that it is by studying matter that we shall find mind."[54] The
reasoning behind this latter claim is five-fold. First of all,
if we can speak of hard facts, the fact that man exists as a
material being seems a harder fact than his existence as mind,
at least apparently. Second, if man does exist as mind this is
not something which is immediately apparent in his development
either individually or historically. It often looks quite like
an achievement on his part to realize mind. Third, because mind
in man occurs only in him as a being of *both* mind and body and
does not manifest itself separately it must in some sense commensurate itself with the material conditions of body. Fourth,
even if materialism cannot provide all the answers, it does offer

a decent explanation of a good share of them. As Weil once
said, "Behaviourism is an excellent explanation--provided one
doesn't believe it." Finally, on a more practical level, if
oppression can be alleviated at all, mind must seize hold of
the material world in order to effect the necessary transformations without which the claim of having rid ourselves of oppression is only an illusion. It is with these reasons in mind that
Weil begins the *Lectures on Philosophy* with the section entitled
"the materialist point of view," which is first of all a study
of the role of the body in action, feeling and thought. It is
only after this study has been completed that one can begin to
investigate the role of the mind in these same areas.

For Weil it is the body which provides the most basic (or
primitive) relations of man to the world. These primal relations consist of reflexes and instincts (instincts being more
complex cases of reflex) which can be congenital and/or conditioned or acquired. Congenital reflexes, on the one hand, are
those which are biologically entailed by the human organism.
Conditioned reflexes or instincts, on the other hand, are a particular adaptation to the environment (i.e. the environment does
not dictate that such or such an instinct is necessary; in fact
others are possible, but nevertheless, these reflexes are the
ones by which an organism does happen to adapt itself). Materially considered, human behavior can generally be classified
under one of these two headings. Their significance lies in
the fact that "thought does not come into these cases; it is the
body which grasps the relations. . . . So when we are on the
point of giving birth to thought, it comes into birth in a world
that is already ordered."[55] On this level, to be human means
no more than to possess these instincts and reflexes.

It is, then, physical human activity which provides the
first objects of thought and the relations between things, and
not any distinct mental ordering of sensations or sensations
per se. In fact, Weil claims, "far from sensations being the
only things that are immediately given to us, it is, as such,
only given to us by an effort of abstraction, and by a great
effort at that."[56] This is not meant to deny that we have sensations; it does deny, however, that any meaningful sense can
be given to 'sense data.' At most "sensation only serves as an

occasion for becoming conscious of what one believes one
feels,"[57] and this belief is founded in human activity.

It is basically the imagination which performs these acts
of perception, and as such, for Weil, is defined as a function
of human activity which by itself does not imply mind. Instead,
as she uses the term, imagination is "the transference into the
object of that which is situated in the subject's body."[58] As
such, imagination itself is a reflex by which humans make their
perceptual way about the world. It is not, however, to be
equated with fantasy. As an organ of human activity, conditioned
by that activity, it is clearly dependent upon the regularity
inherent in activity through which it provides perceptual consistency. It is, therefore not at all arbitrary. As Weil notes,
"when we see two points we are not free to see anything else
except a straight line."[59]

Nevertheless, there is no logically necessary relation between the regularity of perception and the constitution of the
physical world since other equally consistent perceptions are
conceptually possible. Therefore no definite conclusions about
the physical world can be drawn from perception. Here we must
see imagination as an indissoluble mixture of external stimulae
and human reactions which owes its makeup to both. It is "the
link of action and reaction between the world and my thought";[60]
and, in the imagination, "the world and my mind are so thoroughly
mixed that if I believe I am thinking of one of them alone, I
am also attributing to it what belongs to the other".[61]

From all of this Weil then concludes:

> The very nature of the relationship between ourselves
> and what is external to us, a relationship in a reaction,
> a reflex, is our perception of the external world. Per-
> ception of nature, pure and simple, is a sort of dance;
> it is this dance which makes perception possible for
> us.[62]

This account of perception as a reflexive reaction to the
external world which establishes a basic relation between the
world and man is quite consistent, but it still does not give
a full account of human activity. At most, it is so far only a
description of man as conditioned by the environment. Admittedly,
human action has been found in the very act of perception, yet
this is basically no more than reaction to the world and implies

neither any distinct human initiative nor any sort of creation
by man of his own conditions of existence. And, yet, man is not
simply conditioned by the material conditions of existence external to him, even on a materialist point of view, nor is he
limited to immediate contact with the world in order to have
knowledge of it. For in so-called intellectual operations, men
are able to deal with a world that is not immediately present,
and thus, are able to some extent, create their own conditions
of existence, both vis-a-vis the world and themselves in a society.

It is by the means of language, Weil contends, that man can
be split into a dual nature of an active and passive being, who
can create conditioned reflexes in himself and examine his own
ideas. We shall treat each in turn.

If some sort of idea of pre-societal man were to prevail,
then perhaps all that could be said of such a creature, according
to the account of perception given above, is that his action
would be simply a reaction to his physical conditions of existence as entailed by his biological needs. But such a creature
has never existed; or, if he has, he would be thoroughly inaccessible to us now. Man is at his roots a social being, as
Aristotle quite rightly claimed, and if he organically possesses
some innate reflexes and instincts, the greater part of his behavior is conditioned by the human environment in which he ma-
tures. The major tool of this conditioning is language, and in
this sense, man possesses through language the means of creating
conditioned reflexes for himself.

What makes language particularly human is its very artifi-
ciality and social nature. Other than spontaneous ejaculations
and onomatopaeia, words bear no natural connection or resemblance
to the things of which they speak; rather, "the relation of words
to things are conditioned reflexes"[63] and conditioned solely
through the society. In this sense, language is "artificial in
relation to the individual (but natural for the society)."[64]

It is important here that the relation between a society
and an individual be elucidated in order to understand Weil's
contentions about the way that man creates his own conditions
of existence. She claims that "society is not an aggregate of

of individuals; the individual is something that comes after
society, who exists through society; it is society plus something
else."[65] The reasoning behind this claim is based in her belief
that general ideas naturally precede particular perceptions, and
in this sense Man precedes men. Because no primal individual
can be found, it makes no sense to speak of him; rather, in any
reference to either Man in general or men in particular one must
first speak of both being biologically and socially conditioned
in a common way. In this manner, then, no individual can ever
begin to come to light until his most general aspects have been
considered, i.e. what he is as Man, and this means Man as he has
created himself through social structures as well as what is
biologically entailed for him. The breadth of this consideration
is as wide as the language of any society under examination. As
Weil notes, "language itself already contains thoughts. . . .
So due to language, we are steeped in an intellectual environment. . . . Insofar as we give expression to a state we are in,
it becomes something that belongs to the experience of all men."[66]
The argument is two-armed; philosophically, we are obliged to
speak of Man before we consider individuals; socially, every
individual finds, through existing in a society, a primary order
of general ideas already set for him and in which he participates
through his use of language.

Despite this insistence on a temporal priority of society
over the individual, Weil does see individuals arising out of
it by the means of the ability to see particulars as particulars,
and not simply as general ideas or occasions for a pre-determined
reflexive action. "It is the contemplation of particular things
that elevates a man and distinguishes him from animals. Animals
never distinguish between an object and its utility."[67] If it
were otherwise, human language would be no more than a complicated
version of the ritual dances that bees go through as a call for
mating. And, in fact, human language does not always call for
action for it may only call for further words, and quite often,
an examination of language itself and the appropriateness of
certain words. It is only the individual who can so apply words
in certain particular orders, although the words may have a
general logic of application, to describe things. A child who

is reared using the language of Shakespeare will hardly produce
King Lear; it is only Shakespeare who can do that, even though
the language he spoke was accessible and understandable to everybody. It is in this sense that Weil makes the claim, which is
only apparently paradoxical, that "the individual only exists
through society and society derives its value from the individual."[68] Every man is first conditioned by his environment, physical and social, but at the same time by arising to individuality
through examination of particulars he is, in turn, able to create
and be something of value for the society. It is in this same
vein that Weil claims in her analysis of oppression that "the
enlightened goodwill of men acting in an individual capacity is
the only possible principle of social progress."[69] Society, by
itself, cannot change its general ideas whether oppressive or
not; an individual, however, can examine these ideas and provide
a new order for them from which the society can benefit.

   Because language is capable of creating reflexes and thus
establishing a relation of words to things by its fixed, permanent and artificial nature, it also possesses a reality of its
own in the sense that through language we can deal with a world
that is not immediately present. It, in effect, constitutes a
second way other than physical action in which we come to grasp
the world, and a second kind of relationship between ourselves
and things. Whereas action *simpliciter* possesses no inherent
order insofar as the relations which it establishes are subordinate to bodily needs that are immediate and contingent, "language enables us to lay down relationships which are completely
foreign to our needs."[70] It alone can give us method and order
so that through language we can "construct an order of things
which depends entirely on ourselves."[71] Strangely enough, this
order which we construct then appears to us as that which is
most objective and necessary, for it is this order established
by the convention of language that creates our responses to the
world. Thus our most immediate needs can be set aside in the
face of this higher objectivity and necessity.

   This view of language would allow man to live in a world
completely ordered to his existence were it not for the fact
that the material reality of the world external to him and his
social being constantly impinged on it. For this reason Weil

insists on a distinction between the order given by language
and the reality of which it is an order.[72]   Language provides us
with a world ordered to ourselves to which our action is made
to correspond, but unless language in turn is reinformed by
action it loses any real order it might have.   Language by itself
exercises no power over the external world; it is only action
that brings the power and reality to it which allows language
to perform an ordering function.   If it were otherwise and language did possess real power by itself, the very saying would be
its own accomplishment and there would be no disjunction between
desire and fulfillment.   In this case, any sort of order would
have to disappear for there would be no problem in literally
having one's cake and eating it, too.   Or, in Weil's words, "If
in actions there was nothing except what we ourselves suppose
them to contain, nothing would ever get done, since there would
be no snags."[73]

A fuller explanation of the relation between method and order in language and action may be made by a clarification of
Weil's notions of reality and obstacles.   Initially, she gives
a negative definition of reality as obstacle when she says, "It
is what is not contained in the problem as such; reality is what
method does not allow us to foresee."[74]   On this account, it
would appear that we have, on the one hand, a perceptual objective order given by language, and on the other hand, a notion of
reality which constantly opposes order.   This would seem to lead
to the paradoxical, if not absurd, conclusion that reality is
not and cannot be objective, nor can objectivity be real.
Whereas man in order to be delivered from the caprices of his
own immediate needs creates an ordered world for himself in language, at the same time he also finds in the laws of nature un-
moving obstacles which are thoroughly foreign to his desires,
ordered or otherwise.   Yet, Weil does not want to claim that the
only alternatives open to man are blindly subjecting himself to
the caprices of nature by abandoning his ordered world, or remaining in his ordered world and finding constant disappointment.
Nor does she want to claim a simple fortuitous coincidence between the two.   Rather, what she does want to claim is that a
third alternative exists, for, although order and reality may be

different things, they, nevertheless, may be brought into a relation with each other by means of reflection. By means of reflection one may encounter unexpected reality and adjust his
responses accordingly without abandoning order.

     A simple example will help to show that in which a relation-
ship is established between order and reality which does not
conflate the two. In a board game, such as backgammon, a formal
order is established (the social order of general ideas), the
following of which will lead a player to bear all his markers
off the board, which is the stated goal of the game. By following these rules, a player's stance towards the board is established and in accordance with the rules he proceeds inexorably
towards the goal. His desires to move backwards or flip markers
about at random are contained; in fact, as long as he can be
said to be playing the game, such desires are completely van-
quished. If this were all that there were to the game, however,
it would ultimately be pointless to begin playing insofar as
the end is necessarily assured. But the player has to meet
reality in the form of another player who creates an obstacle
to the goal and whose stated duty is to thwart the opposition at
every opportunity. The first player has three choices. He may
proceed on his own, acting as if the opposition were not there
(children often play this way, which is one of the major reasons
that they lose and then wonder why). Second, he may completely
forget the object of the game and resign himself to moving only
when forced to do so (a child who has lost many games in a row).
Or, third, he may develop a strategy which is both in accordance
with the formal rules and goals of the game and which takes into
account the play of the opposition (perception of particulars).
In this case he is clearly not just following rules or reacting
to the opposition, nor is he compromising between the two. Instead, he has begun to play in accordance with a method that has
taken all factors into account. One must carefully note what
has happened. Initially, he simply counts the number on his
dice and moves that number of spaces in the indicated direction.
This may be no more than a stimulation response which any higher
primate could be taught. He then encounters the opposition,
but rather than ignoring it or regarding it as an evil force,
he is able to conceive it as also operating according to certain

rules and within set limits. With this in mind he then juxtaposes
the possibilities entailed in the rules for both himself and his
opponent and decides on an appropriate course of action which
either circumvents his opponent's obstacle (because the opponent
is obliged to wait his turn or only to move in certain ways) or
to use that obstacle to his own advantage. In short, in building
his strategy he has begun to reason. In doing so, he has not
simply acted according to the order of his first ideas (the
rules of the game) but has examined these ideas by means of other
ideas (his conception of his opponent's play and his knowledge
of dice probability). He has not done this idly, however, but
rather has done it because of the obstacle his opponent has set,
and thus the obstacle becomes the critical object for thought
and reasoning.

It is through the examination of his own ideas that man's
nature of mind and body first appears for man is not only able
to create his own conditioned reflexes but is also able to stand
back from this conditioned activity and judge himself and his
ideas. Yet, it is not the case that all that goes by the name
of reasoning or mental operations entitles one to infer or assume
that mind is a distinct substance from matter. In fact, most
ordinary reasonings, which are generally syllogisic, are no more
than the rules of language, and as such, are conditioned responses.[75] As such, this view of reasoning fits quite nicely
with the assumptions of materialism. But this is not the sort
of reasoning by which Weil claims to indicate mind; rather, for
her, mind first shows itself in man's ability to understand his
own understanding and to impose an order upon it in accordance
with standards of necessity and perfection which cannot be derived from any material considerations whatsoever. For Weil, it
is only reasoning that conceives and judges according to necessity that bears the hallmark of mind. Two things, however, are
required to back this claim; one, that a person can conceive an
actual infinity, perfection or necessity; two, that this idea
cannot be derived from the material conditions of existence.
Weil's demonstration of these points are, in the main, to be
found in *Science et Perception dans Descartes*.[76]

In this essay Weil undertakes a meditation as a "new
Descartes . . . who has in common with (the first Descartes) only

being a human being and of having the resolve of believing only in oneself."[77] This 'new Descartes' begins an examination of how she knows the world through the senses and ideas. But in both cases, she finds only chaos and contingency. On the one hand, as regards knowledge of the world through the senses, all that can be said of the matter is that it is an experience of pleasure or pain. "These things which are so intimately present to me are only there by the presence of a inseparable feeling of my own existence. . . ."[78] On the other hand, knowledge by ideas "is no less a chaos than the world of sensations,"[79] for absolutely nothing seems to assure her that there is any correspondence between things and the properties that ideas would impose on them.

> Why is the fact that two pairs of oranges make four
> oranges something graspable by me and two pairs making
> five, not? I am thus. But why I am thus I do not see
> any way of apprehending since I recognize that my thoughts
> cannot inform me about anything, except myself.[80]

There is not really any doubt here about the existence of a world external to her, just as there is not in Descartes. What is at stake, however, is what she can truly say about that world, or, more accurately, what she can say about the relation between its appearance as her experience and that which is in the external world that causes the particular reaction. Both biological factors and the customs and prejudices given by society in language set up a screen between her and the world through which she cannot peer. The external world thus exercises a continual power over her and whatever power, in turn, she exercises over it is quite determined by the appearance which it makes upon her. The external world is not illusory; where illusion enters in is in the belief that the appearance has anything to do with the reality. As she says: "Man begins, not by ignorance, but by error."[81] Any action taken on this belief can only have contingent results, for the power inherent in any action undertaken through the screen is only indirect, and insofar as it is based on a belief that may well be illusory, has only illusory power.[82]

Nevertheless, in one thing she does find a power in herself that is not illusory nor the result of illusion, namely the

power that she can exercise over belief, for she has the power
either to refuse or neglect it. The sensations and ideas im-
pressed on her do not have to correspond to anything; they may,
indeed, be the work of an evil demon. As such, while she has
little control over the fact that she has such sensations and
ideas she can still deny that they correspond to anything and
in this sense she does have a power over them. Through this
exercise of the power of doubting she then comes to recognize
her own individual existence, for "I can, therefore I am. . . .
Existing, thinking, understanding, are only aspects of a single
reality: being able (pouvoir)."[83] This is to say, she exists as
a substantial agent and not simply as the confluence of otherwise unrelated impressions and ideas. She exercises a genuine
power over these things, for if they impress her in a certain
manner, or more simply, are in her head, and tend her towards
the belief of their real existence, having the properties of
their appearances, she has the opposing power to deny that belief. Although the agency of the self has been demonstrated
solely in a negative fashion, it would be a false inference to
conclude that the self is therefore non-identifiable. The doubt
which is implied here is neither the doubt that there are
thoughts nor the doubt of existences independent of the self,
but rather is a doubt of the connection between the two. (In
fact, to doubt the connection makes doubting independent existences absurd, for once the connection is gone so is the possibility of saying anything about independent existences one way
or another.) In this way, the self has a certain power over external existences, not in terms of their existence *per se*, but
over their power to determine completely our thoughts and be
both subject and object of those thoughts. Therefore in the
'pouvoir' of doubting belief about things, the self can be identified as a thinking being, or the subject of thought.

The transition from doubt to the identification of the self
as a thinking being is effected because, whereas the self cannot
create or destroy the objects of its thought, but only deny the
belief connecting them with the properties which thought would
give them, there has never been such a belief that thought *qua*
thought has any independent existence from herself. Thus the
relation of thinker and thought in the subject does not depend

on any sort of illusory connection. If it were otherwise, doubt
could deny itself, which is a manifest absurdity. In this case,
then:

> Insofar as it is only a question of my thought and not
> of the things which I think, willing is self-efficacious,
> and it does not have any other effect than willing
> itself. Willing and acting here are but one.[84]

Because of the power of doubt and the consequent identification of the self as the subject of thought, she discerns
through thought that she is a unique witness to her own existence. "The things that I think cannot testify about anything
outseide of me. To the self which thinks, I am the unique witness."[85] She can, then, even go so far as to discard momentarily
the supposition that there is any other existence. Even if an
evil demon pressed thoughts on her, she has no need of these
illusions to recognize her own existence, for as long as her
willing to think or not think them remains, as it does always,
she can be assured of her own existence, independent of all
others, which is also to say, whether anything else exists or
not. Self-agency is thus complete and established, for "this
power does not allow degrees any more than existence itself
does. And I have recognized this power to be identical with
existence. I can, as I exist, absolutely."[86] The self as agent,
therefore, finds within itself an infinite power, and its very
reality depends on this infinity of power. In this regard, the
self appears equal to God Himself, for there is no limit to the
willing, positively or negatively, to think desires, sensations
or reasonings.

At the same time, however: "I need to recognize limits to
this ability of mine, infinite in nature. My sovereignty over
myself, which is only absolute when I want to suspend my thought,
disappears when it is a matter of giving myself something to
think."[87] From this, she, therefore, concludes that there must
be another existence separate from herself, for if no real power
by itself is limited,[88] and her self is obviously limited in
some respect (and not degree), it must be limited by another
existence or agent. This agent is God or 'toute-puissance.'
Although Weil does not fully explain why this other existence
or agent must be God, instead of another finite agent like

herself, the reasoning, I believe, goes something like this. As
an agent she is clearly not dependent upon anything in order to
will and therefore exist; but, at the same time, she cannot
create the objects of her thought, and thus her will while absolute with respect to itself, is limited in respect to the
existence of other things, and this limitation can only be made
by another power. Clearly no finite agent could do this, for
it would suffer from the same limitations as she does; the other
agent is limited because it does not create her as the object
of its thought. Similarly, she cannot create herself as the object of any other agent's thought insofar as this would first
require the creation of another agent's existence, which she can
neither do nor be obliged to have belief in. In this case, the
only thing which could then both limit her (and thus make itself
known as another existence or, put differently, make itself an
object of thought) and have its own power as an agent would be
the infinite 'toute-puissance.' In order, then, to understand
one's own self agency in the absolute power of denial is to
recognize the existence of the all powerful, without which the
finite agent's power would be non-existent.[89]

Once the self's agency as a thinking being and the 'toute-
puissance' have been established, both the criteria for the existence of mind are met as well as the discernment of the standard of Necessity for all reasonings of the mind. Although the
materialist refutation of this account would be that the notion
of 'toute-puissance,' perfect being (as complete [τέλειος]
agency), or Necessity is derived from an ever increasing progression of imperfect powers, this objection will not do. As Weil
claims:

> This is right, but the progression in itself necessarily
> contains what is infinite; it is in relation to the
> perfect straight line that one can say that such and
> such a straight line is less twisted than some other--
> and with this the series would not have any sense . . .
> There is a complete break between thought and what is not
> thought, because either one conceives the infinite or
> one does not conceive it at all.[90]

This is to say, the notion of perfection cannot be derived from
material considerations, simply because matter cannot provide
its own standard of judgment. This is an irreducible human

activity, and Mind, therefore, comes into play whenever Necessity
is applied in thinking.

Through judgments rendered according to Necessity, the
self is then given a certain power over the world, for while
thoughts of *things* are not created by the thinking self, the
self has the power of doubt and liberty to deny them, unless it
can conceive of them according to Necessity. In this case they
can be seen to participate in the 'toute-puissance.' To deny the
thoughts which bear this mark is to deny the very ground on which
human agency is founded. To affirm them is to attain true human
agency.

> Said otherwise, on the one hand, as another existence
> has power over me by the intermediary of my thoughts,
> on the other hand, I have power over it by the same
> intermediary . . . I can also indeed say that all thoughts
> that I call clear and distinct are true, which is to
> say, all thoughts of which the 'I think therefore I am'
> is the model. Insofar as I affirm such thoughts I am
> infallible. It is God who guarantees this infallibil-
> ity.[91]

Although one cannot give an answer to the question of "why
these things rather than others" (this reason resides in God
alone) but must simply say that it is so, given that these
thoughts are the ones which we have, so far as they bear the
mark of necessity (such as the relation of cause and effect)
one in assuming them can also maintain his liberty, for that
which gives them this mark is also that which gives the self its
power. Man has power over nature, because in encountering obstacles of his environment, by conceiving them according to
necessity he can then turn them to his advantage.[92] When man
understands necessarily that forces in certain relationships
can be used to balance each other, he can then place his building
materials together in that relationship and construct his machines and houses. Through conceiving of his material conditions
of existence according to necessity, man then takes his rightful place in the world, and not the one handed to him by accident.

> It is only those actions and thoughts which have a
> necessity about them that are truly human. Whenever
> one does not have to act, one must avoid those actions
> and thoughts which have no necessity about them. A

> thought without necessity is a prejudice. But one
> has to distinguish between those prejudices which we
> can do without and those we cannot do without.[93]

3. *Mediation in Thought, Morality, and Work*

We have seen so far Weil's consideratons of man as he
stands in relation to matter and to himself. We have seen in
Weil's critique of Marxism how man from his primitive beginnings
to his present situation has attempted to gain mastery over matter and has only succeeded in making himself its slave. We
have seen how man is conditioned through his material relations
to the external world through his body and how through his society he conditions himself by means of his language and the primary order which it provides for him. But, we have also seen
how the explanations of materialism ultimately fail to explain
all of man's nature, for, on Weil's account, man exists as a
free agent in the world through his will's ability to deny and
affirm the thoughts which are pressed upon him. In this way a
dual nature of man obtains, but one of which the relationship
of the two elements appears as at least paradoxical, if not
thoroughly incommensurate. On the one hand, we see man as existing by the concatenation of material elements, seemingly in
perpetual servitude to them, and on the other hand, as a being
that is essentially mind and born for freedom. Weil's attempt
to reconcile these two disparate factors culminates in her doctrine of mediation, which is an attempt to put mind over matter,
without destroying either end of the problem. This reconciliation will, in turn, lead towards a solution of the problem of
oppression.

Weil was certainly not the first to recognize these problems, and the attempts to solve them have been legion. Unfortunately, Weil contended, that in order to reach their conclusions most offered solutions have either tended to idealism by
suppression of the object of knowledge, or to materialism by
suppression of the knowing subject, despite strenuous dialectical
exercises on the part of everybody involved. In her attempt to
maintain the integrity of the knowing subject and known object
Weil embodies and relates in one position certain elements of
various philosophic schools. She has the 'intentionality' of

the phenomenologists and the material social relations of Marx,
as well as a certain form of freedom of the will found in existentialism. Her position, however, can never be placed totally
in any one of these schools.

This independence is particularly seen in her difference
from Sartre's existential freedom; a difference that is worth
noting since the two of them both have roots in Cartesianism.
For Sartre, man's freedom of will is his all, and in order to
establish his values he must keep himself from capitulating to
the exigencies of his material environment. He says in his famous essay, *Existentialism is a Humanism*:

> All kinds of materialism lead one to treat every man,
> including oneself, as an object-that is as a set of
> predetermined reactions, in no way different from the
> patterns of qualities and phenomena which constitute a
> table, or a chair, or a stone. Our aim is precisely
> to establish the human kingdom as a pattern of values
> in distinction from the material world.[94]

To will freely man must never give in, even if this means the
active desiring to "surpass the limitations . . . of the necessities of being in the world, of having to labor and die there."[95]
Weil presents a strong contrast to Sartre. Where he saw it as
an evil "that hinders man's freedom ever to consider man materially or to make him in any way a material object, "Weil often
quotes Bacon's phrase: "We cannot command Nature except by
obeying her."[96]

> For if one were to understand by liberty the mere absence
> of all necessity, the word would be emptied of all concrete
> meaning; but it would not then represent for us that which,
> when we are deprived of it, takes away the value from life.
> . . . True liberty is not defined by a relationship be-
> tween desire and satisfaction, but by a relationship be-
> tween thought and action.[97]

For Weil there is simply no question of mind operating outside
or despite the conditions of existence. What is a serious question for her, however, is how to get mind to work within the
conditions of existence. In short, it is a question of the
mediation of mind in the world.

Since Kant at least, if any sort of mediation is claimed
it is usually in the sense that either through innate categories
of the mind, intentionality, or linguistic habit the world as

phenomenon is interpreted and mediated by human intellectual or
social activity. This is certainly an idea to which Weil held,
but far more as a given than as a problem. For her, thoughts do
arise from the coincidental influence of an external object and
the way in which this influence is received in the human subject.
In this sense, thoughts are intermediaries between mind and the
world of matter, for they stand between the subject and the
world, and owe their existence to both.[98] Here a major difference with an existentialist such as Sartre appears. Whereas for
Sartre the willing and consequent appearance of the human subject
occurs despite the material world (and almost as spite for it),
for Weil, willing and the appearance of mind only occur through
the medium of matter. For this reason, the chief characteristics
of mind are all purely negative, for

> 1. Its duality does not involve two existent things.
> We can never lay hold of what it is in us that isolates
> our thoughts and makes judgments about them.
> 2. Perfection, infinity. . . . The only mark of God
> in us is that we feel we are not God. We feel that we
> should not be imperfect and limited; if it were per-
> fectly right and proper to be so, then we would not
> think ourselves imperfect; we feel that this imperfec-
> tion is alien to us.
> 3. Necessity points to mind well enough, but what we
> grasp is the necessity of things. There would be no
> necessity if the mind did not bring it to the surface.
> The world appears as an obstacle to the mind.[99]

Neither mind nor liberty appears simply because we have
thoughts; where it does appear, however, is in our ability to
think thoughts clearly and according to necessity. That the
objects of thought appear in thought through the imagination in
such and such a manner, due to our biological sensibilities or
social conditioning, is something over which we have no control.
Where we do have control is in the way in which we allow these
thoughts to be ordered and the consequent action which we take
upon them. One can either act upon the primary conditioned order
given in the imagination which are a mass of confusions and prejudices which continue to enforce oppression as well as common
sense notions, or one can take these thoughts and, through the
working of the mind, attempt to discern a necessary order in
them and then act only on that which mind has deemed necessary.
In a word, man's goal is to reach an understanding of the

relationship between his thoughts, which understanding if denied
would mean a thorough undercutting of his own freedom. In this
sense, man gains mastery over the world only by becoming the
master of his own soul. If man does not have control over his
own thoughts by virtue of his mind, he cannot have anything but
an accidental control of the object of thought. Through thought
as an intermediary between the self as mind and the world, mind
can then gain mastery over the world through that intermediary.

The ideal state of human freedom in this case would be one
in which mind had perfect consciousness and control over thought
and in which actions proceeded quite automatically from that
consciousness of thought. Weil wants to take this as far as the
extent to which the person's thoughts and actions are objective
to himself, which includes the so-called subconscious, for insofar as the subconscious consists of repressed thought and not
'minute perceptions' of which we could not possibly be aware, it
falls under the purview of the responsibility of mind.

> We can say that thought is essentially conscious, but that
> one can always prevent oneself from formulating it com-
> pletely. There is a confusion in such ideas because one
> does not want to make them clear, but in the case of the
> subconscious, the consciousness which one has of these
> thoughts is not obscure. Repression consists in calling
> something by another name, for example, the ambitious man
> will call his ambition "public good". . . .
> One has every right to reproach someone for his subcon-
> scious thoughts; one has the right, and even the duty,
> to do so in one's own case; one has a duty to control
> them. . .
> We are completely responsible for the degree of clarity
> there is in our own thoughts; we do not always make the
> necessary effort to become so. . . . . So in reality,
> psychological and moral consciousness are one and the
> same.[100]

This account of the mediation of mind in thought and action
only presents what the ideal state of freedom would be. As
such it remains slightly abstract and not completely pellucid
regarding how this sort of mediation can be accomplished. Despite the fact that this mediation presents a consistent way of
taking all material and intellectual factors of human existence
into account, it would remain only a "likely story" unless it
can be shown that mind can, indeed, supply a necessary order for
action and make some sense of the mass of impressions and ideas

found in the imagination. This is not a task of great ease, for
of all the sensations and ideas that the imagination presents to
be ordered, there is precious little that is not due to the grip
that the world has on the imagination. None of these sensations
have anything to them in which the mind can find a necessary
order.

"In every way, the ideas that I have indeed represent the
presence of the world to me and not the grip that I have on the
world, for they are formed in me, at least in part, despite
me."[101] What is needed is to find something by which we can represent the world in a necessary order and thus gain a grasp on
it which enables our liberty in the world.

Fortunately, Weil argues, the imagination does have one
means of representing the world which irreducibly belongs to the
human subject; namely, the lines and numbers of mathematics.
Because these mathematical representations are not due to the
constant influence of the world, being rather consistent ways
we represent the world, they are prime candidates for mind to
find a necessary order therein. When a necessary order is then
discerned in mathematics a paradigm case can be established for
the understanding since here we have a grasp on the world that
is not dictated by the world's grasp on us. Two things need to
be noted, though, about the way Weil uses mathematics. First,
the mathematical representations are not separate entities unto
themselves, but are symbols of things, although they are quite
flexible in their application. Second, the order inherent in
these symbols, which is thought by mind, is an order *of* the
representations. While this order is not a part of the set of
representations (it does not appear without the mind thinking
it), neither is it divorcible from it (the mind needs the object
in which to find order).

It is then by thinking the world through the intermediary
of mathematics that a necessarily ordered representation of the
world can be obtained in which we know the world through being
able to see its inter-related limits under the *toute-puissance*
and in which mind has perfect consciousness and control in
thought. This then provides for intelligent, methodical action
upon the world. But here it is important to remember two

things: one, we do not exercise any direct domination over the
world since in thinking even our clearest thoughts we are dealing
with an intermediate and indirect representation of the world;
and two, that mind only appears in an otherwise material being
through its mediation in a necessary order of matter, whether
that matter is in the representations of the imagination or in
the physical action directed by that representation.

The representation of the world provided by mathematics
then provides the subject's grasp on matter which can be formed
by the mind into a necessary order. Mathematics is, then, first
and foremost for Weil, a set of symbols or representations of
the world which are essential tools of mind for mind to grasp the
world. Because mathematics is such a tool, Weil felt that science should not be simply an abstract translation of experience
or experiment, which at its highest levels has itself for its
object; rather science should be that which constitutes mind's
own expression in the world and its grasp on it. While Weil
would not have disagreed with the idea that there is a myriad
of *possible* mathematical explanations of experience at the same
time she felt that some were more valuable, and even more real
and true, than others, insofar as they give us a better grasp
on the world in which we live. The Necessity which mind needs
to find is not just logical necessity, but the necessity of this
world. She says:

> What is in accordance with formal conditions is possible;
> what is in accordance with the material conditions of
> experience is real; that whose [sic] agreement with the
> real is determined according to the general conditions
> of experience is necessary.[102]

When a man clearly analyzes and organizes his thought so
that he understands the necessity of it vis-a-vis his world, he
exists as one who has gained mastery of his own self and who
has created his own conditions of existence as fully as possible.
He has realized the liberty for which he is meant.[103] But it is
important to understand that he has done this, like a first rate
artist, by having undertaken to conceive clearly the reality of
the world in which he lives and to reconstruct and represent it
in a form which makes it human. The truth of his mind's liberty
is found in its ability to conquer and reign over the human realm

on a human scale. In this sense, truth and liberty, as well as
beauty, are, for Weil, a relation between mind, our particular
sensibilities and the world itself. Voltaire's Micromegas would
indeed have difficulty finding the same things to be beautiful
that we do, and a man only a millioneth of a millimeter tall
would certainly have an entirely different physics than ours.
Gulliver discovered this, but even so this does not make truth
and beauty only relative and therein vacuous. What does happen,
however, is that because of our limitations, in order to find
truth, beauty and liberty we must construct our art, science and
other activities to a human measure which allows men to find
them. When such things as productive systems are constructed
on a larger than human scale, as they inevitably are when men
seek only an increase of power, they cannot help but be oppressive since they contain nothing for mind to hold onto that is
within its scope of thought. What is needed then to reduce
oppression is to put things back into scale where workers can
understand their labor. In short, to make work man's own by
allowing him to take charge of his own actions in it.

Once clear and necessary thought becomes apparent as that
by which man takes charge of himself, the entire concept of un-
derstanding-the-world begins to merge with morality, for it is
through this knowledge of the necessity of the world that man is
delivered from the caprices of the influence of matter on him
and finds liberty, truth, and beauty. As Weil notes: "The whole
of morals is to be found potentially in mathematics; one has to
overcome one's tendency to allow oneself to depend on chance,
which is the sin of sins, the sin against the Spirit."[104] In
this her conception of morality strongly (and self-confessedly)
tends towards Kant, the Stoics, and most notably Platonism; commenting on Socrates, she says: "For Socrates, virtue and clear
thoughts come from the same source, from the same power within,
conscience."[105]

It is not immediately obvious, however, why this correlation
of knowledge and virtue obtains, or even what exactly it is meant
to say. Is knowledge virtue because it insures an autonomy to
the action of the person which escapes the heteronomy of
nature? Or, said otherwise, is the goal of knowledge a sort of

mastery of the world? Weil did not think so for she did not
believe that morality arises simply from the power that knowledge
brings. Instead, virtue and knowledge are correlated for a
three-fold reason. They are first correlated because there can
be no human virtue without knowledge, since thinking the world
according to necessity is what makes man an acting subject distinct from pure matter. This exercise of thought gives birth
to knowledge, but, concomitantly, the act of thinking according
to necessity is also man's reaching out for perfection in the
dual sense that such thinking is a perfection of man's being,
and that what is thought is the perfection of the *toute-puissance*
which encompasses the world within its limits making each thing
what it is. It is in this sense that Weil says, "perfection is
a duty"; that is, it is a goal of both thought and action, which
if strived for by a human being produces human virtue and knowledge. Virtue and knowledge thus spring from the same source.
Second, the two are correlated in a negative sense in that not
to think is to deny oneself as the subject of one's own actions.
"A reasonable being is an end in himself insofar as he is a
being who thinks. To sacrifice oneself as a thinking being is
the destruction of virtue."[106] Finally, the two are correlated
because in thinking according to Necessity we not only establish
our own subject, but we also no longer act out of caprice, dis-
regarding the limits of our own being and those of others. As
long as we live in this world we will always act; the choice is
whether we will do so by directing our thought towards perfection and then mediating it into appropriate actions, submitting
to things as they exist in the light of the *toute-puissance*, or
whether we will act as if our desire had no limit.

By this line of reasoning, then, avoidance of heteronomity,
autonomy or mastery of nature *per se* do not constitute the fundamental categories of morality or its goal; rather, at best,
they should be considered as an outcome of the perfection of
thought. If man were constituted by anything other than mind,
or if the force of the world were such that man was always driven
on by nature, they would have no place in human morality.

> One doesn't have to oppose "self-mastery" to "mastery of
> the world"; what one has to do is to oppose "the attempt
> to master oneself" to "the attempt to gain mastery of the

world". That is the meaning of what is said in the
Gospel: "Seek ye first the kingdom of God and His
righteousness and all these things will be added unto
you."[107]

The lines of duty towards oneself and others may be drawn through
this correlation of virtue and knowledge. As regards duties to
oneself, one must "subordinate everything to this highest of
ends; thinking. Even if one were alone in the world there would
be a reason for living."[108] Because perfection is a duty, one
must direct all action from clear thought and never reverse the
relationship such that thought becomes the servant of material
passions or desires. As regards one's duties to others, these
duties are "a mirror image of one's duties to oneself,"[109] although understood in a more negative sense. In the case of our
relations with others, it is obviously quite impossible to undertake to think on their behalf or to be their minds; what is possible, is to respect them as their own subjects and to love the
perfection of which they are capable of as thinking beings. In
this sense, Weil stresses one's moral dealings with neighbors
to be that of treating them always as ends, i.e. as rational
beings capable of perfection, and never as means.

Although this negative sense of one's duties to neighbors
continues throughout even Weil's later works, it is not, I believe, as cold as it may first seem and does require effort on
our part on our neighbors' behalf, even if it cannot extend so
far as to think for them. (For, in fact, to think for a neighbor, if not absurd, does, at least, involve making him the means
of exercising our own virtue.) Our own knowledge of the world
requires us to see other people as subjects of their own acts
who also need to act with conscience.[110] It is also a matter
of our knowledge to see what obstacles prevent others from understanding. It then becomes a duty not only to subject all
things within our own purview to thought, but also "to remove
for others the things which prevent them from understanding
things clearly."[111] The range of removing obstacles to others'
understanding is not at all slight, for one can assume it to
extend from the teacher's duty to present his lessons and
thoughts clearly in order that his students may also become free
rational beings, to revision of a social structure which

presently treats rational beings as means. In this sense, when
Weil claims that "the enlightened goodwill of men acting in an
individual capacity is the only possible principle of social
progress,[112] she is not only indicating the sources from which
one can hope for revision, but is also indicating that the man
of goodwill is the one who does undertake to remove obstacles as
a duty not only to himself but to others as well.

When we understand morality and thought as the proper mediation of mind, we also see the true ugliness of oppression. Oppression is not simply the material deprivation of the poor and
the material advantage of the rich; it is, above all, that which
forces man to act completely upon the material demands of the
undertaking with no exercise, or means of exercise, of mind.
When this exercise of mind is absent, no amount of material surplus will ever be able to compensate for this lack. In this
case even if Marx were correct in asserting a history moving inexorably towards a paradisial state where human needs and material production coincided perfectly, this state would hardly
entail any true freedom or thought whatsoever; at most, the
state would be one in which everybody was thoroughly content and
satisfied with being the complete object of matter. A state that
is concerned only with the material welfare of human beings and
does not rise above the collectivity, even at a level which reflects the optimum of material production, has, for Weil, little
to do with human dignity or freedom. As long as it is solely
material welfare to which one is devoted, whether personally or
for the sake of another, no exercise of virtue can be claimed
to be present.

There is a strong contention in Weil's later works where
Plato's influence is most felt that the necessities of this world
do not lead to goodness. The seeds of this thought, however,
are also present in the early works and it is helpful to note
them in order to clarify Weil's point that material welfare does
not lead to virtue. The idea at this point can be described
thus: On the one hand, there is a necessity in the world external
to man which is first made evident to him through the force and
power it exerts on him. It is not something he can change and
the world will proceed on its course, more or less, with or
without him. On the other hand, man as mind is also capable of

forming an inner representation of the Necessity which governs
all other necessities in his mind and ordering his thoughts and
actions according to it. Given this latter capability, he has,
then, the choice of "either blindly submitting to the spurs which
necessity pricks him on from outside, or else adapting himself
to the inner representation of it that he forms in his own mind;
and it is in this that the contrast between servitude and liberty lies."[113] Through the exercise of mind man finds himself
on the same side of the world as the *toute-puissance* which forms
the limits of the material world. This does not mean that man
can exert unlimited force to meet his material goals, but it
does mean that he no longer has to regard the obstacles of the
world as evil forces since they are what they are by the same
power that allows him his thought. Goodness for man in this
case is then the harmonization of all his thoughts and desires
and actions with the overarching Necessity. Here Weil goes beyond a Kantian ideal of imposing reason and embraces the Stoic
amor fati. For Weil, like the Stoics, reason has access to the
overarching Necessity of all worldly necessities, and this is
to be loved and submitted to, even if it entails suffering.

If is in this sense that Weil's ideal is not a state in
which matter coincided with human desire, but one in which human
desire coincided perfectly with all that happens according to
Necessity, even if this were not totally conducive to the material well-being of humans. Man's goal of exercising his mind
in reason is only achieved when the mind reaches out to discover
infinity, perfection and Necessity in the 'toute-puissance.'
In this way, Goodness is only realized when mind does think according to this standard, which, in turn, is to be loved for
its own sake. Not to love it is to deny one's own proper activity and ultimately to let external forces be one's destiny, even
if these forces themselves operate according to the same Necessity. Even in a materially paradisal state every individual
would find it a duty to love perfection, and this is something
which no social structure can by itself supply. In this sense,
a social structure cannot really even by considered 'good' except in the sense that it may be less oppressive or evil than
some other. Whenever a social structure does make its own

continuance a goal, even when it is materially perfected, it
can only subvert the individual's duty of perfection. In this
vein, Weil then further held that not only is it the individual
alone who, by an act of mind, can be the source of any real
change in the society, but also that the very idea of progress
in goodness and morality can only properly be applied to individuals. Whenever it is applied to either a historical process
or social evolution, the means of thought are illegitimately
substituted for its end. What is needed then for goodness is,
at all times, to exercise critically one's own thought.

> . . . to react against the subordination of the indi-
> vidual to the collectivity implies that one begins
> by refusing to subordinate one's own destiny to the
> course of history. In order to resolve upon under-
> taking such an effort of critical analysis, all one
> needs is to realize that it would enable him who did so
> to escape the contagion of folly and collective frenzy
> by reaffirming on his own account, over the head of
> the social idol, the original pact between the mind
> and the universe.[114]

Weil's insistence upon the mediation of mind up to this
point has been, in effect, the description of an ideal. Weil
certainly understood that it was an ideal, perhaps unrealizable,
which she was describing. But, for all that, she also saw a
genuine need to conceive such an ideal. On the one hand, "it
will be useful to conceive this ideal if we can discern at the
same time what it is that separates us from it, and what are the
circumstances that can cause us to move away from it or approach
near it."[115] On the other hand, it is also useful as "a scale
of values conceived outside time. . . . What one can do is to
refer to this scale such and such an aspect of social life, taken
at a given period."[116] Once the ideal of mind's taking possession of the world through its love of perfection is stated, the
question of the relation between the ideal and the real must
be raised in order to discover that which keeps us from the
ideal, and how, consequently, it may be more nearly approached.

There are at least two major areas in which a disjunction
appears between the ideal of perfection direction of human life
by the mind and the reality of man's material existence; one,
there is a disjunction between necessity conceived in the mind
and physical reality; two, there is somewhat of a mystery

attending the specific relations of mind and body in man himself. To each of these problems, Weil offers a means by which
the opposition between the two can be lessened through the specific mediation of mind in work.

The first problem concerning the disjunction between Necessity conceived in the mind and physical reality actually divides
itself into two problems. Initially, there is what Weil called
the 'infinite error' in the application of reasoning according
to necessity in the physical world. Whereas the mind, in say
the geometrical problem of the sum of the interior angles of a
triangle, is able to conceive clearly the necessity that this
sum is equal to the sum of two right triangles and thus build
further propositions on it, it is quite a different thing to
build houses using this knowledge since neither perfectly straight
lines nor triangles are ever to be found in the physical world.
It is in this sense that the application of reasoning to practice
involves an 'infinite error,' for the inner conception of Necessity formed by the mind deals with representations of the world,
such as straight lines, that have no exact counterpart in the
physical world, even if they are its representations.[117] Furthermore, because of the immense number of factors that comprise
the ensemble of physical problems, in dealing with physical
phenomena as soon as we encounter what we think to be a case of
triangle we also find that the lines of which it is composed
admit curves or are constituted by a series of many smaller
broken lines and that the whole thing is subject to constant
fluctuation by external factors that have never been considered.
In this sense, in building a house upon the clear conceptions
of Euclidean geometry, while we are acting upon an idea of Necessity and thus preserving our actions from contingency, we have
no real control over their results. Fortunately, Weil says, a
certain amount of success can obtain in our endeavors, despite
the 'infinite error,' because of "the relative stability that
persists athwart the blind cross-currents of the universe, on
the scale of the human organism, and which alone enables that
organism to subsist."[118] In this way, 'accuracy' can function
quite well in lieu of exactness.

We gain a certain amount of success in our endeavors because of the relative stability of the world on the human scale.

But the disjunction between exact thoughts and material actuality
which first appears in the attempt to apply mathematics bespeaks
a problem in the harmonization of the different aspects of man
himself. The problem arises because although mind can be found
in man's thoughts when he thinks mathematically, the imagination
has in it any number of other thoughts which are very much due
to the fluctuating influences of the external world. These
thoughts hardly show the operation of mind. Thus when the imagination does show these other thoughts (when it acts as what
Weil calls the *folle imagination*) man's total thought is split
between "the abstract reason which conceives necessity,"[119] which
is the subject's own action, and the thoughts in the face of
which man is passive. It would be one thing if all man's ideas
were mathematically exact, but it does not seem likely that he
will ever perceive the world entirely in terms of numbers and
lines. He will, in fact, always perceive other qualities such
as colors, tastes, etc., and when he does so they will help
determine his action. The problem then becomes how these two
dimensions of man's thought can be joined under the dominancy of
mind. It is not a question of eradicating these ideas of the
folle imagination but of being able to discipline and order them.

        To a certain extent, the mediation of mind in the thought
inherent in geometry and physics is the first attempt to rejoin
the two aspects by establishing a consistent and ordered representation of the world. A physics or geometry, however, cannot
perform the actual rejoining but only direct one how to do it.
The actual rejoining, according to Weil, has to be done through
work, that is, actual methodical action on the world which gives
rise to contingent perceptions. In work the contingent representations of the *folle imagination* are actually, and not just
theoretically, put into a necessary order in action. This has
a double result. First these perceptions can be disciplined
and then reformed through the habits which work directed from
the intermediary of thought gives. Second, through the intermediary of thought mind becomes operative in work and thus the
two aspects can be rejoined under the dominance of mind.

        Work, then, for Weil, constitutes 'the ultimate wisdom'
and the ultimate mediation of mind wherein all is subjected to

it and all shows its marks. It is the ultimate wisdom because
it is the true mastery of self and the sole power which man has
in the universe. But it is also the ultimate mediation of mind
because, even in this final rejoining of the two elements of
man in action, the grasp of mind on the material world does not
proceed directly from mind to satisfaction of the set project,
but rather, always proceeds indirectly through a system of intermediaries which mind discerns in the world outside of itself
and which it, in turn, orders for action. Man, unlike God, does
not attain the fulfillment of his desire, however rational, simply by thinking it. In order for mind to take its rightful
place in the physical world, it must first come down into thought
to conceive the world as it operates according to necessity in
its physical laws and then use those laws for physical action.
Even in such a simple instance as sheltering himself, man must
first understand the relative stability of certain sorts of material and the ways in which it can be organized to build a house.
By that understanding he can then establish a system of intermediaries, such as chopping down trees, piling one log upon
another in a certain order, etc., to be undertaken as action to
achieve his final goal. It is in this context that Weil often
quoted Kant's famous phrase: "The light-winged dove, when in its
free flight, it beats the air and feels its resistance, might
well believe that it would fly better in a void."[120] Man in his
intermediate actions might well believe that his thought would
be far more effective without having to worry about matter; but,
in fact, according to Weil, it is the physical world which provides the very means by which mind can have thought, through
which it can control man's life. Necessity is always necessity
of something, and without the medium of that object, mind would
have nothing on which to live.

It is in this sense that matter finally ceases to be an obstacle to man's freedom and becomes the means by which he achieves
that freedom. The matter of the external world possesses its own
existence independently of man, but once it presses itself upon
the imagination it becomes capable of being understood and ordered by mind. When, in turn this understanding is tailored
for action by establishing a system of intermediaries, man
through his methodical action gains power over matter. In this

way, mind is actually mediated twice; first in discerning the
necessity of certain representations of the world and secondly
by creating an order or strategy which is embodied in action.
Accordingly, the matter of methodical action becomes the complete
mediation of mind through its becoming the tool of mind for
achieving mind's rational goal.[121]

It is here that the description of mediation in Weil's earlier political and philosophical writings is complete. Mediation
in these early writings essentially means to establish man's
essential being as mind which directs all of a person's life.
It is mediation because whereas thought, perception and action
by themselves are only material relations between man and the
world, when mind is brought into play, it descends into them and
makes them intermediates between pure matter and the *toute-puissance* of the universe. Man's most essential aspect is that he
does exist as mind by participation in the *toute-puissance*. But
he also exists as matter and if he is ever to realize mind in a
material world he must bring mind to bear on all his activities
and make it come down into nature. This can be done, Weil
thought, for as she says of beauty: "It teaches us that mind can
come down into nature."[122] From here we shall now pass to Weil's
theological conception of mediation in which God mediates himself to the world, and show how she came to understand that mediation as being rooted in Christ's cross.

Before doing so, it will be worthwhile to indicate a theological area of mediation in Weil's early work which was never
sufficiently resolved by her; in good part, simply because it
was a question to which she did not attach a great deal of import. Within the bounds of the argument concerning the relationship of mind and body, there appears to be a certain leeway
in interpretation of the extent to which mind and body can be
harmonized. Weil saw this leeway as giving rise to two different
views, from which she drew the conclusion that there corresponded
to these views two different conceptions of God as being either
transcendent or immanent.

> Let us think of pantheism in connection with the Stoics.
> The question arises in connection with the opposition
> there is between a transcendent God (who is beyond our
> grasp) and an immanent God. Plato thought of God as

> transcendent. The question is one which is related
> to the ideas one has between the mind and the body.
> One thinks that there is a relationship (for the Stoics)
> of harmony between the mind and body just as one thinks
> there is one between God and the world. . . . (For
> Descartes) God is beyond ideas just as Plato's Good.
> . . . Descartes was a man of action, while the Stoics
> and St. Francis of Assissi were much more contemplative
> by nature.[123]

In Weil's own thinking at the period under consideration,
there is a curious blend of both these ideas. On the one hand,
there is a strong tendency in her, even at this point, towards
a Stoic contemplation of the world and a feeling of love for
that world in which all proceeded according to the mandates of
Necessity. On the other hand, she also has a strong tendency
towards a view of transcendence in which good remains beyond all
attempts to immanentize it completely. Here the immanence of
good may be an ideal, but even if not realized, the good loses
none of its attractive force.

While there is little evidence on which to decide as to
whether Weil definitely held to a transcendent good or an immanent one, if indeed she definitely held either, the early writings
do have a certain practical tendency to picture an ideal that
is more immanent than transcendent. Simone Pétrement writes of
Weil's religious beliefs during her time at the *École Normale*:

> All that one can conclude is that she seems to identify
> religion with morality. At this period, to believe in
> God is for her simply to act correctly. "God is presup-
> posed and posited by the right action, and in no other
> way." Belief is more the effect of courage and virtue.
> Morality is primary and unconditioned.[124]

What is notable about this view is that it very much depends
on the ability that man possesses to act morally and not to be
subdued unwillingly by circumstances. As long as this is within
a man's power, there is no need to go beyond his own powers of
thought to find goodness or truth; in fact, to do so might seem
like cowardice. But if the situation is such that man cannot find
goodness on his own, or if courage will not suffice to make the
'critical effort' of analysis, then, if goodness is to be found,
it must come from elsewhere. Weil found such a situation shortly
after finishing *Reflections concerning the Causes of Liberty and
Social Oppression*. This, in turn, paved the way towards her seeing goodness in human life as the mediation of the one transcendent good.

CHAPTER II

CHRIST THE MEDIATOR

It would be helpful in demonstrating an overall coherency
to the thought of Simone Weil if documents could be produced
from her writings which showed a clearly argued transition from
the impersonal God of *toute-puissance* to the God who meets all
who earnestly desire his salvation, and a similar transition from
mind to a religious conception of soul. Unfortunately, there
are not any such documents. This lacuna, however, is not accidental, for as Weil herself candidly wrote to Father Perrin in
1942:

> I may say that never at any moment in my life have I
> "sought for God" . . . As soon as I reached adolescence,
> I saw the problem of God as a problem the data of which
> could not be obtained here below, and I decided that the
> only way of being sure not to reach a wrong solution,
> which seemed to me the greatest possible evil, was to
> leave it alone. So I left it alone.[1]

It is evident in the light of this confession that in order
to show the transition from Weil's early years, so caught up in
the problems of politics and labor, to the later years in which
religious issues came to occupy the central place in her thought
we must have recourse to her biography. By bringing this biographical factor into play we can see how the philosophical
principles of Weil's early life led to certain actions, which,
in turn, brought her face to face with two factors that she had
not previously considered, the grace of God experienced through
contact with him and affliction. It was these two factors which
led her to expand the bases upon which the early principles stood
and to assert a theological meaning for them.

There is, I believe, a greater degree of plausibility obtained by this method of procedure than if Weil's conceptions
of God had proceeded strictly from a desire for a more inclusive
logical consistancy in her thought. Affliction, in particular,
presented a real obstacle to many of Weil's early beliefs.

Weil's first thoughts on mediation insisted on man's ability to make use of all that confronted him, at least morally. This, she reasoned is due to the very nature of mind. Even if the brutal forces of nature beset him on every side, man, by conceiving a necessary order to them, has the capability of being the subject of his own actions and never has to regard himself simply as the product of external forces. In Weil's eyes, doubting this is doubting mind itself. Yet, affliction, she found, does not seem to be able to be made use of. Its discovery, then, caused her to see certain limits to the possibilities of good inherent in the early views. The obstacle presented by affliction, however, neither caused her to totally abandon this view nor did she attempt to make affliction fit the early beliefs; rather, she discovered a reality beyond both.

In 1934, shortly after completing *Reflections on the Causes of Liberty and Social Oppression*, Weil took a year's leave of absence from her teaching post in order to work in a factory. Simone Pétrement explicitly states that the reasons for this decision lay mainly in Weil's belief that she had reached an impasse in her theoretical thought.[2] For a long time, Weil had written and meditated upon the problems of work and now felt that she must put her thoughts in this area into action. Furthermore, she felt that she had not found an adequate answer to the question of how one could coordinate factory work without oppressing the workers and, so, "where theoretical thought could not find a solution, actual contact with the object might suggest a way out."[3] In addition, she also hoped to find among the workers a spirit of comaraderie and friendship that she felt could only be had among equals engaged in a common enterprise.

From the point of view of fulfilling the goals set out at the beginning, this grand experiment was a failure. She found neither the solutions for which she was seeking nor the comaraderie she had so earnestly desired. She found, instead, the phenomenon she came to label 'affliction' (*malheur*). Weil was not physically up to the wort of work that factories demanded. Although she tried very hard, she was naturally clumsy and it was a small miracle that she escaped the experience with all of her limbs intact. Beyond clusiness she also suffered constant migraine headaches which racked her body and soul. In time, the

torture of the physical grind, plus the inhumanly appalling rate
of expected piecework, and the desire of her fellow workers simply to survive under any conditions wore her down and caused her
to question the sense of dignity which she had previously
thought herself to possess. She describes the effect of the experience in one poignant example:

> Upon leaving the dentist's office . . . and in getting
> on the W bus, a bizarre reaction. How is it that I, the
> slave, can get on the bus and ride it for 12 sous just
> like anybody else? What an extraordinary favor! If
> someone brutally forced me off, saying that these con-
> venient means of transportation were not for me, that I
> could only walk, I believe that would have seemed entirely
> natural to me. Slavery has made me lose all sense of
> having rights.[4]

By the end of the year in the factory, Weil, by a concen-
trated effort, managed to regain some sense of human dignity,
but a new one which fully comprehended the fragility of the elements that are commonly thought to compose it. She summarizes
the experience in a letter written to Albertine Thevenon in
1935:

> What working in a factory meant for me personally was
> as follows. It meant that all the external reasons
> (which I had previously thought internal) upon which
> my sense of personal dignity, my self-respect, was based
> were radically destroyed within two or three weeks by
> the daily experience of brutal contraint. And don't
> imagine that this provoked in me any rebellious reaction.
> No, on the contrary; it produced the last thing I expected
> from myself--docility. The resigned docility of a beast
> of burden . . . Slowly and painfully, in and through
> slavery, I reconquered the sense of my human dignity--a
> sense which relied, this time, upon nothing outside my-
> self and was accompanied always by the knowledge that
> I possessed no right to anything, and that any moment
> free from humiliation and suffering should be accepted
> as a favour, as merely a lucky chance.[5]

Previous to the factory experience Weil had understood that
much of the human psyche is based on the blind interplay of natural and social forces. She had then sought a way in which man
through mind could establish his seemingly rightful place in an
otherwise material world. In one way, the factory year did not
alter this belief. What it did do, however, was to make her
realize the extreme degree to which the human personality owed
its workings to force and power. It also implanted the notion

in her that these very forces and powers might very well be
capable of annihilating the human soul altogether. She left the
factory in a wretched state after a year; was it possible that
somebody who could neither leave nor who had her will-power might
not be able to keep his soul at all?

Shortly after she finished her year in a factory Weil went
with her parents to Portugal for a brief vacation. She was, as
she wrote to Father Perrin, "in pieces, soul and body."[6] It was
in Portugal that she had the first of "three contacts with
Catholicism that really counted."[7]

> In this state of mind, and in a wretched condition phys-
> ically, I entered the little Portugese village, which,
> alas, was very wretched too, on the very day of the
> festival of its patron saint. I was alone. It was the
> evening and there was a full moon over the sea. The
> wives of the fishermen were, in procession, making a
> tour of all the ships, carrying candles and singing
> what must certainly be very ancient hymns of a heart-
> rending sadness. Nothing can give any idea of it . . .
> There the conviction was suddenly borne in upon me that
> Christianity is pre-eminently the religion of slaves,
> that slaves cannot help belonging to it, and I among
> others.[8]

Already we can see that the connection between affliction
and Christianity had been formed in Weil's mind. The other two
contacts reinforce this bond, particularly the third. Weil
writes only briefly of the second experience in which "something
stronger than I compelled me for the first time to go down on
my knees."[9] The third contact occurred in 1938 in Solesmes
while Weil was following the liturgical services of Holy Week
there. She describes it thusly:

> I was suffering from splitting headaches; each sound
> hurt me like a blow; by an extreme effort of concentra-
> tion I was able to rise above this wretched flesh, to
> leave it to suffer by itself, heaped up in a corner,
> and to find a pure and perfect joy in the unimagineable
> beauty of the chanting and the words. This experience
> enabled me by analogy to get a better understanding
> of the possibility of loving divine love in the midst
> of affliction. It goes without saying that in the
> course of these services the thought of the Passion
> of Christ entered in my being once and for all.[10]

While at Solesmes Weil also met a young English Catholic,
whom she says chance made a messenger to her. He introduced
her to the English metaphysical poets, and taught her George

Herbert's *Love*, which she learned by heart. She would often re-
cite this poem to herself "as a beautiful poem, but without my
knowing it the recitation had the virtue of a prayer. It was
during one of these recitations that . . . Christ himself came
down and took possession of me."[11]

    This was something totally unexpected. She wrote of the
experience:

> In my arguments about the insolubility of the problem of
> God I had never foreseen the possibility of that, of a
> real contact, person to person, here below, between a
> human being and God . . . Moreover, in this sudden
> possession of me by Christ, neither my senses nor my
> imagination had any part; I only felt in the midst of my
> suffering the presence of a love, like that which one can
> read in the smile on a beloved face.[12]

    Three elements in the description of this course of events
in Weil's life clearly stand out: the contact with affliction
and recognition of it as a factor in human life; the association
of affliction with the Passion of Christ; and actual contact
with God in and through affliction. All three of these elements
are unheralded in Weil's early thought. At the same time they
are hallmarks of her later work. Yet, there is not an absolute
disjunction between the two periods. In both periods, Weil believed in an ultimate good and sought the means to realize this
good. In the early days, she found these means in the mediation
of mind in the world. In the mature years, she found good to
live in one alone but which is mediated to men in the Cross of
Christ. She found through the love in this latter mediation that
not even affliction need ever finally separate a person from
good, and, in fact, affliction through Christ's mediation could
be the means of experiencing the perfect love of God. But, moreover, she also found that Christ's mediation also supplied the
ultimate basis and truth of all other mediations which have to
do with good.

    The three elements--affliction, the connection of afflic-
tion with the Passion of Christ, and contact with God (indirect
as well as direct)--are all inextricably mixed in Weil's religious philosophy. Because of her own experience one can easily
see why this is so for Weil. But Weil was not intent on describing her own experience; in fact, it is surprising how

infrequently she refers to it in her writings. Instead, she
meant to give an analysis of human life in relation to the world
and to God with these three things as central elements. Because
this analysis, however, deals with the transcendent and the
limits of human thought and experience, it will be helpful to
consider briefly how Weil meant it to be taken.

The key to the analysis lies in a form of mediation. Mediation is that which specifically binds the elements of Weil's
thought internally, but, more generally, it is a doctrine which
allows her to forge a link between the world and the transcendent. Weil carefully distinguished between the realm to which
the discursive intelligence has access and the realm of transcendent mystery into which that intelligence cannot penetrate.
She considered it quite illegitimate to use the explanations and
entailments of the one to account for the other. This would
seem to leave a radical disjunction between the two realms as
well as a disjunction in the being of man himself between that
part of him which is touched by grace and that which exists in
the quotidian world. The breach is healed, Weil believed, by a
faith which distorts neither realm, but which also has the capability of establishing a definite relation between the two.

Weil was quite specific in the meaning she attached to
faith. Faith, for her, is not the affirmation of the intelligence to the mysteries and teachings of the Gospel "as one af-
firms facts of experience or theorems of geometry."[13] Neither
is "Faith (itself) . . . a contact with God, otherwise it would
not be called a night and a veil. It is the submission of
those parts which have no contact with God to the one which
has."[14] She goes on later to explain:

> . . . faith is an indispensable intermediary for making
> the body an arbiter in the spiritual conflict of the soul
> with itself.
> Faith creates the truth to which it adheres. The
> certainty that a rite or ceremony gives spiritual re-
> generation confers that efficacy on it; and this is not
> the effect of a phenomenon of suggestion, which would
> imply illusion and falsehood . . .
> The domain of faith is the domain of truth created by
> certainty. It is in this domain that faith is legitimate
> and is a virtue. A virtue creative of truth.[15]

Faith, is, then for Weil, neither a belief in the ordinary
sense nor a state of man's soul. It is, rather, an attitude

towards God and a relation between the reception of his grace
and the rest of man's existence. This relation is discerned in
the *obedience* of man's existence to God. It then becomes creative of truth insofar as this relation establishes an order for
action. Just as in the early period when Weil was concerned
with the thought of an active being and, consequently with how
thought could inform action, so too here she is attempting to
establish an order, which is the intermediary of faith, for action undertaken in perfect harmony with God's goodness. In
short, Weil is attempting in her philosophy, like the Apostle,
"to take every thought captive in obedience to Christ."

Weil's method is admittedly an indirect one, but this is
due to the very nature of her subject, and her philosophy, therefore, need not be considered to be literally descriptive in any
area in which it touches the divine. What it should be seen as,
however, is a work of obedience to that reality outside the
world. In this way it also attains significance for her audi-
ence. Weil did not expect anybody to believe what she wrote
"likd a geometrical theorem"; what she did expect was that her
work would be helpful in establishing an order through which one
could live life in God's light. There is no claim on Weil's
part to any sort of special or esoteric knowledge, nor does she
expect any such knowledge on the part of her reader. All that
is required is that one recognize a need for an absolute Good
which cannot be met by this world and that any talk about it or
action undertaken in accordance with it not be reduced to any
this-worldly factors. In this way, the philosophy itself becomes
a matter of obedience to the transcendent.

1. *Affliction*

There are certain irreducible traits to the thought and life
of Simone Weil which are common to all periods of her life.
They are her complete certainty in an ultimate good and her un-
dying commitment to find the means of that good in a human life
which is beset by woes and evils of varying degrees. She firmly
believed that this good is accessible to the spirit of man and
that it is a duty belonging to his very essence to participate
in this goodness in every way allowable to him. This led her

to assert two further principles in her work: that there is purpose in life and that man can make good use of whatever befalls
him. In the early years, these two principles closely coincide.
There, the goal of human life is centered in man himself for
his perfection consists in subduing all his thoughts and actions
to an intelligent discernment of an order embodying necessity.
By so doing, he can make use of whatever befalls him by preserving his thoughts and actions from contingency, and by acting
only in a way that leads to the full exercise of reason in himself and others. Even when external circumstances batter him
very roughly he can make moral use of them by seeing their necessity and submitting to it. In her mature years, Weil goes
beyond the immanent possibility for man to do this on his own
and locates purpose in a transcendent creator. Nevertheless,
she still holds to the belief that there is purpose for the
world and good use to be made by man of it. In one of her finest
pieces, *The Love of God and Affliction*, she writes:

> God created through love and for love. God did not
> create anything except love itself, and the means to love.
> He made love in all its forms. He created beings capable
> of love from all possible distances.[16]

And:

> It is our function in this world to consent to the
> existence of the universe. God is not satisfied with
> finding his creation good; he wants it to find itself
> good. That is the purpose of the souls which are at-
> tached to minute fragments of this world . . .[17]

Thus, for Weil, it is "man's essence to love God," and God
himself provides the very means by which he can be loved. The
next obvious step is to describe the nature of that love and
its various means. Yet, Weil did not see this step as so very
easy; for if all things can be found to have a purpose, then so
must affliction, the extreme case of evil in human life. What
must first be done, then, is to reach some understanding of affliction and then to reconcile the enigma it presents with a
perfectly good creator.

The fact of suffering in human life is deniable only for
the morally dead and insensitive. It pervades any number of
the relations man has to his natural environment and to other

men. When Weil spoke of affliction, however, she was not speaking of suffering in general but, rather, of a separate, specific
and irreducible form in the realm of suffering. Affliction, unlike any other form of suffering, has the ability to take possession of man's very soul "and mark it through and through with
its own particular mark, the mark of slavery."[18]

There are two critical factors in affliction. The first is
pain, or physical suffering. Affliction cannot be identified
with pain, but neither does it ever occur without it. Pain by
itself is not an affliction, for by itself it does not leave any
mark on the soul. It is essential to affliction, however, in
that it forces the one who is afflicted to be ever conscious of
his condition. Without pain, human imagination retains its
ability to flee into illusion, as it inevitably does at the onset
of affliction. "Thought flies from affliction as promptly and
irresistably as an animal flies from death. Here below, physical
pain and nothing else has the power to chain down our thoughts."[19]

Affliction, however, goes beyond the disruption of the physical organism; it is a "humiliation of the whole being" and an
"uprooting of life, a more or less attenuated equivalent of
death."[20] Here pain can pass into an affliction if severe and
prolonged, for it may then completely dominate the rest of man's
life. But because affliction is such a thorough uprooting and
destruction of the whole person, it includes all the parts of a
life, social and psychological as well as physical.

The social factor is absolutely essential. Every human being's personality[21] is due to the interplay of natural forces
and social powers, either as their subject or their object. His
very *sense* of worth, of who he is, depends on this interplay.
Yet, as forces and powers have combined, either fortuitously or
by the device of the subject, to yield a personality, so too can
they be disrupted to destroy it. For example, Lycaon, that once
haughty Trojan who gained his reputation and prestige in the
eyes of his fellow citizens and himself by his strength of arm,
has this reputation and personality destroyed when he finds himself on his knees imploring Achilles for his bare existence.
This disruption of the essential social factor of human personality can be described both from the viewpoint of observer and
from that of the afflicted himself.

Affliction, because it destroys all that is normally ac-
counted to compose a human being, has the capability of making
a man into a mere lump of matter. The victim is "reduced by affliction to the state of an inert and passive thing."[22] His
humanity is non-existent and thus invisible to those who surround
him. "Humanity does not exist in the anonymous flesh lying inert
by the roadside."[23] It is not at all surprising in the parable
of the good Samaritan that the priest and Levite walked by the
beaten man, according to Weil, for if they had been asked about
their indifference, they most likely would not have been able to
remember that anything except stones were lying at the side of
the road. Among men, the afflicted can exist for years in this
condition without ever being noticed, except perhaps "only that
they sometimes behave strangely, and we censure this behaviour."[24]

Yet, the afflicted do not go away and hide. They do come
into contact with other more fortunate human beings. But they
do not come into contact with others as men, but rather as
things, and they are treated as such. They have no power of
self-movement, the lack of which is the very property of matter.
Accordingly, the strong find no need to consult either the will
or dignity of the afflicted, for they have not either; the strong
simply command.

> When there is a strong and a weak there is no need to
> unite their wills. There is only one will, that of the
> strong. The weak obeys. Everything happens just as it
> does when a man is handling matter. There are not two
> wills to be made to coincide. The man wills and the
> matter submits. The weak are like things. There is no
> difference between throwing a stone to get rid of a
> troublesome dog and saying to a slave: "Chase that dog
> away."[25]

The regard of the fortunate for the afflicted would be appalling enough if it were simply left at the treatment of the
afflicted as things. But it is not left at that. There is a
sense in which the afflicted are invisible to the fortunate because they count no more than a lump of matter. Yet, there is
a further sense in which the afflicted are invisible because the
fortunate do not want to see them, since they cannot bear the
sight of affliction. The afflicted are a reminder of their

own fragility and mortality and this they must flee in order to
continue to expand their own power. Recognition of affliction
as affliction is thus a human impossibility, and because recognition is impossible so too is compassion. "The sympathy of
the strong for the weak . . . is against nature."[26] Even apparent cases of compassion for the afflicted are all too often simply the result of regarding the afflicted as something to be
bought and as an occasion for doing good to elevate the moral
self-esteem of the buyer.

If the dealings of the fortunate with the afflicted are
equivalent to the dealings of man with matter, the feeling and
repulsion for the afflicted run deeper. Because one who has
never experienced affliction cannot recognize the phenomenon he
is forced to see it as something else and call it by another
name. This is due to the fact that the natural sensibility of
men towards affliction is one of scorn, contempt and revulsion.

> Men have the same carnal nature as animals. If a hen is
> hurt, the others rush up and peck it. The phenomenon is
> as automatic as gravitation. Our senses attach to af-
> fliction all the contempt, all the revulsion, all the
> hatred our reason attaches to crime.[27]

Contact with affliction brings about a sense of defilement
to the non-afflicted. This defilement then becomes a contamination and sullying of any purity the non-afflicted might have and
thus the evil of affliction is transferred to the beholder.
But as long as he retains any power whatsoever he then returns
this contamination to the afflicted in the form of his contempt.
The evil must come back on itself.

> Men think they are despising crime when they are really
> despising the weakness of affliction. A being in whom
> the two are combined affords them an opportunity of
> giving free play to their contempt for affliction on the
> pretext that they are despising crime. He is thus the
> object of the greatest contempt.[28]

Weil saw the attitude and behavior towards the afflicted
by the non-afflicted as presenting us with an example in the
extreme degree of the cycle of evil. Because we feel horror at
the evil inherent in suffering and sin we project that evil into
objects external to us and then act as if the evil came from
them. In turn, they reflect it back onto us through our having

to come into contact with them. The afflicted are necessarily
weak and incapable of repelling any projections and so they must
receive the full brunt of the evil that others project upon them.
Contact with the afflicted reflects that evil back and the cycle
of defilement and contempt is begun again.[29]

One would wish that some respite from this cycle could be
gained. Weil, however, holds out no hope for this on the natural
level of force and power. To do so would require that one be
able to let the evil within himself go no farther than himself.
Furthermore it would require that one be able to not extend his
own exercise of power beyond humane limits and even be able to
remit the debts of what might be considered rightfully his. But,
unfortunately, power also brings with it an illusion of invin-
cibility to its wielder. Weil often quoted Thucydides to the
effect that "Power necessarily commands wherever it can." This
is no less true in the dealings of the fortunate with the afflicted than in any other sphere. The afflicted have lost all
power and can no longer check its exercise upon them. In this
way, there is nothing which can stop the powerful from extending
their power wherever they can, much less make them take less
than they might legitimately expect if there were an equality of
power. If then they do have any sort of claim upon one who is
afflicted they feel perfectly within their rights to exact their
pound of flesh. Ironically, however, the crime is then punished
in inverse proportion to the degree of power exhibited in that
crime.

> There are exceptions only where there is a crime which
> for some reason has prestige, as is often the case with
> murder on account of the fleeting moment of power which
> it implies, or where the crime does not make a vivid im-
> pression on those who assess its culpability. Stealing
> is the crime most devoid of prestige, and it causes the
> most indignation because property is the thing to which
> people are most generally and powerfully attached.[30]

The afflicted are not necessarily the innocent. In fact,
other than a few rare examples such as Christ and Job, most are
not perfectly innocent. Undoubtedly, even the victims of con-
centration camps stole and betrayed each other. There is, therefore, a certain justice employed by those who weigh down the
lives of the afflicted. Irony of ironies, it appears to them

necessary to do so! In a perverse sense they are not incorrect
for without the administration of punishment the good of a social
order cannot be maintained. But one must be careful to distinguish what has really happened. On an abstract level injustices
and sins are reprobated. On another level, however, this administration of justice is only the justification for bringing the
entire force of the social order's contempt down upon the necks
of the afflicted. This is something that not even the most
fastidious administrators of justice can see, particularly in
any legal system in which right is rooted in social privilege
and prestige, the two things of which the afflicted have none.
It is rarely the actual guilt of the afflicted which is being
punished since the illusions of power and the inherent non-
recognition of affliction keeps anybody from seeing that, in
reality, it is the affliction which is being held in contempt.
The cycle of evil is evidenced precisely in its activity of
conjuring up illusions that have the persuasion of reality to
all those under its sway.

If the analysis of affliction stopped at the description
of the attitudes and actions towards the afflicted, i.e. that
of a society towards an afflicted individual, affliction could
be regarded simply as a most hideous and severe form of oppression. When affliction is considered from the point of view of
the victim, however, it shows itself to be something quite different from oppression and inexplicable by the mechanism of that
phenomenon. Two important factors combine to make this so: the
hatred of the individual for himself and the ultimately blind
causality responsible for affliction.

Weil believed that in a case of oppression one could escape
the contagion of folly and collective frenzy by reaffirming on
his own account, over the head of the social idol, the original
pact between the mind and universe. This is something impossible
for the afflicted for they share with the rest of humanity the
same contempt and revulsion for the condition of affliction.
The guilt and defilement which others feel towards affliction is
internalized by the victim.

> Everything happens as though the state of soul appropriate
> for criminals had been separated from crime and attached
> to affliction; and it even seems to be in proportion to

the innocence of those who are afflicted . . .   This
law of sensibility (i.e. the hatred for affliction) also
holds good with regard to ourselves.   In the case of
someone in affliction, all the contempt, revulsion,
and hatred are turned inwards; they penetrate to the
centre of his soul and from there they color the whole
universe with their poisoned light . . .   The first
is of the very essence of affliction; there is no affliction without it.[31]

Men hate and revile the afflicted. The afflicted insofar
as they are men, or rather, once were men, maintain this same
attitude. They cannot believe that they are anything and they
feel as if there is a certain justice that they be treated as
they are. They even go so far as to render themselves incapable
of receiving help for "another effect of affliction is, little
by little, to make the soul its accomplice, by injecting a poison
of inertia into it."[32] Affliction is, at least, the destruction
of the empirical personality and the removal of all power from
the person, being that on which which personality rests. This
is something from which no one is immune. If, however, one believed, as Weil certainly did, that man is mind or soul as well
as personality, one might also believe that *this* might be spared
the terrors of affliction. In turn, it could be that by which
an afflicted man might re-establish a chain of intermediaries
to raise himself. Unfortunately, as Weil saw it, affliction
holds such a grasp over the whole being that, in time, the one
part of man which could conceivably save him becomes drawn into
a complicity and total belief in his affliction.

This complicity impedes all the efforts he might make
to improve his lot; it goes so far as to prevent him from
seeking a way of deliverance, sometimes even to the point
of preventing him from wishing for deliverance. Then he
is established in affliction, and people may get the
impression that he is quite contented.[33]

When this state is reached the afflicted cannot help pro-
jecting the evil of his affliction into the world at large and
seeing it as an evil place, just as others have projected their
evil into him to make him seem evil. In this state the afflicted
cannot or will not receive benefaction for they necessarily hate
those who, by their attentions, remind them of their state.
They must also hate anyone who can touch the uncleaness they believe themselves to be; "this is the cause of certain inexplicable

acts of savage ingratitude."[34] When a person has reached this
state he is as close as possible to literally losing his soul
while yet continuing to breathe.

A second reason exists why the afflicted cannot raise themselves. This is the very inexplicability and absurdity of affliction. This inexplicability is one of the chief hallmarks of
affliction.

> There is a question which is absolutely meaningless and
> therefore, of course, unanswerable, and which we normally
> never ask ourselves, but in affliction the soul is con-
> strained to repeat it incessantly like a sustained mono-
> tonous groan. This question is why? Why are things as
> they are?[35]

It is not that the *causes* of a person's affliction cannot
be laid out before him, even if they are the result of a complex
set of interacting circumstances. These things can be explained.
Human crime is, in the main, the responsible factor for most affliction. This crime often enough has its causes as does the
suffering causes by it. But this explanation is not an answer
to the sort of why? the afflicted ask. Their question pertains
to the purpose of affliction and not to its causes of which there
may be many. Weil writes of this:

> There can be no answer to the "why?" of the afflicted,
> because the world is necessity and not purpose . . .
> Whenever we look for final causes in this world it re-
> fuses them.[36]

The introduction of necessity throws a great light on what
affliction is. In her early years Weil regarded man's ability
to conceive a necessary order in things as that which marked him
off from other creatures. If this necessity cannot be called
friendly, it is at least useful for man's taking his proper place
in the world. In those early years, Weil, like the Stoics, believed that as long as one clearly exercised his mind on things
by discerning the necessity inherent in their order he could
thereby ennoble himself and his race. Even when the external
world operated contrary to his wishes and desires and consequently battered him very roughly, he could always make moral
use of the situation by consenting and approving of the order
he could so clearly see into. In this way not even severe forms
of oppression need thwart his destiny. Affliction, however, is

entirely different for it is a case brought about by the interplay of forces blind to human wishes, an interplay in which man
is supposed to see necessity. Yet, affliction does not seem to
have any possible good use which can be made of it. Even the
ennobling moral use of consent to fate is excluded in affliction
for there cannot be consent made to guilt and defilement. By
definition the state of affliction is one that makes the afflicted ridiculous and not noble. To consent to it is to consent to the extreme example of evil in human life.

The relation of necessity to affliction requires further
clarification for there are two aspects to this relation. On
the one hand, affliction is the result of the interplay of blind
forces. These forces are capable of having necessity discerned
in them. On the other hand, however, affliction appears as a
chance result of these forces. This is to say, while all of the
forces can be seen to embody necessity and a chain of these
necessary forces can be discerned as the cause of affliction
there is no conceivable necessary relation between the cause and
its effect. In order to explain this it is a prerequisite to
first come to some understanding of what 'necessity' means for
Weil in this context.

As we have seen previously, Weil's ideas of necessity present themselves under two faces: as an obstacle and as an order
of matter conceivable only by an act of mind. For her, the
world is a play of forces and man is one of them. Man, however,
as an actor and as a wielder of force attempts to fulfill and
satisfy his needs and desires and is met by the resistance and
reaction of external forces. He thus meets the world as an obstacle. Fortunately, these external forces do not display an
amorphous and chaotic character but differentiate themselves
generically and specifically by operating within certain discernible limits. Man, in turn, by presenting these obstacles to
thought can by an act of mind conceive a necessary order to them
and then turn them to his own use. Moreover, because he can
conceive of a single, actual and infinite *toute-puissance* he can
confidently assume that all phenomena operate within limits,
subject to an overall and pervading necessity.

This view does not exclude chance, although all things can
thus be seen to come to pass in accordance with necessity. Here

we must be careful to distinguish chance from arbitrariness and
chaos. Arbitrariness and chaos are precisely those things that
do not operate within limits, whereas chance does. Weil explains
chance thus:

> (Chance) is not the contrary of necessity, nor incom-
> patible with it. The truth is the opposite: Chance never
> appears except at the same time as necessity. Suppose
> there are a certain number of distinct causes which pro-
> duce effects while conforming to a rigorous necessity;
> then if the effects appear as an aggregate with a cer-
> tain structure and if the causes cannot be grouped to
> form an aggregate of the same structure, what we have
> is chance. Dice are so made that they can fall in six
> ways; but there is no limit to the various ways of
> throwing them.[37]

But does this not give the definition of chance a slightly
Pickwickian sense in that it depends on human ignorance of all
the data in a necessary chain of events, albeit one that might
need tracing to the day of creation? Weil did not think so.
She did believe that there is never

> . . . the slightest break in the tissue of mechanical
> necessities and that the human mind, because of its
> finite capacity for data must remain ignorant of all
> the data. But it is not this ignorance that gives me
> the feeling of chance. It is given solely by the image,
> while I am throwing of an indefinite number of possible
> similar movements, whose effects are distributed in six
> classes.[38]

This is to say, that a certain definitely described throw will
necessarily yield a six, but, also, any number of throws might
be definitely described as well. The indefinite number of six
throws when taken together, however, will only yield an aggregate having a common structure that is defined by possible hand
and arm movements. Once this structure is contemplated it will
be discovered that it is suddenly capable of yielding any one
of the five remaining numbers. The structure of the aggregate
of an indefinite number of throws--the continuum of causes--
therefore cannot be seen to yield any particular number, although, given a cube, it necessarily has only six possible results with any particular throw being capable of being seen in
a necessary relation with the resultant number.

This understanding of chance may now be applied to affliction. It is not a theoretically impossible matter to give the

chain of causes which has led to a particular person's affliction
nor to demonstrate the necessity of their order. Yet this does
not exclude the element of chance for, although the chain has
led to affliction, and is a necessary chain, it is by chance that
it was *this* chain that produced affliction in *this* person. Any
number of chains might have exactly the same effect, but a chain
producing affliction might not always produce that state. This
is due not only to the nature of the chain but also to the individual nature of each man. A set of circumstances may produce
suffering, and if prolonged and intense exceed a limit beyond
which suffering becomes affliction, but "this limit is not purely
objective; all sorts of personal factors have to be taken into
account. The same event may plunge one human being into affliction and not another."[39] A warrior who had previously set his
stock in his power of arms and who is now taken prisoner and made
a slave might easily be plunged into affliction whereas the slave
Epictetus might have a difficult time finding the situation even
mildly inconvenient. It is under the sway of Necessity that
forces come together in such a way and in a particular person.
It is therefore the case that no person is ever immune from affliction os some degree, no matter what his state of preparation.
It is also the case that no person can ever be regarded as marked
out for affliction. Because of the element of chance which excludes final causes, affliction is all the more readily seen as
being in an anonymous and invisible state to other human beings.

It is also this element of chance which causes Weil to differentiate sharply between affliction and martyrdom. Martyrs
know exactly why they suffer. Their suffering is endured in full
consciousness of this fact. The afflicted, however, never know
why they are treated as they are. Even if they may have pro-
voked some vengeance on themselves, the affliction exceeds all
reasonable bounds. They can never feel themselves to be making
a sacrifice for some higher cause.

On a level above the specific human actions and reactions
to affliction, the condition can now be seen to be an occasional
occurrence which is the sometimes unfortunate result of living
in a world bounded by necessity. This Necessity works blindly,
but it is for all of that, recognizable by the human mind. This

recognition of Necessity is, in fact, the sign that there are
human minds. Yet, by itself it gives no more. The reasons for
"why these things?" remain impervious to the human intellect.
Yet, once affliction becomes an understood factor in human life
this question becomes the most important of all if there is to
be any purpose or good use in human life. But the question about
final causes and purpose asked by man is asked by a creature
who is himself under Necessity and who, therefore, cannot find an
Archimedean standing point outside the world from which he can
judge the whole. The only answer he is capable of affirming is
one that embodies Necessity and this is precisely what he is
questioning. "Whenever we look for final causes in this world
it refuses them. But to know that it refuses, one has to ask."[40]

2. *The Crucifixion of Christ*

The lack of an answer to the why? of the afflicted is not
without significance for it indicates that if goodness is real
then "the place of the good is in the other world." Good is
transcendent, and therefore, Weil concludes, there is an inescapable distance between Necessity and Goodness. If we want to
escape the cycle of evil, so forcefully demonstrated in affliction, then "we must either confound 'the essence of the necessary with the good' (Plato, *Republic*) or else go out of this
world."[41] The first alternative is, of course, taking refuge in
the illusions of power which affliction so forcefully shatters,
and we are honestly only left with the second. The lesson we
can learn from this is never to represent the transcendent good
under the conditions of necessity for "every single thing which
has properties is not only the good, but something else besides.
And on this account it is not the complete good, nor is it good
always and in every respect."[42] Any good which can be represented under the conditions of necessity must also be subject
to destruction by it. Because affliction shows us that there is
no final good in this world it can have a use and even be a
blessing. As Weil writes: "If there were no affliction in this
world, we should be able to believe ourselves in Paradise. Horrid possibility."[43]

Unfortunately, the lesson to be learned from affliction is
all too often wasted on both the fortunate and the afflicted.

Because the fortunate tend to confuse the necessary with the
good, they do not see affliction as a real possibility of human
life. The afflicted, on the other hand, are in no condition to
make any use of this lesson, for while they are the first to see
that good transcends necessity, their state of affliction "causes
God to be absent for a time, more absent than a dead man, more
absent than light in the utter darkness of a cell . . . During
this absence there is nothing to love. What is terrible is that
if, in this darkness where there is nothing to love, the soul
ceases to love, God's absence becomes final."[44] The awful truth
of affliction is that just when one's illusions about necessity's
capability of delivering any ultimate goodness are broken and
one, for the first time, discovers transcendence, at the same
time he finds nothing in himself to love it. He consequently
turns back to the world of necessity to find goods on the level
of his pain. These goods, however, are only compensatory and not
eternal. This fact leads Weil to assert the real enigma of affliction.

> The great enigma of human life is not suffering, but
> affliction. It is not surprising that the innocent are
> killed, tortured, driven from their country, made desti-
> tute or reduced to slavery, put in concentration camps
> or prison cells since there are criminals to perform
> such actions. It is not surprising either that disease
> is the cause of long sufferings which paralyze life and
> make it into an image of death, since nature is at the
> mercy of the blind play of mechanical necessities. But
> it *is* surprising that God should have given affliction
> the power to seize the very souls of the innocent and
> to possess them as sovereign master.[45]

Weil felt that one could make use of suffering and often
quoted Aeschylus' words, 'learning comes through suffering,' to
that effect. Affliction, however, she did not feel to be "a
divine educational method." Affliction may very well be a window
on transcendence, but it is this only because it forces man to
a realization of his own creatureliness. When he does realize
this the entire realm of necessity stands between him and God,
with God above it and with him at the extreme end of its force.
On this account there cannot be any question of man's rising to
meet God, for the weight--the gravity--of the entire world of
necessity rests on his back. The only possible way, therefore,

of there being any good in affliction is if both its purpose and
use are found in God alone.

> The infinity of space and time separates us from God . . .
> We are incapable of progressing vertically. We cannot take
> one step towards the heavens. God crosses the universe
> and comes to us.[46]

Weil therefore can find a purpose and use for affliction,
through grace in which God comes and touches the soul of the
afflicted. But this evokes numerous questions as to the possibility of this contact for it is, in fact, contradictory.

Because Weil's notion of 'contradiction' plays such a crucial role in her philosophy as indicating where mediation is
needed, it is important to understand what she means by it. Unfortunately, Weil uses the term 'contradiction' in a very loose
manner and alternates it with the terms 'contrary,' 'incommensurate,' and occasionally, 'mystery.' Furthermore, her usage
has little in common with the standard logical meaning of contradiction that a statement (*p* & not *p*) is a contradiction. She
does not dispute this formula, but simply does not consider it.
In fact, there is very little sense of propositional logic in
Weil's use of contradiction.[47]

What then is 'contradiction' for Weil? In the first instance, it is an opposition between perceptions, thoughts, ideas
or the predication of terms in regard to their referents that
evokes thought to contemplate truth; as Weil says, "every truth
contains a contradiction."[48] This is a plainly paradoxical formulation, but one that is not devoid of meaning or of hallowed
usage. What Weil means here is that 'contradiction' occurs when
our intellectual expectations, at no matter what level, come up
against an unforeseen obstacle which forces us to recast our
thoughts in order to think it in truth. In this sense, 'contradiction' is necessary for us to begin to think on our own. This
is a usage Weil unquestionably derives from Plato, when in the
Republic he has Socrates say:

> perception no more manifest one thing than its con-
> trary (τὸ ἐναντίον), alike whether its impact comes
> from nearby or afar.[49]

Weil's use of 'contradiction' in this sense is revealed by
the remark: "Method of investigation: as soon as we have thought

something, try to see in what way the contrary (sic) is true."[50]
This remark helps to explain a great deal of Weil's indulgence
in paradox throughout her writings. "Contradiction . . ." in
this sense is a valuable heuristic device for "emerging from
the point of view."[51] Here we may expect that so-called contradiction is used by Weil as a means to a more inclusive and insightful way of conceiving our existence and its conditions.
Contradiction can, in this special sense, be seen as another way
of putting Weil's definition of reality as an obstacle, for the
obstacles set by reality oppose our conditioned thoughts and
force us to re-think them. Noting this opposition can therefore
be a gateway to a fuller encounter with reality.

The sense of opposition Weil intends by the term 'contradiction' does not stop, however, with paradox or what are only
apparent contradictions. Instead, there are two increasingly
stronger meanings, namely, incommensuration and mystery. We
shall treat each in turn.

In Weil's writings 'contradiction' and 'incommensuration'
are essentially equivalent and she often uses them interchange-
ably. In fact, often incommensuration offers the clearest sense
of how Weil uses 'contradiction.'[52] Here it is important to see
the difference between incommensuration and apparent contradictions, for apparent contradictions can be resolved by analysis
and proper predication of the opposing terms involved whereas in
incommensuration the terms cannot be so resolved. For example,
there is an apparent contradiction between our perceptions of
the earth's place in space and a heliocentric theory of the
earth's movement. The contradiction is resolved, however, by
the heliocentric theory's ability to explain both the anomalies
of planetary motion presented by a theory developed solely in
accordance with our perceptions, and why we would have those
perceptions in the first place. In incommensuration the two incommensurate elements are *both* necessarily conceived. If, then,
one wants to take seriously any set of ideas in which surd elements appear, he must discover a unity to the set which is on a
higher plan than the one on which he was working before the discovery of the surd. This point can be shown with the help of an
illustration in mathematics, one that Weil herself found enlightening. In early Greek mathematics when numbers were

represented by lines, each line could be expressed as a natural
number by virtue of the ratio (λόγος) it had to another line
when both have a common measure, no matter how small. This expressible λόγος was in fact the very definition of number and its
applicability embraces all the natural numbers. However, it was
discovered that not all lines have a common measure, such as the
sides of an isosceles right triangle and its hypotenuse, and
therefore have no λόγος. These lines are incommensurate (ἄλογος)
and no amount of manipulating can discover a λόγος in the prescribed sense. The consequence of having no λόγος threatens the
very rationality of the most rational science. But with Eudoxus
it was found that by extending the sense of λόγος to cover the
relative magnitude of lines that one could include the natural
numbers with the irrationals in the one real number system. A
λόγος ἄλογος[53] (a ratio involving incommensurates) is not definitely expressible, but it is a perfectly rigorous relation between incommensurate numbers. The new theory of numbers does
not in the least change the incommensuration between two numbers
having no common measure; what it does do, though, is to transcend the limitations of the natural and irrational numbers by
conceiving an order of numbers that incorporates both, but is
not reducible to the definitions of either.

The applicability of this way of reasoning goes further than
just the proportions between lines. It can also be extended to
other incommensurate elements such as weight, time and distance
to yield important formulas in physics. Weight, time and distance are all distinct things, but once we introduce an overriding concept of number they can be combined to yield force
equations. Weil understood this, and introduced it as a principle of reasoning in many realms.

> The system of Eudoxus, by which a ratio between weights
> can be equalled to a ratio between times etc.--How is it
> we allow ourselves not to refer to it in education? If
> it is a case of rational ratios--3 hours are to 2 hours
> as are 3 kilos to 2 kilos--at bottom the notion is the
> same but concealed by the numbers . . . Since it is pos-
> sible in this way to equalize the notions in the case of
> two completely different pairs of magnitudes one could
> hope to be able also to apply the notion of ratio to
> psychological and spiritual matters.[54]

When incommensurates are reconciled into a higher unity, this unity can be a witness to aspects and dimensions of our existence of which we may not have been previously aware, or, at least, are confused about. The force equation mv^2 is example enough of this. We do not see force as such, nor, strictly speaking, do we feel it as 'force'; nevertheless, we understand it to exist and can understand it quite clearly by means of the equation. Weil believed this sort of understanding was also possible in psychological and spiritual matters wherein surd elements of our common experience could bespeak a need for unity on a higher plane, which need if met could give us a clearer understanding of our lives and thus a firmer grasp on them. It was on the basis of reasoning such as this, I believe, that Weil found incommensuration such a valuable tool. It led her to assert: "All veritable good involves contradictory conditions, and is therefore impossible. He who keeps his attention really and truly fixed on this impossibility, and acts accordingly, will carry out good."[55]

There is, however, a further sense of incommensuration which cannot be covered by the Eudoxean system, and that is where two incommensurates are not of the same kind nor are possibly describable as being of the same kind (time and distance are obviously not of the same kind, but they can both be described numerically which for purposes of the equation does make them of the same kind). This sort of incommensuration can only be unified in infinity. Weil does not specifically note this kind of incommensuration, but indicates something of the sort when she says: "What is contradictory to natural reason is not so for supernatural reason, but the latter can only use the language of the former."[56] It is here that Weil brings in the notion of mystery as being the most absolute sense of what she means by contradiction. Mystery involves a final sense of incommensuration and is not to be used for any and every opposition the mind encounters in thinking; instead, Weil has criteria for the legitimate and illegitimate uses of mysery. The use of mysery is legitimate when it involves: a) two strictly conceived terms which are in contradiction (incommensuration) with each other; b) when suppression of one term negates the meaning of the other; c) when suppression of the mystery itself leads to a loss

of the light shed upon the intelligence. This last criterion
indicates a supernatural unity of the two lines since if they
were not linked there would be no loss of light by suppressing
one end of the opposition. She writes:

> The notion of mystery is legitimate when the most
> logical and most rigorous use of the intelligence leads
> to an impasse, to a contradiction which is inescapable
> in this sense: that the suppression of one term makes
> the other meaningless and that to pose one term neces-
> sarily involves posing the other. Then, like a lever,
> the notion of mystery carries thought beyond the impasse,
> to the other side of the unopenable door, beyond the
> domain of intelligence and above it. But to arrive
> beyond the domain of the intelligence one must have
> travelled all through it, to the end, and by a path
> traced with unimpeachable rigor . . . Another criterion
> is that when the mind has nourished itself with mystery,
> by a long and loving contemplation, it finds that by
> suppressing and denying the mystery it is at the same
> time depriving the intelligence of treasures which are
> comprehensible to it, which dwell in its domain and
> which belong to it.[57]

Once these sense of contradiction are sorted out and placed
on their relative levels we gain a better grasp of Weil's metaphysics. On the one hand, we can see that Weil does not have an
irreducible dualism since evil and the supernatural good are
not truly contradictory, that is, they are not commensurate and
on the same level of understanding. On the other hand, we can
also see that Weil does not envisage pantheism either, because
there is real incommensuration and not just unitary Being which
appears in manifold forms. This is particularly seen in affliction, for the so-called contradiction of affliction is not simply
that the level represented by Necessity provides no final good,
but that there is a void--"an internal tension to which nothing
external corresponds"[58]--between necessity and Goodness. This
void indicates an absolute incommensuration that cannot be
bridged by finite thought. To be on either side of this void is
to be totally other than what is on the opposite side.

From the consideration of this distinction, Weil then draws
a series of 'contradictions' which need harmonization. The first
deals with there being a creation at all, for

> . . . creation is itself a contradiction. It is con-
> tradictory that God, who is infinite, who is all, to
> whom nothing is lacking, should do something that is
> outside himself, that is not himself while at the same

time proceeding from himself. (Pantheism which consists in a suppression of one term of the contradiction
is useful as a transition for bringing home the contradiction.) The supreme contradiction is the creator-
creature contradiction . . . This contradiction reaches
its supreme expression when the creature is reduced to
the selfsame quantity of matter which constitutes
it . . .[59]

Secondly, because God has created, and assuming that he has
done so out of love and in order to be loved as the supreme
good, another problem arises. On the one hand, viewed from the
opposite side, it appears impossible that the transcendent and
universal good could touch a particular individual soul in any
way but a universal one. But even this universal way is problematic for God's goodness. It is one thing to find a deity
creating a natural order which provided through its general
workings for creatures, but quite another when that natural order includes affliction where Necessity cannot provide any good.
Weil's resolution to these problems is found in her doctrine of
the Mediation of Christ's Cross.

Our researches to this point have taken us through an examination of affliction to recognize the inescapable void between God and creatures. This distance is an omnipresent factor
in all human life, but it is most evident and seen as a problem
in affliction. The unafflicted can easily ignore the distance
and believe that they can bridge it by their own efforts.
"There are people whose manner of seeking God is like a man
making leaps into the air in the hope that, if he jumps a little
higher each time, he will end up by staying there and rising
into heaven."[60] But this illusion is not open to the afflicted,
weighed down as they are by the entire force of gravity with
the attendant pain to prove it. Here there can be no question
of man bridging the chasm between himself and God; if the chasm
is to be bridged it must be done by God, and then through his
grace man is given the wings to mount above necessity.

There are two somewhat different ways of describing this
bridge. The first is from the viewpoint of God himself, and
the second deals with how and where we see this mediation in
human life. These two descriptions are not disparate elements
in Weil's thought, but are, rather, strongly correlated

throughout it. The first, as Weil certainly understood, is
basically symbolic, as indeed it must be unless one could see
perfectly into the thought of God himself. It is, nonetheless,
valuable and essential for the symbol is the form of the soul's
transcendent spiritual certainty which provides, as nearly as
possible, both a way of construing divine purpose and an object
of thought by which man can make use of that purpose. It is,
therefore, a structure of faith. But this structure of faith
is not arbitrarily constructed; instead, it is discovered *in*
the activity of the incarnate and crucified Christ who is in the
world and who is also in obedience to the transcendent good.
And it is discovered *by* beings who act similarly. It is at this
point that the two descriptions are correlated for the descent
of God's mediating activity is met in the how and where of certain human activities. In this way, if an empirical anchor is
required for the symbol or belief expressed in it it is to be
found in human activity, and the efficacy of the belief rests
in the efficacy of the action. Its certainty is experimental.[61]
Because, however, Weil posits a void between the fullness of
God's goodness and man's necessity, it is not possible to argue
from man's activity *per se* to an inference of God's being. We
shall, therefore, describe the symbol first and then center it
in the action taken upon it.

Weil begins with a consideration of God before the act of
creation. He "produces himself and knows himself perfectly."[62]
He is All in All, and outside of himself there is nothing. Yet,
above all he is love, and in the persons of the Trinity there is
a unifying love. It is this love between the three equal persons which gives God his very definition of unity for "between
the terms united by this relation of divine love there is more
than nearness; there is infinite nearness or identity."[63] The
Father loves the Son and the Son loves the Father and the bond
between them forms a third person which is both love itself and
loved. There is no inequality in the various terms of the relationship for the love of either the Father or the Son is in no
way diminished by their love for the Spirit which binds them.
The Trinity, therefore, is a perfect harmony which is equality
and perfect joy.

There is no more fullness of being or goodness than the
Trinity. Yet, although God is all perfection, he chose to create
a world of creatures who are not God and who have an existence
independent of him. Here Weil asks: "Why did God create? It
seems so obvious that God is greater than God and creation together."[64] However, to see the how? of creation is to begin to
understand the why? In creating God willed that beings other
than himself might live. If he is All the only way in which he
could do this is by abdicating the full exercise of his power.
In this way, Weil saw creation not as an act of power or as an
expansion of God's power, but as one of the renunciation of
power.

> Because he is the creator, God is not all powerful.
> Creation is an abdication. But he is all-powerful in
> this sense, that his abdication is voluntary. He knows
> its effects, and wills them . . . God has emptied him-
> self. This means that both the Creation and the Incarna-
> tion are included with the Passion.[65]

Thus, in the very act of creation there is a 'crucifixion'
in God. But, if creation is an abdication what then is the stuff
of which the creation is made? Here we must tread carefully for
there is at least a tendency in Weil towards a terminological
confusion between two different sense of 'necessity' and a conflation of two steps into one in the description. On the one
hand, creation, while a renunciation, is also an abandonment to
the forces of matter and to necessity which is the stuff of this
world. "God abandons our whole entire being--flesh, blood, sensibility, intelligence, love--to the pitiless necessity of matter and the cruelty of the devil . . ."[66] In this sense, creation has an independent existence and necessity is truly distant
from goodness. On the other hand, she views necessity, as in
her early writings, as an order or tissue of immaterial connections without force. It is the duty of all intelligent creatures
to recognize this sort of necessity and to submit to it in the
manner of the Stoic *amor fati*. If these two elements are taken
together, however, the resulting ensemble, (if it were not
thoroughly confusing), would, at least raise serious questions
about either the possibility of transcendent goodness ever entering into creation or freedom, depending upon whether the major
emphasis is laid on necessity as abandonment or as the inflexible
tissue of material relations.

Resolution can be obtained, however, by distinguishing not only the two sense of necessity but also two of 'renunciation.' In creation, God does abandon the world and allows it its own existence by withdrawing in favor of a 'conditional necessity.'[67] This sort of necessity can be equated with natural forces *per se*. It is conditional, however, in that it depends on God's withdrawing in order for it to exist. It consists of forces without limits and is a type of unregulated chaos. Nonetheless, Weil did not see creation only in this sense where God simply withdraws to an inaccessible corner of the universe. At the same time that he withdraws and renounces the full exercise of his power there is also a crucifixion within God himself whereby the Son is separated from the Father and incarnated in the body of the world. When the Son is so crucified he then becomes the Λόγος, or order of the world, which is precisely necessity in Weil's second sense; " . . . God turns himself into Necessity."[68]

We are now in a better position to understand Weil's notions of God's governance of his creation through a providential necessity which he furnishes for it. The creation has its own proper forces, but through the crucifixion of God these forces have rigorous limits imposed on them. They then admit of an order through the interaction of limits for "limit is only inscribed in a relationship between several conditions which compensate each other, in an order."[69] Weil often used the balance to symbolize this idea, for a balance puts two opposing forces into an equilibrium around an immaterial mathematical point. The point, being without magnitude or force, exercises no force while at the same time being a necessary relation between forces which forces invariably obey. When this principle is then applied on the cosmic scale, the Λόγος Necessity is seen as "an ensemble of laws of variation which are determined by fixed and invariant ratios."[70] Because the ensemble is capable of being regarded as a single entity pervading all the laws of variation and one, in fact, from which they all proceed, Weil feels justified in taking this immaterial structure as the Λόγος of the world.

In this way, Weil, like Plato, postulates a dual causality of goodness and necessity to all created phenomena.[71] There is,

on the one hand, the causality of conditional necessity which
is the individual blind forces making up the matter of phenomena.
On the other hand, there is the causality of the good which is
reflected in the form and order of the matter. The form and
order, however, are not the good itself, which, in Weil's terms,
must always be transcendent. The form and order are caused by
the good, though, insofar as they bear a relationship to it which
can only have proceeded from the good itself. This is the
Λόγος, the crucified Son of the Father. Weil pithily expresses
this by paraphrasing Plato with her own emphasis: "a *wise* persuasion convinced *necessity* to turn the majority of things toward
the *good*."[72] This is to say, the Λόγος, taken in relation to
conditional necessity creates a new Necessity which bears a
mediatory relationship to the transcendent Good. She also puts
it this way: "*In order that Good may pass into existence, Good
must be able to be the cause of what is already entirely caused
by Necessity.*"[73] This cause, *per se*, is seen in the order of
the world which cannot be divorced from the world of which it is
an order nor can it be equated with any part of it.

Weil sees the significance of her Λόγος theory in two areas.
There is initially the docility and obedience of the forces of
matter to the created order. Although they are blind and without
intelligence, by instinct or by external compensation "every
nature moves across the tide of the great sea of being to its
own port."[74] This, to Weil's eyes, reflects the perfectly just
equanimity of God's providential care of the creation. In this
regard, she often quoted Christ's two sayings in the Gospel of
Matthew, "where we are told to contemplate and imitate the lilies
of the field and the birds of the air, in their indifference as
to the future and their docile acceptance of destiny; and another time, he invites us to contemplate and imitate the indis-
criminate distribution of rain and sunlight."[75] But, secondly,
and just as important, there is added significance here for
creatures of intelligence. Insofar as they are creatures of
matter, intelligent beings, like matter, are subject to the same
form of creation, however, they have the gift of intelligence
which allows them the possibility of conceiving the order of
the world and freely consenting to it. This is a liberty no

other creature possesses. Man thus has the choice of how he is
going to obey necessity; he can either be continually buffeted
by natural forces and let his thought be under necessity, or
he can exercise his intelligence in the sphere of the immaterial
order and accept that order as good. In time and through a
methodical transformation of himself, the person who so conceives and consents to the order of the world makes it, as it
were, a second body.[76] He becomes, as the Stoics said, a citizen of the world.

But doesn't this lead to interpretations similar to the
worst sort of notions held about Stoic apathy and resignation?
What, in fact, is the good in this situation if the only difference between the fool and the sage is one of perspective?
Weil saw the difference to lie in the beauty of the order of
the whole universe which is perceived and reflected by the wise
man. Beauty, like affliction, can be a sign and window of the
transcendent good. Unlike affliction which is pure sorrow,
however, beauty is an image of the pure joy of the Trinity. The
person who conceives and consents to the order of the world and
who loves it--who does not wish it to be anything other than it
is--participates in the Λόγος, who is the order of the world by
obedience to the will of the Father whom he loves. This participation of the wise man consists not only in his appreciation
but also in the perfect order of his own life. The presence
of love here is the critical factor, for it would be entirely
possible to conceive a necessary relation between things without
loving it. When there is love for this order, however, beauty
appears, and as a good precisely because love finds the order
fitting and appropriate. Weil writes:

> . . . beauty is perfect order. So likewise, the abso-
> lutely obedient soul is in a perfect order.
> The world is only beautiful for him who experiences
> *amor fati*, and consequently *amor fati* is, for whoever
> experiences it, an experimental proof of the reality
> of God.[77]

In this way, then, the transcendent universal good which
can only be contradictorily be spoken of as touching the creature, can do exactly that through the mediating function of the
Λόγος. By loving the Λόγος, a person takes on a life similar to

the Λόγος for he both attempts to imitate it in his own thoughts
and actions, and does so out of sense of love for the good which
the Λόγος also loves and obeys. In turn, he participates in the
love of the Father and Son in beauty and joy, even when his love
may occasionally involve suffering.

Unfortunately, there are limits to this sense of the goodness of beauty which strictly correspond to the limits of human
capability of consenting to the world. Beauty is, as Kant said,
a finality without finality; or, as Weil adds, a *promise* of
transcendent goodness. One can through a system of intermediary
steps--an 'apprenticeship' as Weil calls it--gradually align and
unite one's soul with the woul of the world (or Λόγος) and find
one's own will in the cosmic order. To do so requires a disin-
vestment of all one's personal interests, or rather, a coinciding
of one's interests with those of the world. Problematically,
however, a final and full consenting love to the entire order
of the world must finally include a consent to affliction, or at
least its possibility. This is precisely that to which no person can consent, for to be afflicted is not to rise and find
one's soul above the world but to be at the very bottom of it,
under the entire weight of necessity. If, then, there is to be
any final good for men, they must be linked even in affliction
to the *summum bonum*. This requires a form of contact and mediation that is more particular than the order of the world which
is accessible to intelligence. This mediation is found in the
Cross of Christ.

In the Incarnation, Passion and Crucifixion of Christ--the
Λόγος become flesh--Weil finds a further separation between the
Father and the Son. If the Λόγος theory described above paints
a picture of the original separation in God where the Son stands
as mediator *between* matter and the Father, in the Crucifixion
it is quite different, for the entire world of necessity stands
between the Father and the Son. The Son is, in fact, afflicted.
Like every other person who is afflicted Christ must endure the
scorn and calumny heaped upon him (the mocking and scourging),
he wants to avoid his inexorable fate (the Agony), his power of
self-movement is denied him (being nailed to the Cross). Moreover, the sight of his affliction causes even his disciples and

friends to flee the wretched sight of him. Finally, he intensely
feels the absence of God and of any final goodness when he cries
out "My God, my God, why have you forsaken me?" One may even say
that Christ is at the very extreme end of affliction, a point
which nobody else ever quite reaches, for there is no possibility of hope. "When Pity herself becomes affliction, where can
she turn for help? It would have needed another Christ to have
pity on Christ in affliction."[78]

     Yet, there are two essential differences between Christ's
affliction and that of other men. On the one hand, from the
Incarnation to his death Christ was perfectly pure and perfectly
innocent. Nobody else, however, can make such a claim, and perhaps we even deserve affliction, insofar as it can be deserved
at all, through our complicity in crime and in our "crime of
ingratitude in paying no attention to the world's beauty."[79]
On the other hand, Christ did not cease to love the Father and
to obey him, even when the Father was perfectly absent and when
obedience meant submitting to an undeserved and unwanted punishment. In regard to the latter, Weil insists that we should not
think of Christ as a "martyr for the truth," as Hegel did, but
quite literally as one of the afflicted. With these two differences in mind, Weil can then see Christ's Cross as expiating,
redeeming and mediating.

     Human beings can love and consent to the order of the world
because of its beauty, even when like an overly strong handshake
of a friend it presses them quite hard. What they cannot accept
is affliction nor can they even recognize it because of its contradictory nature, which is that while the beauty of the world
invites love and consent and promises good it also possesses
the very means of destroying that in mean which is to accept it.
The will simply cannot will to will no longer. Furthermore,
the contradiction appears in that man seeking perfect good
through the order of the world, instead, receives, almost quite
mechanically, all the evil projected into him by those around
him when he is plunged into affliction. He, in turn, cannot
help but project it back. Thus the order of necessity brings
the very opposite of what it promises. Christ, however, from
his very incarnation has had no will for himself other than that
of the Father. Because even to become incarnate implies for

Christ full and total consent to whatever the Father should will,
there is no question of undergoing an 'apprenticeship' and consequently *gaining* in full consent. He consents and loves the
Father's will as being his own, including the possibility of
affliction. When he is then actually afflicted, although he is
tempted, he continues to obey perfectly the Father. This does
not lessen the affliction, but it does abnegate the moral evil
of that condition. In this way he expiates evil's cycle of
projection and reflection, for the evil in sin and suffering
which is heaped upon him in his degradation goes no farther.

Once the contradiction has been accepted and the evil ab-
sorbed, one then no longer has to consider affliction as an irreducible evil and can accept its existence as a distance between God and God. But how, one may ask, is so considering it
to make it mediatory and therefore redemptive? Weil establishes
the point on an analogy of love in friendship.

> There are two forms of friendship; meeting and separa-
> tion. They are indissoluble. Both of them contain the
> same good, the unique good, which is friendship . . .
> As both forms contain the same good thing, they are both
> equally good.[80]

In Friendship, the two friends desire the same good of
loving each other so much that they, as it were, form one being,
just as the halves of humanity in Aristophanes' *Symposium* myth
desire to be united. But, if they are true friends, they also
can consent to a separation and yet continue to love each other
"so much that, having half the globe between them, their union
will not be diminished in the slightest degree."[81] In fact,
the separation itself is an act arising out of the union of
love. In this way, the separation itself, insofar as it entails
certain actions on the part of both parties, is a new form of
that union and must be regarded as real. Weil then applies this
reasoning to the persons of the Trinity. In the immanent Trinity
there is "more than nearness; there is infinite nearness or
identity."[82] In the economic Trinity, in Creation, Incarnation
and Passion there is infinite distance. Yet while there is this
infinite distance imposed by all of time and space, as long as
the Son continues to love the Father, even while afflicted, and
oppressed by all evil there remains the unity of love. Thus

affliction, if submitted to in loving obedience to the Father's
will, while indeed a separation from the Father is also the occasion for a perfect love wherein the Son is joined in perfect
unity with the Father. Affliction need no longer be considered
a final evil, but a state in which love may be perfected in act.

> The love between God and God, which in itself *is* God, is
> this bond of double power; the bond which unites two beings
> so closely that they are no longer distinguishable and
> really form a single unity, and the bond which stretches
> across distance and triumphs over infinite separation.
> The unity of God, wherein all plurality disappears, and
> the abandonment wherein Christ believes he is left,
> while not ceasing to love his Father perfectly, these
> are the two forms expressing the divine value of the
> same love, the Love which is God himself.
> God is so essentially love that the unity, which in a
> sense is his actual definition, is a pure effect of love.
> And corresponding to the infinit virtue of unification
> belonging to this love there is the infinite separation
> over which it triumphs, which is the whole creation
> spread throughout the totality of space and time, con-
> sisting of mechanically brutal matter and interposed
> between Christ and his Father.[83]

When Christ continues to love the Father even in affliction
he accepts the entire weight of necessity on his shoulders, as
the Father's will, even when despair and flight would be the
most natural reaction. In being afflicted, however, he not only
receives the weight of physical force, he also receives all
the calumny and evil that man heaps upon him as one afflicted.
He is, as St. Paul says, cursed and made sin. Yet, even in this
degraded condition, he continues to love and with that love a
unified and blessed contact is established between the Father
and the creature.[84] Christ's love thus bridges the most horrid
of chasms between man and God and redeems even the greatest
separation between the two. In this Christ is the Mediator for
his act of unreserved consent and love on the Cross makes the
very means of greatest separation the means of contact with God.
This is something no one else could do, since we flee from affliction, a flight that makes it difficult to consent to the
Father's will as being the rule of Necessity. "Because no other
could do it, he himself went to the greatest possible distance,
the infinit distance."[85] Without the Son's crucifixion we would
continue to flee affliction, but with it we can see that even

affliction can contain a good, indeed our greatest good, and
thus a purpose and a use. If we consent to the possibility of
affliction we give our radical consent to God's goodness, and
if we actually undergo it and continue to love as Christ did,
by God's love we are joined to Him in perfect love.

> As for us men, our misery gives us the infinitely pre-
> cious privilege of sharing in this distance placed be-
> tween the Son and his Father . . . For those who love,
> separation, although painful, is a good, because it is
> love. Even the distress of the abandoned Christ is a
> good. There cannot be a greater good for us on earth
> than to share in it. God can never be perfectly present
> to us here below on account of our flesh. But he can
> be almost perfectly absent from us in extreme afflic-
> tion. For us, on earth, this is the only possibility
> of perfection. That is why the Cross is our only hope.[86]

Because Christ is at the extreme distance, a distance
farther than ours could ever be, we can then see that there is
no occasion or state in life that is unredeemable or excludes
God's love. But Christ is not the mediator simply because he
is the prime example of loving God even in affliction, although
he is that, too, for Weil. Rather, he is mediator because the
state of affliction is his originally. As Weil so often quoted
the Apocalypse, he is "the lamb slain from the foundation of
the world." This thought lends itself to a particularly Weilian
interpretation of St. Athanasius' principle of mediation; "God
became man so that man might become God." Weil, like St.
Athanasius, can be assumed to claim that in God's becoming man
we suddenly become like God since God is now a man. By being
men we are quite automatically in his image. Her own particular
contribution to this conception of mediation, however, is that
the likeness we bear to Christ is in our ability to consent to
the entire order of creation and to love it unreservedly. In
short, it is in our Christlike renunciation of having any particular claim on the goodness of the universe in favor of the
divine will which created it and which is the source of all its
goodness. Weil expresses the mediation of Christ in this way:

> Man has sinned in trying to become God (on the imaginary
> plane), and God has redeemed this sin by becoming man.
> By which means man can really become *sicut deus*. Thus
> the serpent had spoken truly.[87]

It has often been the case among Weil commentators to say
that Weil sees no actual need for the Incarnation of the Word,
and thus no need for the actual crucifixion. Jacques Cabaud
argues: "There is no necessity for the Incarnation of the Word.
Christ has become an example, a paradigm, a living doctrine,
but he is not the source or the necessary condition of salvation."[88] This, however, is incorrect for given a creation nothing is more needed than the Crucifixion in actuality. Cabaud's
reasoning is based on the idea that for Weil affliction submitted
to in love and consent in any time or place of history can have
the effect of contact, and this was certainly Weil's view. But
what he misses is Weil's point that in the so-called contradiction of affliction there is a chasm between ideas which cannot
be bridged mentally but only in the act of God himself. This
act is needed, else we should have no way of being able to submit
to affliction. Weil herself says:

> We needs must have a just man to imitate so that the imi-
> tation of God does not simply remain an empty phrase; but
> it is also necessary so that we may be carried beyond the
> boundaries of the will, that we should not be able to
> desire to imitate him. One cannot desire the Cross.[89]

Without the actual Incarnation and Crucifixion of the Word not
only could we not conceive affliction and as something to be
submitted to, we also could not submit to it since, in Weil's
view, it is the love of Christ that empowers our very souls to
give consent. Similarly, without the Cross, we could not even
give unrestrained consent to the beauty of the universe, since,
as we shall see, all consent to God's will is a participation
in the Cross.

If my interpretation of the mediatory value of Christ's
Cross is correct for Weil, it forces two conclusions which I
contend give Weil's thought its overall cohering value. The
first conclusion to be drawn is that Christ's Cross for Weil
represents the absolutely central fact of her entire religious
thinking. This is to say, that her acceptance of Christianity
in Christ's Cross is not the *terminus ad quem* of an argument by
other principles she held previously (although up to now it has
been described as such) but that it is the *terminus a quo* she
centers every other argument and insight. As a correlate to

this, the second conclusion is that Weil's elaborate symbol of
Christ's mediation first as the Λόγος and then as the Incarnate
and Crucified Christ is capable of being read backwards and all
that pertains to mediation needs to be read in the light of the
Cross. Metaphysically, of course, the Incarnation is a specification of Christ's mediating Λόγος function and the Cross is a
further specification. Yet, there can be little doubt that the
spiritual hub of the description of either the renunciation in
Creation or the self-emptying of the Son in the Incarnation is
what happens on the Cross since both are described as a free
renunciation of the Son in obedience to the Father's will. The
Cross is obviously the center of Weil's doctrine at least in
this descriptive sense. But, even metaphysically, God's own
love and purpose is not seen as complete except in the Cross
where the Son actually undergoes what we must undergo. It is
an act ordained from the Creation.

Weil's 'symbol' of the three-fold Christ as Son of God,
Λόγος, and Incarnate Mediator is, in fact, more easily understandable if read from the Cross. There are certain fundamental
difficulties if one begins with the Trinity and then *in time*
proceeds to a first split and Incarnation in the Λόγος, which
gives the world its order and beauty. The problem is mainly
that affliction then appears as a sort of errant and uncontrolled
phenomenon ignorantly caused by the order of the world. In this
case, consent is impossible to the entire order because it includes affliction. The full truth and beauty of the world cannot
be accepted because affliction cannot be accepted and affliction
is a part of the order. This would then make the Cross a sort
of patch work to cover the weakness of Providence. If, however,
the separation in God is infinite from the very beginning, the
Λόγος would originally include the mediating use to be made of
affliction. In this case, loving God and consenting to his will
even in affliction will always be possible and will always include the possibility of full contact with him and the revelation of the full beauty of the world, as Weil, indeed, says it
does.

> So it was that to Job, when once the veil of flesh had
> been rent by affliction, the world's stark beauty was
> revealed. The beauty of the world appears when we

recognize that the substance of the universe is necessity and that the substance of necessity is obedience
to a perfectly wise love.[90]

Also:

> God is love, and nature is necessity; but this neces-
> sity, through obedience, is a mirror of love. In the
> same way, God is joy, and creation is affliction; but
> it is an affliction radiant with the light of joy. Af-
> fliction contains the truth about our condition. They
> alone will see God who prefer to recognize the truth
> and die, instead of living a long and happy life in a
> state of illusion. One must want to go towards reality;
> then when one thinks one has found a corpse, one meets
> an angel who says "He is risen."[91]

The Cross as an actual event can only take place in time
with a before and after. But if from Creation itself Christ
submits to become incarnate and crucified in time, and Creation
is based on this obedience, then the Λόγος not only originally
contains the mediating use to be made of affliction, it is itself the effect of the primal mediating renunciation of Christ.
On the basis of this reasoning Weil says: "In this world, necessity is the vibration of God's silence."[92] In the *Notebooks*
she also says that "the necessity contained in this contradiction (i.e. of a creature loving the transcendent God) represents
the whole of Necessity in a nutshell."[93] Affliction can therefore lead to perfect love just as the beauty of the world can
lead one to love God in affliction. The two are completely
inter-related such that the intimation of joy found in beauty
is nothing more than the effect of the love between the Father
and his infinitely separated Son, appreciated on a level above
affliction. Thus the beauty of the world, its order, is formed
by Christ's being "slain from the foundation of the world,"
and, in turn, all intermediate actions undertaken in accordance
with necessity can be said to be the result of this order formed
by the Cross.

    We can now therefore make some sense of Weil's claim that
the cross is the principle of *all* life, and particularly intelligent and loving human life, no matter whether that life is
lived before or after the historical Crucifixion.[94]

> The idea of necessity as the material common to art,
> science and every kind of labor is the door by which
> Christianity can enter profane life and permeate. For

the Cross is necessity itself brought into contact
with the lowest and highest part of us; with our physical
sensibility by its evocation of physical pain and with
supernatural love by the presence of God. It thus
involves the whole range of contacts with necessity which
are possible for the intermediate parts of our being.
There is not, there cannot be, any human activity in
whatever sphere, of which Christ's Cross is not the
supreme and secret truth.[95]

The Cross, being the very principle of creation, is that
which establishes all order and orders of Necessity. In this
way, we can see why Weil understands diverse aspects of intellectual and spiritual life to depend on the Cross. It shall now
be our duty to pass on to see how these various aspects can and
do lead to the Cross in actual human practice, and to what degree.

3. *Mediation and the Love of God*

Weil's 'symbol,' based as it is in the mediatory value of
Christ's Cross presents a wonderfully constructed picture of
how God's goodness can be present at all levels of life, even in
the depths of affliction. We can see through the Cross that we
receive a guarantee that nothing need separate us from the love
of God. But Christ's Cross is meant to be more than a guarantee;
it also contains a love which is to be the end of all human
activity. Furthermore, the Cross is also the door and key to
that end.

It is in this sphere of human activity that Weil's doctrine
of mediation takes on its full significance, for here she ela-
borates on how we *become* like Christ and thus participate knowingly and willingly in the divine love. But it is also here that
the most difficult problems arise. It is one thing to show how
God's love can be present throughout human life but it is quite
another to show how humans recognize divine activity and then
act on that recognition. This is particularly so when humans
by nature or perversity are not inclined to either recognize
divinity or to follow it in their lives. For this reason it is
necessary to show Christ's mediating activity from the human
perspective in order to see how it is recognized and how it provides the means by which humans can be led to the Cross. This

description involves a series of considerations. It first requires a consideration of what the conditions for good are within
the world of necessity. Secondly, it requires showing what it
is in human life that keeps goodness from being realized in it.
Third, it is required to be shown how Christ fulfills the requi-
site conditions. Finally, it needs to be shown how in fulfilling
these conditions he is the Mediator who is present in the activity of men so that they may also fulfill these conditions so
that they may ultimately direct their love towards God with
all of their heart, mind and soul.

A. *The Conditions of Good*

Weil argues that true goodness in this world presupposes
doubly impossible, or contradictory, conditions. Initially,
when the matter is objectively considered, the accomplishment
of any positive good entails a negative evil. This is to say,
that insofar as any good must be the result of an act in a world
which includes matter, that act because it requires the expansion of power or force in one direction necessarily means a
diminution of power in another. In order to realize a good G
it is necessary that either one act to gain G from somebody else
or, even more accurately, direct one's forces to gain G such
that one cannot at the same time gain G'. Second, Weil continues, there is also another impossibility when the matter is
regarded subjectively, for "the accomplishment of a good act
implies a way of behaving which constitutes from another aspect
a disposition toward evil . . ."[96] This is not only because of
the objective correlation which dictates that desiring a good
involves a correlated evil and thus insofar as the desire is for
a whole it is also for the evil as well as for the good, but
because, to *act* is to go beyond desire and to therefore plot
the means of accomplishing the act. This includes a *deliberate*
diminution of some force. Weil thus concludes; "evil is the
shadow of good. All real good, endowed with solidity and den-
sity, projects evil. It is only imaginary good which does not
project any."[97]

Despite the fact that these subjective and objective correlates of good and evil are descriptive of action in this

world, it is at least paradoxical that a free willing being
capable of moral action should always be bound to will evil con-
commitantly with good. The problem, Weil believes, is in the
subjective correlates in the *way* we will good, for inevitably we
do so from an ego-centered perspective. In order to show this
Weil argues that thinking beings always act on a system of
values "for at each instant our life is oriented, in fact, according to some system of values . . ."[98] If then there is a
set of values in the eternal and we do act on a set of values,
clearly we ought to ensure that the values we act on are the
eternal ones. This action can then possess a value in itself.
Not so to act is at least the sin of ingratitude. The problem,
however, enters because we act unconditionally on a set of values
when we can naturally have only a conditional knowledge of them.
Because the true values are eternal and therefore immaterial
and outside conditional necessity, and because we are limited
and act from a particular perspective they are inaccessible to
us. Nevertheless, because we do always orient our lives toward
some value, and do so unconditionally, we inevitably end up by
denying the value we set out to accomplish. We thus give unlimited love to limited values, and give limited, if any, love
to the ultimate good. Once again, the original sin is error
and not ignorance.

> A criterion for values is the supreme necessity for all
> people; but it is also something that no one will
> achieve. For all knowledge is hypothetical; demonstra-
> tions proceed from previously demonstrated theorems or
> from axioms, facts constituted thanks to the sense
> organs are only facts insofar as they are entailed by
> other facts. But value cannot be a matter of hypothesis.
> A value is something one admits unconditionally . . . a
> system of values, at the moment when it orients a life,
> is not accepted on conditions, but is, purely and simply,
> accepted. Since knowledge is conditional, values are
> not susceptible of being known.
> But one cannot renounce knowing them, for that would
> be to renounce believing, which is impossible because
> human life cannot not be oriented. Thus at the center
> of human life there is a contradiction.[99]

Egotism then becomes the case because whereas each soul
capable of knowing God is created with a value and a perspective
on creation--a window to God's sight of his creation--that soul
exercises its power and gains its knowledge *from* a perspective

instead of understanding that its life *has* a perspective which
is merely one of many. When this happens the perspective of the
creature becomes a point of view, or, otherwise said, the center
of a field of vision.[100] This center, Weil claims, is nothing
other than the self or ego. The moral fault then does not lie
so much in the ignorance of other values but in the spiritual
error of acting according to a false set of values in which the
supreme value is the perspective of the agent.

Oddly enough, the situation arises from the three-fold facts
that human beings have a value, that they always desire an ultimate good, and that other things also have a value both in themselves and for us. The egoist unfortunately conflates the value
of his individual existence with that of the ultimate good and
then, in turn, organizes his systems of values according to this
conflation. The highest value he knows is his own existence,
and hence he reasons all other values must be ordered under it.
In part, he is not incorrect insofar as his own value is partially
constituted by the ability to recognize what else is valuable and
by his ability to act on this knowledge in order to bring good
into existence. Where he makes his mistake, however, is in not
seeing that the value of his own existence comes from a higher
good, and that the value of other existents can have that value
without him. He, therefore, like the black horse of Plato's
tripartite soul, seeks to rush upon and possess whatever intimates value to him, when he should respect the common source of
goodness and the integrity of the beloved. It is as if he believed that in order to have good he must expand his own existence to the utmost and encompass everything else under it. Unfortunately, this self-expansion leads to a proportionate decrease in regard for other values. The egoist, in short, plays
a role in regard to the rest of existence which could only be
proper to God.

It would ba a mistake, however, to understand Weil to be
saying that egoism is a fully conscious celebration of the self
which finds its full happiness in a self-absorbed existence,
although this might be the extreme extension of the idea. Her
point is far more subtle. It is only the maddest sort of mega-
lomaniac who believes that he has no need of anything external

to his own ego in order to exist. Weil argued that men do understand a perfection that they either are not or have not; else
why would they consistently try to improve their undertakings,
or, for that matter, undertake them at all? In order to fill
this void of their desire's lack of fulfillment they seek to
represent to themselves what such fulfillment would be like and
invest the things required to achieve this goal with a sort of
ultimate worth. Thus the miser expects his infinite happiness
in gold, the tyrant finds it in power, and the lover in his beloved. Already, there is a confusion of the Necessary with the
Good. But no one is content simply with knowing that gold,
power or a beloved exists; he wants to possess them, believing
that control over them will constantly direct the energies of
the object his benefit. By a strange inversion exactly the
opposite happens, for the worth of the possessor becomes bound
up with the fate of the object. Finites, because they are subject to necessity, do not provide the longed for good, but simply
drag one alone with them.

> We are drawn toward a thing, either because there is
> some good we are seeking from it, or because we cannot
> do without it . . . In time it often comes about auto-
> matically that the second motive takes the place of the
> first . . . A man smokes opium in order to attain to a
> special condition, which he thinks superior; often, as
> time goes on, the opium reduces him to a miserable con-
> dition which he feels to be degrading, but he is no
> longer able to do without it.[101]

Thus, the blessing of some value, if adhered to unqualifiedly,
soon becomes a demon.

The case of a miser or opium smoker is obvious enough,
involving as it does an addiction to a single object. But, Weil
argues, these are basically extreme examples of the attachment
we naturally have for our own personalities which are made up
of a number of objective attachments and desires. A person at
birth has various innate capabilities. He may have the genetic
disposition to intelligence or to strength. He also has various
internal and external environmental dispositions. Finally, he
has certain needs such as food which are common to the race.
All of these things, in varying combinations according to the
individual's choice of which of them he exercises, and how, go
to make a human being's personality and his objective existence

within the realm of Necessity. All of them imply some human
exercise of power, or lack of it. As such they may be the deliverance of a necessity persuaded by goodness, and thus a sort
of gift, but the fact that any soul has exercise of any of them
is purely contingent. But rather than understanding them simply
as the blind play of forces and accepting the limited value they
might bring, men inevitably seize them as if they belonged to
them by right. Most men do not have their sense of existence
and personal worth invested in any one single object, like the
miser. But even if their attachments are spread over a number
of things, the supreme value remains that they are able to subsume all other values under their personal control. Furthermore, they cannot help but do so because to give up control would
seem to thwart their own sense of self-preservation. Other
values, then, are values only insofar as they contribute to the
extension of power and the prestige which power brings. It is
in this sense that every way of behaving to accomplish a good
"constitutes from another aspect a disposition toward evil," for
to read and use a value from a necessarily limited perspective
inevitably implies the diminution of that value from any other
perspective. Theologically, this makes the original sin a seizure of the gift of existence.

> In relation to God, we are like a thief who has burgled
> the house of a kindly householder and been allowed to
> keep some of the gold. From the point of view of the
> lawful owner this gold is a gift; from the point of view
> of the burglar it is a theft . . . It is the same
> with our existence. We have stolen a little of God's
> being to make it ours.[102]

Thus Weil sees a self-centered love for our own existence
and the seeming impossibility of renouncing perspective as being the fundamental stumbling blocks to any sort of human action
designed to bring unblemished good into the world or to return a
pure love to God. The original sin of the seizure of existence
is in a strictly logical sense not entailed but it is omnipresent and inevitable in human life whenever we exercise a will
other than God's, which we do as independent creatures. The
question then is how a transition is to be effected from our
present state to one in which God's goodness may be present in
human life. Weil accomplishes this transition in three steps

by showing how Christ meets the contradictory conditions of good
in this world, how through his action grace enables other men
also to meet them, and finally, what the intermediate steps are
towares coming to an explicit and finally a perfect love of God.

B. *Meeting the Conditions of Good*

As we have seen, Weil contends that the presence of real
good in this world presupposes contradictory objective and subjective conditions. The objective connection between good and
evil, she says is irreducible. She does see, however, a two-
fold way of reducing the evil in the subjective correlates, for:

> It is possible, by clearly conceiving the connexion be-
> tween the good one is pursuing and the evil attached to
> the way of behaving involved by this pursuit and to
> the conditions of behaving involved by this pursuit and
> to the conditions and consequences necessarily bound up
> with its accomplishment, to direct the attention towards
> the good only.[103]

Second:

> Since all good has some evil attached to it, it follows
> that if one desires the good and if one does not want
> to spread the corresponding evil around one, one is
> obliged, since it is impossible to avoid this evil,
> to concentrate it upon oneself.[104]

The man, however, who desires only good inevitably finds
himself in opposition to the law of the world which links good
with evil, for by so directing his energy to the good alone, he
must lessen the force which he uses to realize that good. He,
then, "inevitably falls under the stroke of affliction,"[105] because he willingly deprives himself of the force he would normally use to ward off that terror. Consequently, Weil says,
"the absolutely pure desire for the greatest amount of possible
good implies the acceptance for oneself of the last degree of
affliction . . ."[106]

Unfortunately, affliction is precisely that which is impossible for a man to desire or will for himself. It would be
possible if the acceptance of affliction constituted only an
offering and a sort of martyrdom, but it is not just an offering.
It is also, by definition, a form of suffering which can never
be willed, for it is, in fact, that which completely destroys
the ability to will at all.

> The *irreducible* nature of suffering, which makes it im-
> possible for us not to have a horror of it at the moment
> when we are undergoing it, is ultimately designed to ar-
> rest the will, just as an absurdity arrests the intel-
> ligence, or absence, non-existence, arrests love.[107]

Thus affliction appears as the prime evil for any being who
would desire pure good. The possibility of pure good is nil,
because desire of it involves desire of an unacceptable evil.

The argument may be transposed to God as well, for the
contradictory conditions of good are as applicable to him in a
world of particular forces as they are to humans. In fact, they
may be regarded as primarily applicable to God because he is
the source of all real good. God, in creating a world, created
existences other than himself. This involves a certain amount
of what is commonly called metaphysical evil, which simply indicates that the world is not the perfection of God. As Weil
says: "God alone is pure good. Creation being both God and
other than God is essentially good and evil."[108] It becomes
problematic for Weil, however, when this metaphysical evil is
made manifest, not metaphysically, but in the physical clash
of forces, for the expansion of any force towards the fullness
of being entails the diminution of other forces. It may, then,
quickly be seen that metaphysical evil leads to natural evil
(evils caused by factors other than intelligent intention), particularly affliction, and finally to the moral evil of human
agents, who, in order to escape what they perceive as threatening
their existence, resort to particular expansion of their own
power. Thus it appears that there is a certain amount of inescapable evil in simply creating a world; and because of it,
there also appears a contradiction between a perfectly good God
and the creature, for the former is, by nature, incapable of any
evil, and the latter is incapable of achieving real goodness.
And yet, Weil insists, it is man's very essence to love the Good.

If the problem arises as thorny in the first instance as
one of creator-creature, it becomes all the more so when the
claim is made that it is the cause of the Good which governs
Necessity and finally acts to redeem man. Any *act* of governance
or redemption in a world constituted by forces would seem to
fall prey to the above described contradictory conditions. In
order to be at all real within this world the act would have to

be both particular and exerting a force. This, however, could
only go to make up another force among others which would be
subject to the same expansion and diminution of forces as natural
attempts at good. Similarly, the subjective correlates would
appear as well.

It is in the Cross, however, that Weil sees all of the
contradictory conditions met, for the Cross "is at the same time
an offering freely consented to and a punishment undergone entirely against his will."[109] Christ freely offers himself to
the will of the Father, even when this means the undesired affliction. His desire for the good of the Father is such that
not only does he find himself in opposition to the good-evil
correlates by desiring and acting only on what is good, but he
also accepts the entire imposition of affliction upon himself.
Weil writes: "God can only come down to earth, become incarnate,
and continue to be pure good, by undergoing the extremest form
of affliction."[110] But, second, not only does he fulfill the
subjective conditions in this way, he also on the Cross fulfills
the objective ones as well. The act of his crucifixion is real
while yet not exerting a force nor constituting any change in
the forces of necessity. Thus, Weil claims: "Absolutely pure
good must be both real and ineffectual. What is ineffectual is
nearly always imaginary. But the Cross is certainly not something imaginary. It alone can fulfill the two conditions."[111]

In meeting the contradictory conditions Christ becomes the
mediator because on the Cross he is subject to the same laws as
the creature while at the same time he is perfectly obedient to
the pure good outside of the world of good-evil correlates. He
partakes of both the nature of God and of man by being subject
and acting according to the laws pertaining to both of them.
His mediation is that of a geometrical mean, as it were, between
the two incommensurate entities of divine and human nature; but
he is also mediator because through his affliction he becomes
the means by which human nature can partake of the divine goodness. This he accomplishes in a two-fold way. In the first
place, he becomes the prime example of a perfectly good man.
In this way, he is the revelation to us of God's nature and he
also reveals to us the fundamental constitution of our own

nature. Without Christ's perfect obedience to the Father which
is manifested locally in the Cross, Weil claims, there would
not be the grace to teach us about affliction and the fragile
limits of our own power. This is because, second, the Cross reveals perfectly, and is, the eternal nature of perfect goodness;
that is, the renunciation of power. This renunciation, however,
is not simple ceasing of the exercise of power in order to acquire higher goods beyond the realm of power; it is, instead, a
renunciation of one's power in order that another might live.
In this way, the significance of the Cross goes beyond example
and revelation, for by renouncing what is his prerogative by
right of his divinity, Christ dies in order that men might live.
In his renunciation he is able to carry those who love him beyond
what human nature could desire or accept if left to itself.
Without Christ's actual renunciation, the simple example of the
just man would not be able to enable us to do any more than give
an abstract recognition to affliction.

> We needs must have a just man to imitate so that the
> imitation of God does not simply remain an empty phrase;
> but it is also necessary, so that we may be carried
> beyond the boundaries of the will, that we should not be
> able to imitate him. One cannot desire the Cross.[112]

The truth of the Cross, however, is not simply an "historical
anecdote refracted into eternity":[113] rather, it is the eternal
truth about the world and God established from the foundation
of the world which finds its localization in time and space in
Christ's crucifixion. When God created the existence of a world
which was not of his own essence, he did not do so by the expansion of his power; instead, he accepted his own diminution in
order that something different from himself might live.

> On God's part creation is not an act of self-expansion but
> of restraint and renunciation. God and all his creatures
> are less than God alone. God accepted this diminution.
> He emptied part of his being from himself . . . God per-
> mitted the existence of things distinct from himself and
> worth infinitely less than himself. By this creative act
> he denied himself, as Christ has told us to deny our-
> selves.[114]

Because the creation of a world of self-expanding forces
brings metaphysical evil and, in turn, natural and moral evil,
these evils could easily be attributed to the creative act if

that act and the consequent governance of the world were in some
sense a force itself. Furthermore, evil could be directly attributed to God by claiming a lack of providence if creation were
purely and simply an abdication. Neither, Weil contends, is the
case. God withdraws himself so that there may be a creation,
but he does not totally abandon it (although Weil occasionally
speaks this way). Instead, there is a separation of the Father
and the Son. All of the evils of the creation are then concen-
trated on the Son from the very act of creation. Whatever evil
is attendant upon there being a creation--a sort of counter-
shock to the making of a world and a shadow cast by the pure good
intended--is expiated and redeemed originally by the Son's suffering. His suffering of the world's forces, then, in effect,
forms the ordered immaterial limits of all forces beyond which
no force will go. Because he suffers and accepts those forces
he establishes limits to the evil which they can do, for they
cannot become infinite and destroy the Son's love for the good
of the Father. But once their evil is seen as finite they can
also be regarded as capable of being "persuaded by the good" and
obeying, each in its own way, the order formed by the Son's suffering of them. The *way* in which he suffers each force, a suffering which checks the tendency of each force towards infinite
self-expansion, gives a correlate value to each which is found
in Christ's acceptance and willingness to allow each force its
own proper existence. In this way, both beauty and truth are
capable of being discerned in the physical world, and the Son,
in turn, becomes its Λόγος.

God's perfect goodness consists in his renunciation of his
own divine right in favor of the existence of other creatures.
For this reason, Weil argues, the existence of evil does not
count decisively against his goodness; rather, she feels, it
reveals it.

> Pure goodness is not anywhere to be found (in this world).
> Either God is not almighty or he is not absolutely good,
> or else he does not command everywhere where he has the
> power to do so. Thus the existence of evil here below,
> far from disproving the reality of God, is the very
> thing that reveals him in his truth.[115]

In the renunciation of creation God allows other beings to
exist, even if they are not perfectly good and their existence

does involve a certain amount of evil. For Weil, this allowance
is the chief mark of God's own goodness. Yet, God in giving
creatures their own existence does not abandon them, but gently
persuades them towards goodness and gives them value.

Goodness and value for unintelligent creation consists in
its blind, unknowing obedience to its limits. For intelligent
creation, goodness, at least, consists in knowing obedience to
limits. But moreover, for creatures of spiritual nature, it
consists in their active participation on the Cross. Human beings, as being creatures of necessity cannot help but obey the
limits of the matter of which they are composed. They, however,
do have a choice as to whether they will obey these limits as
matter does or whether they will freely consent to the existence
of other beings. In short, their ability to receive good, as
spiritual beings, consists in their ability to renounce themselves, like Christ, so that others may live. This renunciation
is their participation in the Cross, and in that participation
they are then made in the image of the forsaken Son, through
whose mediation, God's full goodness is revealed in perfect absence.

C. *Attention and the Seeds of Grace*

If we, by grace, renounce our self-perspective in favor of
obedience to God and then are afflicted and yet continue to love
there is a final and irretractable giving back to God's own love
the existence of which he made a gift to us at birth. We cannot
will or desire affliction, but we can consent to its existence,
and if affliction should beset us and we continue to love and
consent even in the void, then affliction may be the occasion
for a perfect love.

> Affliction is a marvel of divine technique--It is a
> simple and ingenious device to introduce into the soul
> of a finite creature that immensity of force, blind,
> brutal and cold . . . The man to whom such a thing
> occurs has not part in the operation . . . But through-
> out the horror he can go on wanting to love. There is
> no impossibility in that, no obstacle, one could almost
> say no difficulty. Because no pain, however great,
> up to the point of losing consciousness, touches that part
> of the soul which consents to a right orientation . . .
> The man whose soul remains oriented towards God while
> a nail is driven through it finds himself nailed to the

very centre of the universe; the true centre, which is
not the middle, which is not in space and time, which is
God.   In this marvelous dimension . . . the soul can
traverse the whole of space and time and come into the
actual presence of God.116

Affliction thus appears as a sort of radical experimental
application of Cartesian doubt.   In affliction, all in man--
personality, finite attachments and will--is stripped away leav-
ing only the essence of man, for all that is left is the love
of the soul for God.   But two questions arise.   Does this mean
that God's goodness is only present in affliction consented to?
Furthermore, even if we understand this limit of perfect love to
exist, how does one move from repulsion of affliction to its
acceptance?   Christ did so because his will was that of the
Father from his birth, but that is not the case with us.   The
answer to this latter question helps provide an answer to the
former.   Weil certainly understood that "affliction in itself
contains no gift from above,"[117] and that to be afflicted was
not automatically to feel contact with God through Necessity.
Without preparation, she claims, affliction can be almost equivalent to hell.   "If the soul stops loving it falls, even in
this life, into something which is almost equivalent to hell."[118]
The union with God on Christ's Cross can only come if we have
already, like Christ, renounced our self-perspective and then
when affliction has beset us and stripped away the last vestige
of the self, if we continue to wait fo God alone, he will come
and join the infinitely distant creature to himself.   For the
soul which is not prepared and which has continued to invest
ultimate worth in the things of necessity, however, a screen is
erected thorugh which the love of God cannot pass.   What is required, then, is to show how we can become prepared through
gradual renunciations of the self which imitate and participate
in varying degrees of Christ's own renunciation.   Each of these
renunciations then becomes a part of God's goodness incarnate
in the world.

Perspective, bound up as it is with our sense of worth and
existence, is not something we easily give up since the dissolution of our perspective ultimately involves an acceptance of
death.   For this reason, Weil believed in Socratic fashion, that

if philosophy is the search for unconditioned values it is also
learning how to die. But our very instincts of self-survival run
contrary to this idea and keep us from ever willingly renouncing
our perspective. It was St. Augustine who said, "My love is my
weight"; Weil, in similar fashion, contended that our natural
attachment to our terrestial existence is weighty and constitutes
a sort of spiritual gravity to which we are constantly subject.
Consequently, she argued, that as long as we remain subject to
this gravity there is no way from man to God. In fact, she continues, we cannot even legitimately make the decision to believe
in God in this state, for the object of this belief will involve
a certain degree of falsehood as long as it is at all tied to
our present conceptions of value. If, then, man is ever to
overcome gravity, clearly he needs the help of something beyond
his own powers. He must rely on the grace of God's descent.

> The infinity of space and time separates us from God. How
> can we seek for him? How can we go towards him? Even if
> we were to walk for endless centuries we should do no
> more than go round and round the world. Even in an aero-
> plane we could not do anything else. We are incapable
> of progressing vertically. We cannot take one step
> towards the heavens. God crosses the universe and comes
> to us.[119]

Whatever possibility of real good there is in our lives
must be the result of the operation of supernatural grace which
overcomes our natural gravity; a grace which does not bypass human faculties, but enters them and transforms them. What does
happen is that God "comes like a beggar" and "we have the power
to consent to receive him or to refuse."[120] This is not to
glorify the role of the will in the drama of salvation. It is,
rather, an idea which is consistent with God's activity. God
never acts with the force of compulsion. He has created through
an act of renunciation which allows creatures an existence worth
less than the fullness of his goodness. If he should reveal the
fullness of his goodness, they could not exist, being so much
less than his goodness. In order, then, to decrease humans and
finally, to recreate them, he comes in a fashion which respects
what they are as intelligent creatures with a certain degree of
free will. To create an attitude or disposition in them without
their consent would be to violate them. When and if they consent,

they then, in turn, accept his goodness for what it is. His
goodness is then incarnated in them. That goodness has the virtue of a seed which grows in the human soul until it is finally
united with God.

> If we remain deaf he comes back again and again like
> a beggar, and also, like a beggar, one day he stops
> coming. If we consent God places a little seed in us
> and he goes away again.[121]

Consent to God's goodness, however, already seems to presuppose an act of renunciation of which we are not supposedly
capable according to our natural loves. The implantation of
the seed of God's goodness is the implantation in us of a *via
renunciationis*; yet without the seed we could not renounce ourselves and without renunciation of our own claims to peculiar
benefits the seed cannot be implanted. The seed, in order to
be placed in us, requires that there be some kind of void in us
so that it may have room.

The paradox can be explained if it is realized that the
consent and the implantation are not two actions, or an action
and a reaction, but two aspects of the same action. One aspect
belongs to the operation of grace, the other to the receiving
human subject. Weil gives this reasoning by postulating an
'uncreated' and 'divine' part of the human soul which is destined
for the love of God. This postulation, however, easily lends
itself to the misinterpretation that there is something already
formed in the human soul which simply requires liberating in
order that it may spring fullformed and without alteration into
a communion of equals with God. This is not at all what Weil
really means. What the 'uncreated and divine' part of the soul
is, is something unformed. It is, in fact, basically a bare
expectation and desire for a good that cannot be satisfied by
any particular good in this world. Weil herself explains it in
this way in at least two different places. She writes:

> At the bottom of the heart of every human being, from
> earliest infancy until the tomb, there is something
> that goes on indomitably expecting, in the teeth of all
> experience of crimes committed, suffered, and witnessed,
> that good and not evil will be done to him. It is this
> above all that is sacred in every human being.[122]

Further, she writes in a manner that makes it clear that this

expectation is not for terrestial goods; but for God's goodness
alone.

> There is a reality outside the world, that is to say,
> outside space and time, outside man's mental universe,
> outside any sphere whatsoever that is accessible to hu-
> man faculties.
> Corresponding to this reality, at the centre of the
> human heart, is the longing for an absolute good, a
> longing which is always there and is never appeased by
> any object in this world.[123]

Because there is this divine part of the soul, the soul has
a capacity of standing in the attitude of waiting for its desired
good. Moreover, it also has the possibility of recognizing and
loving particular manifestations of goodness.[124] All this is
due to God's own grace of creating such a part of the soul. A
void can then be introduced in human willing when it recognizes
a value which intimates a descent from the source of all goodness. This void, however, can only come about when a value is
presented for recognition. Again this is the result of divine
causality. In both the existence of the value and the recognition of it there is evidence of a dual causality where Necessity
cooperates with Goodness, for in the creation, through the mediation of the Son, Beauty and Truth, the first offspring of the
Good, become qualities of the world and its contents. Our
recognition of them as values indicates a similar cooperation of
what there is in us that is capable of recognizing values for
themselves and the part of us that wills, for in recognizing
them as values the will submits to the higher part of the soul
and respects the independent existence of the value. Both Beauty
and Truth can therefore create a chink in the armor of our egos--
a chink created by the operation of the good. In this chink,
God places the seed in our souls. This is the first step of
decreation.

     To say, however, that it is Beauty and Truth which is the
first entrance of the seed of God's goodness into men makes the
situation sound far more grandiose than Weil actually conceived
it to be. She believed that this first recognition comes in
much smaller things and that each created thing, having a value,
is capable of being the first means of our introduction to God.
In this sense, very particular beauties or truths can be what

she called μεταξύ, or intermediate means, of God's love in the
world. For example, she cites the beauty of a Gregorian chant
or Romanesque architecture as being capable of persuading us to
give our consent to the existence of realities outside of ourselves. They are, as she says, snares set for the soul by God
so that he may place the seed in us--the seed which in time, if
unbetrayed, grows into the tree of the Cross. Similarly she
sees other μεταξύ in our understanding of the truth that the
world is composed of forces that are quite distant from goodness.
In this sense, the real heartfelt understanding of human fragility and recognition of the eventuality of one's own death can
also serve as a μεταξύ.

Once the seed has been planted, it grows solely according
to its own virtue until the substance of our being becomes nothing
but the love which God bears for us and which we bear for him.
There is nothing we can do directly to promote this growth, except wait, and continue to consent to the growth of the seed
within us. But because full contact with God does not occur
until the growth of the seed is complete, our consent is not un-
shakeable and cannot be until our lives are derived only from
God. Rather, we must stand in faith, which Weil says, citing
St. John of the Cross, is "a dark night of the soul" because
God and the soul are not full united. In this night, there are
activities which need to be undertaken; activities which are
illumined by the light of the soul's first intermediate contact
with God but which do not yet have the fullness of God's goodness in them. These activities of the life of faith are two-
fold.[125] On the one hand, they consist of the soul's spiritual
waiting. On the other hand, they consist of the duties which
the will performs in obedience to light received. The interplay
of these two factors is what Weil called 'non-active union.'

The activity of the part of the soul destined to receive
God consists in a sort of spiritual immobility. This spiritual
immobility, however, is not purely passive in the sense that it
does nothing. It is, rather, an activity of waiting and expectation, or in the biblical phrase Weil so often employed, it
is waiting ἐν ὑπομένη. The soul cannot take one step on its
own accord towards God; it must patiently await his descent.

But to wait for God alone implies then the refusal on the part
of the soul to become attached to anything less than God, or
to accept any finite good in his place. This, accordingly, gives
at least negative criteria to this activity. Weil writes:

> To believe in God is not a decision we can make. All we
> can do is to not decide to give our love to false gods.
> In the first place, we can decide not to believe that
> the future contains for us an all-sufficient good . . .
> In the second place, we can decide not to confuse the
> necessary with the good. A thing everyone can do is to
> keep his attention fixed upon this truth.[126]

If these negative criteria constitute the truth of where
we are not to expect full goodness then positive criteria must
be adduced to give us some indication of what we are to wait
for. Waiting (*attente*) implies an orientation of our desire and
a direction of our sight to the place where we are to look while
waiting (*attention*). Our souls are so made that they do desire
good and direct their attention towards that which they believe
will provide it. Unfortunately, "a part of the evil that is
within us we project into the objects of our attention and desire; and they reflect it back to us."[127] When the necessary
and the good are confused, our attention is directed towards
that which will serve the continuance of perspective, for unless we love what is completely pure we cannot avoid having our
loves tainted by self-interest. The object of our attention
then receives the projection of whatever evil is within us because we desire them for a reason which is less than good. When,
in turn, the object does not provide the expected good, a good
which is due to our illusion in the first place, we come to
feel our own evil. Thus the cycle continues. But, Weil adds,
"if through attention and love we project a part of our evil
upon something pure, it cannot be defiled by it; it remains pure
and does not reflect the evil back on us, and so we are delivered
from the evil."[128] As examples of things which possess this
purity, Weil cites such things as the Lord's Prayer, the Sacra-
ments, sacred texts and the beauty of the world. In a lesser
degree she also includes inspired works of art and human beings
"in whom God dwells."

These objects of purity, Weil argues, can only have this
quality through God's mediated presence in them. They are

"remembrances of himself; that is to say, things in which he is
present, for otherwise their purity would fade away through
being in contact with evil."[129] By directing our attention to
these μεταξύ our love is oriented towards God and a sustaining
intermediate contact is gained with him. But this contact is
also more than sustaining for it also provides the means by
which the soul is transformed and drawn closer to God. For the
soul which has not yet given its prime consent to God, by ab-
sorbing the evil directed upon them and not reflecting it back,
these μεταξύ provide an incommensurate element in human experience which is witness to the loving renunciation of God. In
this way, "all the soul's horror at the evil it harbours is
changed into love for the divine purity."[130] For the soul which
has given its first consent there is a continued absorption of
evil and transformation in the soul towards the love of God.

     In Weil, this dissolution of the evil in us and transforma-
tion towards righteousness is actual and not just juridical or
imputed. Here, while the efficacy of any sacramental μετοξύ
derives from God alone, the effect must also correspond to an
actual change in man and this change is in the increased renunciation of the ego. In this sense, Weil understands there to
be a direct correlation between attention and the transformation effected in us by the sacrament, for attention, in her
technical use of the term, is a renunciation of the ego in order
to see the world without perspectival interference. Miklos
Veto in commenting on the idea, says: "The essence of attention
is not the gain it brings us, but the fact that it is in operation which makes us turn ourselves outward by ridding our minds
of the self."[131] When we first direct our attention to a sacramental μεταξύ we do so because a void has already been created
in us and we have consented to the existence of something outside the purview of our wills. But, moreover, our continued
direction of attention towards the object means our continued
consent to its good. Through this continued attention, in which
we are already participating in the goodness of God's renunciation, the effect of the sacrament is to further attract us and
increase our attention. It takes away our evil and transforms
us because our attention and consent increases and deepens.

Attention, then, is basically of the same virtue as prayer and
in fact, often is prayer. We pray because we find God good, but
one of the prime benefits of prayer is to increase that appreciation and to submit further our wills to God, until in the
activities of life we begin to "pray without ceasing." Our attention, then, constitutes a mediation of God's love in the
physical world. It is something which is at first engendered
by God and which finally returns to him in the form of human
lives lived perfectly according to his will, but which is mediated because it takes place through us and with our consent.

Weil, however, understood that while these sacramental
μεταξύ are sufficient for God's operations on the soul that men
do not spend the majority of their lives in churches or in contemplation of the beauty of the world. For this reason, she
found it necessary to conceive "symbols making it possible to
read the divine truths in the circumstances of daily life and
work . . . For this purpose the symbols must not be arbitrary
but must be found inscribed, by a providential arrangement, in
the very nature of things."[132] Through these symbols it then
becomes possible to establish an entire range of secondary
μεταξύ by which through attention man can order his life. Each
thing in the world can therefore be a means of evidencing God's
love and through which we, by renouncing our self will in respecting its value, can love God.[133] Once such a system is
established it can then be seen how the entire world order can
serve the goodness of God.

Despite the fact that it is loving attention and pure desire for the Good alone which raises the soul, the growth of
the seed does not always proceed smoothly and continued consent
to its growth does not come entirely automatically. Elevation
of the soul through the increased attention which renounces any
particular claim on the object of attention necessarily implies
a correlated decrease and death of the pre-eminence of the more
mediocre parts of the soul. These mediocre parts of the soul
are sensitive to that which impends the cessation of their
dominance in human life. They naturally recoil from it, just
as the flesh quite instinctively jerks away from fire. Because
of this instinct, then, there is a very real conflict within

the soul of man which must be won by the part meant for God before one can be united in perfect love with him. In this conflict the will plays a very definite role. Like the divine part
of the soul there are both negative and positive criteria attached to it.

     Negatively considered, there is an effort of the will in
"keeping one's gaze directed towards God, bringing it back when
it has wandered, and fixing it sometimes with all the intensity
of which it is capable."[134] This effort, in effect, is a sort
of uprooting of all the tares that threaten to choke the growth
of the seed. Furthermore, this negative effort is the hardest
of all because the mediocre parts of the soul which do not want
to die "fabricate every falsehood that can possibly divert our
attention."[135] They do this easily, for our attention, while
it should be directed towards the Good which is unrepresentable
under the conditions of necessity, also needs a particular object. In this area, falsehood can arise in any number of ways
by making a particular mediated good an absolute one with which
the mediocre parts of the soul are perfectly comfortable. They
can, therefore, divert attention and unless there is a definite
effort made to suppress whatever prevents us from looking towards
God, the higher part of the soul runs a very definite danger of
committing the treason of choosing to attach itself to this world
instead of the goodness of God for which it is meant and for
which God has begun to prepare the soul.

     The positive aspect of the role of the will is found in
the duties it undertakes according to the light in the soul.
Here certain distinctions must be carefully made. The duties
which are acted upon are not initiated by the will; rather, they
are the obligations enjoined upon it by God. Neither is the
performance of these duties to be confused with legalism for
the duties and obligations are not a set of prescriptive ethical
dogmas applicable in all states and circumstances in the same
way. Although Weil insisted on a final perfection, she was not
a fanatic and, in fact, abhorred ethical fanaticism as a sort of
idolatry which confuses the state of one's own soul with the
transcendent good. What these duties are, then, are the fruits
of attention borne out in action. The will can neither create

good nor can it act in a fashion better than the state of the
character formed by love from which it derives.[136] To do the
latter is like trying to pay a debt when one has only an amount
of money less than the debt. But it can act on whatever good
it receives through attention. In this way, through the mediated
love which God bears us in attention our love becomes a mediated
love which he bears to the rest of creation through our actions
derived from attention. Similarly, through the performance of
our duties the light shed upon our attention can increase because in our actions we become more and more obedient to God.
Without the performance of these duties there can only be back-
sliding and treason.[137] Finally in time as the actions of the
entire human being become more and more harmonized with the light
received from God, and their conflict ceases, these actions involve less and less deliberate effort and become quite automatic.

> The model is the crucifixion of Christ. Even though
> an act of obedience when seen from the outside, may seem
> accompanied by a great expenditure of activity, there
> is in reality, within the soul, nothing but passive
> endurance.[138]

D. *Implicit and Explicit Love*

Once the soul has attained to 'non-active action it might
be expected that it has reached a point of direct and explicit
love of God wherein God's reality is known directly by the soul.
This, however, is not quite the case, for Weil argues, there
cannot be an explicit love of God until God becomes fully present
to the soul and this only occurs when God himself "comes in person to take the hand of his future bride."[139] Yet, she continues, because the commandment to love God is laid on us so impera-
tively, a permanent obligation is implied. Because of this,
there must be an indirect or implicit love of God. The term
"love of God," she says, is permissible for this indirect love
because of the development bound to follow latter.

Technically, the phrase "implicit love of God" can be applied to any action in which that action proceeds from the light
of loving attention, and, therefore, to all that has been previously discussed under that point. A certain confusion ensues,
however, in treating the essay *The Implicit Forms of the Love*

of God unless it is understood that in that essay an implicit
form of the love of God is already a highly developed and altru-
istic form of love. Without this understanding it would be easy
to assume that what Weil says in that essay is meant to be a
starting point for love of God. Because the discussion takes
place at such a high level, however, it is all but impossible
to use what she says there as a starting point for the spiritual
life. What the best way of taking the discussion is, then, is
to assume that just as the loves in that essay are implicit because of their indirect participation in God's goodness, so then
are the lesser loves also implicit because they embody another
weaker form of the implicit love, which is seen by their also
embodying a form of God's presence.

According to Weil there are four things here below which an
implicit love can have as its immediate object and in which love
God is really, but secretly, present. They are the love of
neighbor, love of the beauty of the world, love of religious
practices, and love of friendship. All of these loves, Weil
says, have a virtue that is "exactly and rigorously equivalent";[140] a virtue which is imitative of God's own love in the
crucifixion. It is Weil's claim that "the soul is not ready to
receive the personal visit of its Master, unless it has in it
all three indirect loves to a high degree."[141] Nevertheless it
is purely contingent upon circumstances and temperament which
is the first to enter the soul. But once one of these loves
has entered the soul it can easily lead to the others, for each
of these loves is a participation in one of the ways that God
himself loves; therefore to begin to love in a way that God
loves is to soon incorporate the other aspects of his love as
well. When the soul finally comes to love God in the fullest
and most explicit sense, these loves, although preparatory, do
not disappear; "they become infinitely stronger and all loves
taken together make only a single love."[142] We shall treat each
in turn.

Love of our neighbor, Weil contends, is strictly equivalent
to treating him with justice, for, she says, "The Gospel makes
no distinction between the love of our neighbour and justice."[143]
In making this equation, however, she intends each term to be
informed by the other. On the one hand, the charity which we

bear towards our neighbor has to be informed by considerations
of justice, which is to say that in recognizing the need of our
neighbor we recognize that it is our obligation to aid him, and
that we are not simply to regard him as the means toward increase
of our own virtue. We recognize in him the claim that he has
upon us to be treated as a person and not an object. On the
other hand, justice has to be informed by love so that the benefaction of our neighbor includes the obligation of giving whenever he is in need, and giving abundantly. Where justice is
divorced from charity, it dispenses with the obligations of him
who possesses from giving. On the side of the recipient, a just
charity obliges him to express gratitude while allowing him to
do so as a person and not as a 'servile animal.' The obligation
of gratitude is as incumbent upon the recipient as the obligation
to give is on the benefactor.

Weil found the symbol of the balance to best exemplify her
concept of justice, because it indicates a proportional equality
between two parties. Justice on the natural level well reflects
this idea, for there, there is a certain balance between forces
which tends to equalize them. In the realm of natural human
justice this is shown in the mutual consent of two parties to
a proportional balance between their powers. When there is no
proportion of force, however, there is never need to consult
justice. The strong simply command and the weak obey; in the
realm of nature there is no need for the former to consult the
latter. This is particularly evident in dealings with the afflicted, for in the natural realm they are nothing but lumps of
matter.

In dealings with the afflicted, however, Weil saw that
natural justice could be superceded by a supernatural love which
establishes a proportion where there naturally is none. "The
supernatural virtue of justice consists of behaving exactly as
though there were equality when one is the stronger in an un-
equal relationship."[144] But this equality can only be established on two counts; that we direct our attention to the afflicted and see humanity in the lump of matter by the side of
the road, and that, consequently, we renounce our right to command. In turn, the attention directed towards the afflicted

creates him, *ex nihilo* as it were, once again as a human being.
The afflicted, in their turn, can then have the possibility
through this newly established proportion to give their gratitude
and thanks, which is to say they are allowed once again to act
as human beings. The attention which seeks to benefit them does
not do so by coercion. Rather, it always respects their free
consent and in this way allows them to be human once again.

Man by loving his neighbor in this way imitates the very
creation of the universe by God and God's saving incarnation,
for in those cases God directed his attention towards that which
did not exist. In doing so he renounced his power and consented
to the existence of beings worth infinitely less than himself.
But moreover, in so giving them existence he also gave them the
means by which he could be thanked and loved as an equal. This
he did by becoming the mediator--that is, one of them who took
on their sufferings on the Cross. In the same manner, the one
who loves his afflicted neighbor becomes a kind of mediator
through his unblinded recognition of the state of affliction and
his solidarity with those undergoing it. By this means he accepts the affliction as his own and gives up his own being to
the man who has lost his. And he does so quite automatically,
for in his solidarity the need of the afflicted is felt as his
own. To the person who loves with this kind of love, giving
of himself follows as inexorably from the recognition of affliction as eating does when he is hungry.

> The actions that follow are just the automatic effect
> of this moment of attention. The attention is creative.
> But at the moment when it is engaged it is a renuncia-
> tion . . . The man accepts to be diminished by con-
> centrating on an expenditure of energy, which will not
> extend his own power but will only give existence to a
> being other than himself, who will exist independently
> of him. Still more to desire the existence of the other
> is to transport himself into him by sympathy, and, as
> a result, to have a share in the state of inert matter
> which is his.[145]

The love of the beauty of the world involves the same renunciation "that is an image of the creative renunciation of
God."[146] It is thus a complement to love of neighbor for whereas
loving our neighbor involves "imitating the divine love which
created us and all our fellows, by loving the order of the

world we imitate the divine love which created this universe of
which we are a part."[147]

There is, of course, a certain dissimilarity between the
two for there is no question of giving our attention to the
beauty of the world in order to create beauty where there was
none before. Nor can we, in this case, renounce our power to
command the universe, because we have never possessed it. The
act of renunciation in both cases, however, does bear other
similarities, for in both cases the direction of our attention
involves giving complete consent to the existence of something
external to us. In regard to beauty this renunciation amounts
to giving up the sort of imaginary divinity that perspective
confers on our thoughts and actions. To give our attention to
the beauty of the world, therefore, involves giving up being an
imaginary center of the world and accepting reality for what it,
in truth, is.

> To give up our imaginary position as the center, to
> renounce it, not only intellectually but in the imagina-
> tive part of the soul, that means to awaken to what is
> real and eternal, to see the true light and hear the
> true silence. A transformation then takes place at
> the very roots of our sensibility, in our immediate re-
> ception of sense impressions and psychological impres-
> sions. It is a transformation analogous to that which
> takes place in the dark of evening on a road, where we
> suddenly discern as a tree what we had at first seen
> as a stooping man . . . We see the same colors; we
> hear the same sounds, but not in the same way.[148]

When we give up our positions as centers we can then see
that other things in the universe are also centers of existence.
This renunciation is also to consent to the rule of mechanical
necessity in matter, and finally, it is a recognition and love
of the free choice at the center of each individual soul, which
respects that choice as free and independent of our own wills.

Properly speaking, Weil adds, only the world as a whole deserves the name of beauty. Therefore, our recognition of it and
consent to it must be total if there is to be an implicit love
of God. But there are also secondary beauties which reflect
the sense of proportion and divine inspiration. Through these,
we can gradually come to appreciate the full beauty of the universe, if we do not arrest our love in any one of them. In this

sense, particular beauties can attract us to good whether they
are found in nature or art. In fact, in art and science we are
actively to express the beauty of the universe.

The best art, Weil contends, is that in which the beauty of
the world is expressed without the perspective of the artist's
ego and imagination. "A poem is beautiful, which is to say the
reader does not wish it other than it is. It is in this way that
art imitates the beauty of the world. The suitability of things,
beings and events consists only in this, that they exist and
that we should not wish that they did not exist or that they had
been different."[149] Similarly, true science must do the same
sort of thing for "The object of science is the presence of
Wisdom in the universe, Wisdom of which we are the brothers, the
presence of Christ, expressed through the matter which constitutes the world."[150] The object of science is this Wisdom and
science must search for the real truth and beauty of the world
and attempt to reproduce it in thought. To know matter and
to seek the wisdom which governs it is to understand the beauty
of the world. Science is not just an abstract sort of attention
to facts, although this may be helpful, but a real desire for
goodness.

The love of religious practices is also an implicit love
of God, for although the name of God enters into it, there is
still not yet a direct presence of God. Once again his presence
is mediated. But unlike other implicit forms of love, the love
of religious practices is instituted by a specific revelation of
God himself. To understand why this is so goes to the root of
Weil's understanding of religion.

As we have seen previously, Weil believed that it was only
through contact with an object perfectly pure that the evil in
us can be gradually purged and our souls transformed. Moreover,
she contends, we cannot do without this contact with purity, for
it is by desire for the good alone by which we are saved and
this desire needs to be directed. Religious practices correspond
precisely to this need in a way that nothing else can. She
writes:

> Religion . . . corresponds to this desire, and it is
> desire that saves . . .
> Attention animated by desire is the whole foundation of
> religious practices. That is why no system of morality
> can take their place.[151]

But because the object of attention must be perfectly pure, and because no object with which we come into contact naturally possesses this purity, she then argues, that the object must be instituted by divine convention.

The use of the term 'convention' unfortunately is slightly suggestive of ritualistic fuss and arbitrariness. This clearly is not what Weil means. What she does mean is that in order for an object to have the needed purity, it must have it by right and by definition, such that no matter what the state of the priest, or particular theology of the church or religion, the object in question retains its saving power. This sort of convention can only be instituted and ratified by God. The two conventions which she then cites are the Name of God and the Eucharist. Both have the power to deliver the soul from evil, by virtue of God's own implicit presence in them, when the soul directs its full gaze upon them. Neither have any essential properties attached to them except this power to save. They have neither beauty of sound or shape nor anything else that would give any indication of their power. Thus, their power can only be verified experimentally and never by argument.[152]

The love of religious practices embodies an element of renunciation just as do the two previously described loves. Unlike them, however, the renunciation of this love does not strictly involve a consent to another's existence except in the sense that the soul through attention puts its life in the hands of God. It is a renunciation, however, in the sense that in directing its attention towards God, the soul recognizes that it has no claim to any goodness on its own and that its desire for good can only be nourished and satisfied through God's own love. In this way, an additional indispensable love is provided which must take place in order for salvation to occur.

All three of these implicit forms of love of God have an impersonal character. This Weil felt ought to be the way it should be until there is a direct and personal contact with God. In part, this is due to the fact that if "our souls are hid in Christ with God" we can never understand fully the true meaning of personhood until we have reached full contact with him. From another side, it also helps us avoid confusing God's universal goodness with particulars. But there is another form of implicit

love which does involve a particular love and that is friendship.

The particular love for another human being also reflects
and intimates divine love. The form of divine love there embodied, however, is not that of the crucifixion but rather that
of the joy found in the love of the persons of the Trinity. It
is a love that is only found between equals and which consists
in the rejoicing in the good of the beloved. Furthermore, it
is an active wish that the autonomy of the beloved be preserved
at all costs.

Weil distinguished between this sort of friendship and that
which is formed simply by the bonds of necessity, although the
former may first occur through the workings of necessity. Any
number of things can cause the bond of affection by creating
a material or psychological need that can only be met through
the bond. Often enough, friendships that have mutual consent
can degenerate into only this need and in all friendships of
this sort, the mark of necessity in the affection is evidenced
by the consideration that the dissolution of the bond "really
causes a decrease in the vital energy"[153] in at least one of the
parties. When this happens, if there is no mutual consent, the
party who suffers the loss inevitably gives up the affection,
not wishing his friend to have a good he does not have, or he
reconstitutes the bond along lines in which he becomes quite
servile so that he can meet his need.

> When a human being is attached to another by a bond of
> affection which contains any degree of necessity, it is
> impossible that he should wish autonomy to be preserved
> in both himself and in the other. It is impossible by
> the mechanism of nature. It is, however, made possible
> by the miraculous intervention of the supernatural.
> This miracle is friendship.[154]

In true friendship there is an attraction to another because
of some good he possesses. But there is also a respect for the
autonomy of the friend, and a consent that he should keep this
good and dispose of his soul according to his own attention.[155]
Without this respect and consent there can be no true equality
between the parties, for in that case, whatever equality there
might be consists only in a standoff of powers. When there is
respect for the autonomy of the other "there is equality because

each wishes to preserve the faculty of free consent both in himself and in the other."[156] Thus the equality is formed of the
bond of supernatural love.

This bond of friendship which represents the autonomy of
the other unites the two only over distance. In the mutual consent, "the two friends have fully consented to be two and not
one, they respect the distance which the fact of being two distinct creatures places between them."[157] But in their respect
of this distance they can be united, just as the persons of the
Trinity are through love. Weil concludes:

> "Where there are two or three gathered together in my
> name there am I in the midst of them." Pure friendship
> is an image of the original and perfect friendship that
> belongs to the Trinity and is the very essence of God.
> It is impossible for two human beings to be one while
> scrupulously respecting the distance that separates
> them, unless God is present in each of them. The point
> at which parallels meet is infinity.[158]

At the end of the period of preparation constituted by the
implicit loves in which God's presence seems absence, God comes
to the soul "to possess it and transport its center near to his
very heart."[159] When he does so the soul is wedded to him.
After this nuptial union, however, the loves for neighbor, the
beauty of the world, etc., do not disappear; rather, "these first
loves continue; they are more intense than before, but they are
different . . . Love in all these forms has become a movement
of God himself, a ray merged in the light of God."[160] Weil
describes this moment in a letter to Joë Bousquet, using the
ancient image of an egg:

> The egg is this world we see. The bird in it is Love,
> the Love which is God himself and which lives in the
> depths of every man, though first as an invisible need.
> When the shell is broken, and the being is released, it
> still has this same world before it. But it is no
> longer inside. Space is opened and torn apart. The
> spirit, leaving the miserable body in some corner, is
> transported to a point outside space, which is not a point
> of view, which has no perspective, but from which this
> world is seen as it is, unconfused by perspective. Com-
> pared to what is inside the egg, space has become an
> infinity to the second or rather the third power. The
> moment stands still. The whold of space is filled,
> even though sounds can be heard, with a dense silence
> which is not an absence of sound but is a positive object
> of sensation; it is the secret word, the word of Love who
> holds us in his arms from the beginning.[161]

Once this explicit love is described and posited as a goal
of spiritual activity, however, a question arises concerning
the relation between explicit love of God and the love of God in
affliction. On the one hand, Weil talks of this union as if
there were none greater. This would seem to make explicit love
perfect love. Yet at the same time, in *The Love of God and Affliction*, she makes it clear that it is only in actual affliction
and total absence that one can perfectly love God, irretractably
giving back to him all of one's being.

In order to clarify the relation between the two it is
necessary to consider briefly two models Weil had in mind when
describing the spiritual progress of the soul, namely, the "dark
nights" of St. John of the Cross and the Analogy of the Cave of
Plato, the two of which Weil felt coincided in their description
of the spiritual life. The Cave Analogy, Weil says, describes
two periods of void, the first being when one is unchained and
walks out of the cave without being able to use his customary,
but illusory, bearings, and the second is when one emerges from
the cave and is blinded by the light. Weil says, "These two
periods correspond exactly to the two 'dark nights' described
by St. John of the Cross, the night of sense and the night of
spirit."[162] After these 'nights' the soul comes into the explicit presence of God. "The final moment, when the emancipated
being looks upon the sun itself, the good itself, that is to
say God himself as he really is, corresponds to what St. John
of the Cross calls the spiritual marriage."[163] This spiritual
marriage is Weil's explicit love. But this is not the final
stage, for, as Plato indicates and Weil says St. John of the
Cross also indicates, once the soul has contemplated the sun it
must return to the cave. Here the explicit love of God must be
incarnated and bear fruit within the world. It is in this incarnation that love is perfected.

Weil's point is that while we are still alive we continue
to have gravity and act in this world, even if we have totally
consented to our death and the possibility of affliction, and
therefore have been decreated in spirit. It is not until actual
death, whether in affliction or not, that gravity is completely
overcome. The explicit love of God therefore needs to be acted

upon, for God's own love is a love that incarnates itself and
perfects itself in act, even in the extremes of affliction.
Thus it may be said that Christ from his birth explicitly loved
the Father and that in the Incarnation he began to perfect the
love that was perfect on the Cross. Weil says: "Christ was in
that state at birth. And yet it was only on the Cross that he
became complete."[164] If, therefore, the seed has grown into an
explicit love of God, one's actions become God's own actions,
and if, while in this state, affliction strikes and one still
continues to love even when God is no longer present but completely absent, love is perfected. "If the tree of life, and
not simply the divine seed is already formed in a man's soul at
the time when extreme affliction strikes him, then he is nailed
to the same cross as Christ."[165]

Once it is understood that explicit love and perfect love
are not the same thing, and that explicit love while a goal in
itself must be related to the limit of perfection, it becomes
possible to distinguish and relate all the steps of spiritual
life to this limit which is realized in Christ. What Weil is
describing in the process of decreation and incarnation is a
schematization of divine activity which distinguishes and relates the various parts by the ultimate criteria of Christ's
Cross. She does this in two ways. The first is in relation to
God's own activity, wherein the Incarnation and Creation are
understood as the self-renunciation of God. Of course, the
Creation, Incarnation and Crucifixion are part of the same unique
activity of God which is manifest in the Cross, but at the same
time the first two must converge in the Crucifixion to take on
the significance Weil ascribes to them. The second is in human
activity wherein Christ's consent and love in affliction defines
all the steps of human spirituality from the perfect love of
being nailed to his Cross to actual death consented to, to lesser forms of consented suffering. It is for this reason that
explicit love is considered a state that comes upon spiritual
death and that implicit loves are also treated as renunciation
and consent to the Father's will. Each one of these steps can
be distinguished by the degree to which they imitate and participate in Christ's passion. But they are also consequently related to each other by being a form of Christ's love that leads

one on towards perfect love. Each form is, in fact, an act of
God's own love which becomes more and more fully incarnate in the
soul.

Weil certainly understood that spiritual life does not always proceed in this schematized straight line and that the perfect love of God was probably only realized in a few, and, perhaps, that only a few reached an explicit love before death.
She understood that affliction, accidental as it is, may come
before we are prepared, or not at all if we are, in which case
the fruit our love bears is not that of perfection but very
nearly so. She also understood that despite previous degrees of
preparedness, explicit love may come at the same time as death
if one fully consents to undergo it actually. Here the consent
can bear immediate fruit in death which is a participation in
the Cross. But her point is not so much that these steps unde-
viatingly follow each other to the same point, but that in these
steps God's love and goodness is mediated into human life at all
levels. This does not mean that we can ever be satisfied with
only partial forms of good, but it does mean that we and the
world are fed by God's grace through the mediation of the Son;
fed, not to satiation, but to the degree that strengthens us to
realize more and more God's goodness.

Weil's religious doctrine of mediation can be clearly seen
now to rest in her fundamental appreciation of Christ's Cross.
Yet, while the Cross is the primal genius of mediation which
gives the doctrine its meaning, there is also a structure to mediation that needs further uncovering, and this is found in
Weil's understanding of mediation in the ancient Greeks. This
is a structure that will give Weil's work as a whole its overall
coherence. We shall therefore now turn to Weil's Platonic understanding of mediation.

CHAPTER III

THE PLATONISM OF MEDIATION

For Simone Weil, Christ the crucified incarnate Word is the
Mediator between man and God because he has gone to the furthest
distance and taken the entire weight of necessity and sin on his
shoulders. In doing so he establishes a blessed contact between
man and God that is perfected in absence. Without this act,
Weil contends, God could not be held to be perfectly good in
creating a world, and without it we would have to remain eternally separated from God. Yet, Cabaud and others, while they
are incorrect in not seeing the need Weil sees for the actual
incarnation and crucifixion of the Word, are right in seeing
that Christ does play the role of example and paradigm in Weil's
thought. We have already seen this in how Weil makes Christ
the model of spirituality in the implicit loves of God and in
the Son's function as Λόγος, which is a freely willed subjection
to necessity. But the model of Christ's crucifixion is more
than a literary device in these instances for Weil; it also
serves two further purposes. In the first place, it underlines
the importance of Christ's mediation, how all other mediation is
accomplished through him and what the nature of the divine love
is which is mediated. Second, it provides the hub of a definite
schema in which the Mediator is mediated to us in such a way
that spirituality imitates and participates in Christ and ultimately orients itself towards the Cross. The theological
fact of Christ's mediation on the Cross dictates that it is
there that we are redeemed and finally joined to God and thus it
posits a definite end point and perfection of spirituality.
But the schema Weil uses to describe how God's love is mediated
to us on the way to the Cross is not given by the Cross as such.
Instead, there is a clear structure operating here and it is
one that Weil derives from the ancient Greeks.

Here the Greeks are obviously important for understanding
Weil's complete doctrine of mediation. They have this importance

137

because on the one hand, many of Weil's ideas are directly derived from and interwoven with her readings of the Greeks. In
this regard, her philosophy is especially indebted to her readings of Plato and the Pythagoreans, and to a lesser degree,
others such as Aeschylus, Sophocles, Homer and the Stoics. Yet,
on the other hand, they are also important because Weil is not
just borrowing from them because they conveniently provide a
structure. Instead, she uses their thought because she finds it
to be divinely inspired, which is to say, an effect of grace and
a form of spiritual obedience in thought. It is, therefore, she
believed, appropriate for expressing divine truth.

A complicated relationship obtains, however, among the
elements of the historical incarnation, the general structure of
mediation provided by Greek philosophy and the spirituality that
inspired that philosophy. This relationship, unless properly
understood, can often lead to confusion regarding the priority
of the elements, for it can be variously made to appear either
that Christ's mediation is the clearest possible statement of
principles Weil had already discovered in the Greeks, or that
mediation first and foremost refers to Christ's act which is then
related to spirituality and mathematical mediation in Greek
thought and then expressed in the terms of the latter.

The priority of mediation as Christ's act was doubtless
uppermost in Weil's mind since she does see a need for his crucifixion. This priority comes across clearly in her claim that
Greek spirituality was an intuition of the Incarnation and that
this spirituality was responsible for Greek philosophy and, in
fact, was its core. But once the priority is seen it must also
be seen how and why Weil spelled out this relationship in the
first place.

A general overview of Weil's conception of this relationship
with particular regard to mediation is not hard to find. We
have seen in the preceding chapter Weil's claim that wherever
there is affliction there is a witness to the Cross, and that
the mediating value of the Cross is present for anyone who, in
the face of affliction, unconditionally chooses the truth. From
this claim and corollary she was then able to conclude that mediation between man and God obtains even in times and places

where the Name is not known and that in these places there was
sufficient grace, through the Mediator, to choose the truth.
But Weil was not content simply with making this claim; she also
saw it as capable of far reaching application. The Greeks, more
than any others, were the object of this application and it was
in them that she attempted to discern an understanding of mediation that was divinely inspired and which would bear witness to
Christ's mediation. In the Greeks, then, she noted, "the con-
struction of the mean proportional between a number and unity
. . . was the symbol of the divine mediation between God and
man."[1] When she then saw, for example, formulae of mediation
in the Gospel of St. John such as "As my Father has sent me,
even so I send you," which she felt intentionally embodied the
algebraical form of the mean proportional, she concluded:
". . . just as Christ recognized himself in the Messiah of the
Psalms, the Just One who suffers in Isaiah, the bronze serpent
of Genesis, so in the same way he recognized himself in the mean
proportional of Greek geometry, which thus becomes the most re-
splendent of prophecies."[2] Because of this prophetic connection,
Weil felt fully justified in using Greek mathematics and philosophy to structure and develop her doctrine of mediation in much
the same way that theologians will use the Suffering Servant of
Isaiah to understand Christ's role as redeemer.

A certain logical difficulty arises in this account which
concerns Weil's blending of Christian religion with Greek philosophy. The difficulty arises in the form which asks whether
Weil's blending of the two has been gained by committing a *peti-
tio principii* at the very beginning. If the truth of the Cross,
as Weil conceived it, is supposed to be the standard of all mediation , it seems that the Greek sense of mediation already is
included in that standard. If this is so, it would only be
natural for Weil to make the claims she did about the intimations of Christianity among the ancient Greeks.

There is in the final analysis, I believe, a certain circularity in Weil's arguments concerning the mediation of the
Cross and mediation in the Greeks. Although mediation is present
in Weil in a non-explicitly Greek form from her earliest writings,
the Greek form is in the philosophical background. This can be

seen in the general problems of duality such as body-mind and
universal truths versus a world of particulars which the Greeks
solved by mediation and which she also solved through a form of
mediation. Once the similarity of the two approaches became
evident to her, the Greeks could not help but be a great assistance to her for bringing her mature form of mediation to frui-
tion. But for all this, the circularity is not vicious; rather,
it serves to establish the consistency of the assumptions at the
various points. If, then, one can accept the assumption that
Christ on the Cross is the Word Incarnate and also accept Weil's
account of the mediatory value of the Cross as the primordial
means of the deliverance of God's good and gracious love into
human life, what remains to be shown is that what is irreducibly
Greek in the interpretation can be made consistent with the assumption of Incarnation and of gracious love.

In order to clarify the relationships of Christianity and
the ancient Greeks in the thought of Simone Weil, particularly
as they concern mediation, it is necessary to discern what is
actually a three-pronged argument in her writings concerning
this relation. In the argument a certain distinction and priority can be introduced in the usage of the term mediation.
Initially, Weil's concern is with Christ's mediation on the
Cross from which she develops a general theological usage of
mediation by which she can see Christ's redeeming and expiating
activity having effect by God's grace in times and places where
the Gospel has not been preached. Second, she is concerned with
the ideas which are an effect of this mediation. In regard to
the Greeks, these ideas are those which touch on mediation as a
mathematical and philosophical subject. Here Weil finds a wealth
of material she feels she can use for theological argument, inspired as it is by a love of Christ. This material can then be
used to inform the theological idea of mediation and further
develop it. Weil's method here is to allow, for example, the
meaning of the mathematical analogue to be reformed by the divine
anologate and then to use mathematics as a sort of mediator to
the intelligence in which the terrestial relations of which
mathematics speaks can be ordered in relation with the transcendent good. Finally, through this expanded notion of mediation

Weil is able to find a general means of thought in which all
life, secular as well as spiritual can be brought into an unity
which harmonizes the many dualities that beset human life. Once
these distinctions are made, it is then possible to grasp their
use in Weil's thought, particularly as concerns the inter-relationship of the first two.

Weil's interpretation of Christ's mediation strongly empha-
sizes that the Incarnation is "that to which the destiny of man
is related."[3] This is to say, that man's destiny is to be joined
to God in love, and like Christ, to incarnate God's love on
earth. We have been created for the very purpose of this love
which exists eternally in the economy of salvation between the
Father and Son and which is manifest historically on the Cross.
She says: "We have been created because of the Incarnation."[4]
These are claims Weil felt are entailed by the Pauline dictum
that "God wishes to give his Son many brothers."

Weil's view is that Christ's mediation is decreed before the
very creation, and is, in fact, the very *raison d'être* of creation. Weil thus embraces what is essentially a supralapsarian
view in which she did not feel that salvation depends on one's
historical relation to the Incarnation, although the Incarnation
is itself historical. For Weil, redemption is on an eternal
plane and the means of redemption are really accessible, by
God's grace through the Son, at all times and places of human
history. This furthermore means that life in God through Christ
is equally possible for each soul who comes into the world.
Unless this were so, she says, " . . . it would not be possible
to pardon God--if one can use such words without blasphemy--for
the affliction of so many people, so many people uprooted, enslaved, tortured and put to death in the course of centuries
preceding the Christian era."[5] It would be one thing for death
to be an omnipresent factor in human life as the penalty for
actual sin committed by human beings; it is quite another to
find the excessive, accidental and unexplainable phenomenon of
affliction to be omnipresent, determining the lives of all who
come under its sway to the point of forcing them to lie about
reality. If affliction does not have a final purpose and use
to be made of it, which is explicitly found in Christ's mediating
renunciation on the Cross, man would have no choice but to flee

into the sin of illusion and falsehood whenever he encountered
the horrors of affliction. And this would be something for which
he could never be blamed, unless the means of his continuing to
love the good were present to him.

But if Weil saw the possibility of redemption where the
Name is not explicitly known, she also saw that this possibility
depends solely on God's freely given love. This then leads her
to assert the possibility of revelation of implicit Christian
content outside the particular canons of the Church.

> There is no salvation without a "new birth," without
> an inward illumination, without the presence of Christ
> and of the Holy Spirit in the soul. If, therefore,
> salvation is possible outside the church, individual or
> collective revelations are also possible outside
> Christianity.[6]

This presence of God, through grace, in the loves of men which
embody a form of Christ's self emptying, even outside historical
Christianity, is one of the chief effects of Christ's Mediation.
It is an effect which can lead one to be joined with Christ on
the Cross.

But God's presence also influences the very thought of
those obedient to his will, and it was for this reason that Weil
said "the love and the knowledge of God cannot really be separated . . ."[7] Because of this link she expected that some location of the influence of God's love can be found in certain
ideas and texts which show a supernatural light and/or an understanding of God's mediating love.

Once this location is made, however, a three-fold relation
obtains between those ideas and texts, the eternal nature of
mediation and the historical actuality of the Cross. This is a
relation which Weil does not spell out in detail, or is even
always consistent about, although, fortunately, she does indicate her thoughts on the subject. These indications are that
insofar as thoughts and actions are the result of an inward il-
lumination and are obedient to the light they are efficacious
means of bringing the soul towards contact with God and are
capable of expressing, within the limits of human language, the
truth of divine love in the world. But, coincidental with this
view of their inspired nature is the view that they do not compete with nor relativize the actuality of Christ's incarnation
and crucifixion.

An example will help. Weil, in discussing Aeschylus' *Prometheus Bound*, notes a number of similarities between Prometheus and Christ and then claims: "The story of Prometheus is like the refraction into eternity of the Passion of Christ. Prometheus is the Lamb slain from the foundation of the world."[8] This claim, strong as it is, raises a basic question of the level of similarity of which Weil is speaking. The question could be put thus: Is Prometheus henceforth to be considered as a new mediator alongside Christ on the Cross? The answer is an unqualified "no." The story of Prometheus, Weil notes, "never appears as a historical dated fact which might have happened at a certain point of time and at a certain place."[9] Instead, it points to the Cross, for "all that is wanting is its localization in time and space."[10] This is exactly the way it should be Weil felt since "an historical anecdote whose central character is God cannot be refracted into eternity."[11] This is to say, the story of Prometheus is an expression of the eternal nature of God's relations with humanity and the world at large and is painted on an eternal background. In this case, she says, in the resemblances between the story of Christ and that of Prometheus there is none of an 'anecdotal' or historical character; rather, the similarities of the two rest on an eternal plane of ideas. The one is the eternal come down into the flesh and actually submitting to necessity, the other is a statement of the truth that it is in the nature of the eternal to descend. The second is thus a witness to the first. Stories such as that of Prometheus then "can in no case serve as arguments against the historical character of the Gospels. Consequently, they can only confirm, and not weaken the Christian dogma . . . (they are) a haunting of the Passion."[12]

This same line of reasoning can be applied to the philosophic texts which Weil uses to develop the doctrine of mediation. They are not meant to compete with the historic incarnation of the Word; rather, they are general ideas that are inspired by God's eternal love and which speak of that love. These ideas can be used to reason about the divine nature and the relations God bears to the creation through the Son. The Cross does not entail any particular metaphysics, although it may

exclude some, and therefore in order for intelligence to be
able to represent a method and order to itself, an additional
principle of reasoning is needed which is an act of the obedience
of the intelligence. This is in the ancient Greeks the philosophical and mathematical conception of mediation. Weil does
not say that the ancient Greeks had the Incarnate Christ, but
she does say that they did have a divinely inspired spirituality
which is expressed in philosophic and mathematical forms and
these forms are an intuition and witness to the Cross and Christ's
actual mediation. It will therefore be the task of this chapter
to uncover those ideas in Greek philosophy which Weil found to
contain authentic spirituality and then to show how she uses
them to develop her doctrine of mediation so that it might include all relations in one mediated whole God. It will then be
the task of the last chapter to show how Weil intended these
ideas to be acted on in a way that has Christ's Cross at its
heart.

The method of the succeeding sections needs to be noted.
A major portion of Weil's treatment of the ancient Greeks is
concerned with demonstrating her claim that there was a spirituality in ancient Greece that is an effect of divine mediating
activity. Her major means of demonstrating this claim rest on
her idea that "The whole of Greek civilization is a search for
bridges to relate human misery with the divine perfection."[13]
In this regard, her attention is drawn to a number of texts
where mediation is not explicitly recognized. She sees true
spirituality in them, however, because they give an understanding
of the relation of human misery and divine perfection which she
felt could only come through the Mediator since this understanding could not have been derived from Necessity. The best
example of this sort of treatment is her essay, *The Iliad, Poem
of Might*. The *Iliad*, she says, is supernaturally inspired
and contains a divine understanding because:

> The bitterness of it is spent upon the only true cause
> of bitterness: the subordination of the human soul to
> might, which is, be it finally said, to matter.
> The accent is inseparable from the idea which inspired
> the Gospels; for the understanding of human suffering
> is dependent upon justice, and love is its condition.
> Whoever does not know just how far necessity and a

>   fickle fortune hold the human soul under their domina-
>   tion cannot treat as his equals, nor love as himself,
>   those whom chance has separated from him by an abyss
>   . . . Only he who knows the empire of might knows how
>   not to respect it is capable of justice and love.[14]

Other examples of this same sort of treatment occur in numerous
essays and selections from the *Notebooks* which are concerned with
searching out essential spiritual truths in mythology and litera-
ture. Few actually bring up a Greek idea of mediation.[15]

It is not with these essays and *Notebook* selections that
the succeeding sections will deal, however. Because the goal of
the present work is to present an understanding of Weil's own
doctrine of mediation the presentation will be limited to those
works of Simone Weil which deal explicitly with the idea of mediation as she finds it in the Greeks. Furthermore, the presentation will mainly center on Plato and the Pythagoreans since
these figures are Weil's main objects of attention in regard to
mediation and her major sources. The presentation will follow
this order. We shall first show some of Weil's interpretations
of Platonic texts which she feels demonstrate a true spirituality
akin to that of Christianity. From there we will treat her
claims that the love of God is the linchpin of that spirituality,
that this love is essentially a mediation of God and how it is
mediation. In the final two sections we shll see how Weil takes
this mediation of love to be a general principle which in varying
forms allows a metaphysics of mediation.

1. *God, Love, and Mediation in Plato*

Before the twentieth century it was not at all an uncommon
practice for philosophers and theologians to see in Plato a set
of high religious ideals that are remarkably similar to many
points of Christianity. In recent years, however, theologians
have tended to emphasize the difference between Plato and Christianity, and philosophers have tended in a positivistic vein to
regard him more as a major transition from a crude world of
religious myth to a rational and empirical science than as a
religious thinker. Simone Weil presents a direct opposite to
both these tendencies. Whereas Plato is now often thought of as
a major advance upon earlier systems of thought Weil saw him as

the deliberate inheritor and conservator of numerous religious
ideas. Furthermore, she saw in Plato the same sort of religion
as she felt Christianity is. She writes: "My interpretation:
that Plato is an authentic mystic, and indeed the father of
Western mysticism."[16]

The single most important essay in which Weil explains and
demonstrates this claim is her *God in Plato*. In this essay,
through a collation of her translations of the relevant texts
in Plato and her commentary on them Weil seeks to show the
supernatural basis of justice in Plato, how grace is necessary
for this justice in human life, and how love, which Plato conceived as mediatory is the central cohering factor of his entire
religious and moral thought. In this discussion Weil keeps a
careful eye on the relation between Plato and Christianity, and
shows how once the doctrine of love is reached, it occurs in a
context similar to Christian morality and spirituality. It is,
therefore, for Weil an expression of true spirituality, not only
because it speaks of mediation, but also because when it does
speak of mediation it does so in such a way that its beneficent
and divine character cannot be mistaken.

A. *God in Plato*

Weil first examines the divine nature of justice in Plato
through a treatment of the *Theaetetus* 176 sq. In this passage,
Socrates after having described the philosopher as one who is
truly wise but who appears as foolish to the majority of men,
is told that if he could convince everybody of the truth of his
claim that there would be far fewer evils in the world. Socrates,
however, says that it is impossible that evils should ever disappear because by necessity there is always something opposed
(ὑπεναντίον) to the good. These evils have nothing to do with
the gods; rather they hover about moral nature and this world.
For this reason, he says, we should attempt to flee this world
as quickly as possible: "This flight is, as far as possible, an
assimilation (ὁμοῖος) to God, and assimilation consists in becoming just and holy through the aid of reason."[17] The only
good reason for being just, however, is not in wanting to *appear*
virtuous, but because "*God is never* in any way unjust."[18] It

is only the man who is as like God as possible who is wise and virtuous. If one does not make this flight he cannot help but be foolish and wicked. Unfortunately, this foolishness is also the ignorance of one's moral state. Concluding, Socrates says:

> There are in reality two patterns, one of them divine and most blessed and the other godless and most wretched. But they do not see that this is so. Their stupidity and extreme ignorance prevent them from seeing that by their unjust actions they resemble the second pattern and differ from the first. They are punished by the fact that they live the life which matches the pattern they resemble.[19]

In this passage Weil finds three principal ideas: flight, assimilation and the perfect justice of God. These ideas show that in Plato there are two moralities; the morality of nature, subject to the correlates of good and evil in Necessity, and the morality which is supernatural and comes from God alone. This latter morality, she says, is identified with the knowledge of the highest truth. In this sense, she understands the dictum, "Virtue is knowledge," to indicate that it is the virtuous who, because they are like (ὁμοῖος) God, have knowledge, and those who know God to be virtuous. In the domain of Necessity, however, there is neither true virtue nor knowledge, but only the appearance affected by the interplay of natural forces.

> In other words, whereas in the domain of nature (including the psychological) good and evil mutually produce one another, in the domain of the spirit evil produces only evil and good only produces good (The Gospel). And good and evil consist in contact with (contact by likeness) or separation from God. (Therefore there is no question of anything like an abstract conception of God, which can be achieved by the human intelligence without grace; the conception is an experimental one.[20]

So far so good. But two questions need to be asked. What is the specification in human terms of the justice of which Plato is speaking? Second, how can a man be like or imitate God? In Christianity, the Incarnate Word shows the answer to both these questions; but what is it in Plato?

In order to find the answer Weil considers two passages in which the images of nakedness and death are linked to justice. The first is the 'Just Man' passage of the *Republic*[21] in which

Socrates is asked to show the utter worthiness of justice in
itself even when all the appearances of good normally pertaining
to it are stripped away, including the reputation for justice
and salvation for having acted justly. The image is of a man
scourged, tortured, bound, crucified and despised, yet who is
completely just. The second image is the Myth of Judgement at
the end of the *Gorgias*[22] in which Socrates tells the story of
how men used to be judged while still clothed in the appearances
of earthly life. Unfortunately, these external appearances im-
pressed the divine judges which led to the result of many criminal souls entering the Isles of the Blessed. Zeus, however,
put a stop to this unjust situation, requiring that all

> . . . come to the trial naked, so they must be judged
> after death. The judge too must be naked, dead; with
> his soul itself he must contemplate the soul itself of
> each man the moment after his death, without his friends
> or any of his earthly array, if the judgement is to be
> just.[23]

In this way, it is the soul of each man that is judged and "when
it is naked and stripped of the body, its natural dispositions
and the effects upon it of all its attachments to things become
apparent."[24]

    In these two passages, Weil sees Plato deliberately linking
the mystical image of nakedness with death and ultimately with
that of justice. From this she concludes that it is Plato's
thought that not only does perfect justice require living after
the divine pattern but also in renouncing any influence of non-
divine things in morality, for these things all tend to obscure
the divine truth. Truth in Plato, she says, is

> . . . only manifest in nakedness and nakedness in
> death . . . Plato does not say but he implies that
> in order to become just, which requires self-knowledge,
> one must become, already in this life, naked and dead.
> The examination of conscience demands this rupture of all
> the attachments which constitute our reasons for living.[25]

    But even if Plato does not explicitly say that already
being dead in this life is necessary to be just, he does, in the
Phaedo, explicitly make death a condition for knowledge. There
Socrates does say that philosophy is learning how to die. Moreover, he also says:

> If we are ever to know anything purely we must separate
> ourselves from the body and contemplate things by the
> soul itself . . . And it is only then, so it seems,
> that we shall possess what we desire and what we say we
> love, namely reason; that is to say, after death and
> not while we are alive . . . And while we are alive
> it seems that we shall be closer to knowledge the less
> commerce and communion we have with the body, apart from
> strict necessity; not letting ourselves be possessed
> by its nature but purifying ourselves from it until God
> himself releases us.[26]

In all these passages, Weil understands Plato's intent not
to be a naive sort of dualism, but, rather, a recognition of
the distance between necessity and goodness (a distinction which
is originally Plato's). Necessity cannot produce goodness and
anyone who earnestly desires goodness must not look for it in
the realm of Necessity amont things commonly received as good.
In order to find goodness, knowledge and justice it is required
that the seeker look elsewhere than in the realm of appearances.
This must appear as a sort of death to the common conception
which finds life in the things of necessity. What Weil then
claims Plato to be saying is that one finds true life only by
dying to a false life; a false life which everywhere in the
realm of necessity parades itself as true being.

It is in this linking of nakedness, death and justice in
Plato that Weil finds strong similarities to the Christian tradition. As examples from that tradition she cites St. Paul's
notion of having died in Christ (Romans 6) and the spiritual
nakedness so emphasized in the great mystics, particularly St.
John of the Cross and St. Francis. She then concludes: "If
justice requires us to be naked and dead in this life, it is
clear that justice is something impossible for human nature, is
something supernatural."[27] Here Weil finds the first strong
connection of Plato with the truth she found in Christianity.

But is there anything which Plato sees that keeps the souls
of men from being assimilated to God through justice? The
answer to this question is important for establishing any further
connections between Christianity and Plato insofar as it also
requires an answer as to why and how one can be assimilated.
This is to say, that even if Plato recognizes the supernatural
nature of justice it does not mean that he recognizes the need
for all men to be delivered from sin to justice or even that

he recognizes that it is at all possible for such deliverance
to occur. What exactly is the relation between misery and perfection?

Weil notes two things in Plato which keep the soul from
being assimilated to God. The first, of which there are numerous
examples throughout the Platonic corpus, is the perils of the
flesh wherein the divine part of the soul is subordinated to
earthly desires. The second, however, is an even greater obstacle than the flesh; it is society and no man escapes its influence. This notion Weil finds to be most explicitly expressed
in the Great Beast passage of the *Republic*.[28] In this passage
Socrates claims that the corruption of morals is not just the
influence of the sophists on a few young rogues, but occurs whenever a crowd of people is gathered together. These crowds
"tumultuously blame or approve what is said or done." This,
Socrates says, could not help but move the hearts of young men,
and individual education cannot resist being submerged in its
torrent. And so, through the force of the crowd, a morality
of the herd arises, a morality based on the movements of Necessity. As far as the sophists are concerned, they are only men
who teach the opinions which arise when a crowd is assembled.
Socrates then likens this phenomenon to that of a keeper of some
great beast. The handler carefully studies its humors, desires
and whims and so learns how to approach it and handle it in such
a way that it will always be pleased with him and so that he will
be safe. This great beast is the crowd and the teachers of
morality are its keepers.

> But in reality he has no idea as to which of these
> notions and humors is beautiful or ugly, good or bad,
> just or unjust; he applied these terms to the opinions
> of the great beast. Whatever pleases the animal he
> calls good and whatever annoys it he calls bad, and
> this is his only criterion. Things that are necessary
> he calls just and beautiful, for he is incapable of
> perceiving or of explaining to anyone else *how great
> the difference is in reality between the essence of what
> is necessary and of what is good.*[29]

Weil, in commenting on this passage then notes that it is
the social element which is the product of Necessity that is
the main obstacle between man and God. This is an obstacle for
every man because he is born into a social world and has his

thoughts shaped by it. This by itself is not an evil; what is
an evil is when the soul which needs to be made in the image of
God accepts and consents to this morality, as Weil and Plato
thought it inevitably does. Once again, the original sin is error and not ignorance.

But exactly how far does the influence of the beast extend
in Plato and how is one delivered from it? Weil states that the
beast's influence is all-pervasive. This can be seen in the
famous Cave allegory which shows the natural condition of men as
being chained and engaging in a shadow guessing contest which
they mistake for discussions about the true nature of things.
Weil says, "*This is what we are like* (not what we used to be
like . . .)."[30] But if this is the natural condition of men,
how is anybody ever saved from it? Weil's answer is, of course,
by grace, but this is an answer she also sees Plato himself
giving. She produces a text from the great beast passage which
she feels categorically states that the social influence is all
pervasive and that it is by the grace of God alone that men are
saved from it. She quotes:

> For there is not, there never has been, and there
> never will be, any other moral teaching except that of
> public opinion. At least, no other human teaching; the
> divine, as the proverb says, is an exception to all
> rules. It is necessary to know that anything which is
> saved and becomes what it ought to be, in the present
> state of society, must correctly be said to have been
> saved by a divine predestination (θεοῦ μοίραν).[31]

Weil thus finds another strong connection between Plato
and Christianity. She felt that it would be difficult to assert
more categorically than Plato does that grace is the sole source
of salvation and that it comes from God alone and not men. She
writes of Plato, then:

> There are two moralities, social morality and super-
> natural morality, and only those who are enlightened
> by grace have access to the second. Plato's wisdom is
> not a philosophy, a research for God by means of human
> reason. That research was carried out as well as it
> can be done by Aristotle. But the wisdom of Plato is
> nothing other than the orientation of the soul towards
> grace.[32]

B. *Love and Mediation*

Once Weil recognizes that in Plato grace is necessary to
deliver men from the beast and make them just she undertakes an
examination of what this grace consists in, by what methods salvation is accomplished and how man receives grace. The key in
Plato, just as in Christianity is the love of God. She writes:

> The fundamental idea . . . is that the disposition of
> the soul which is granted and receives grace is nothing
> else but love. The love of God is the root and founda-
> tion of Plato's philosophy . . . love oriented towards
> its proper object, that is to say, towards perfection,
> puts the lover in contact with the only absolutely real
> reality . . . the good is above justice and the other vir-
> tues, it is in so far as they are good that we seek the
> other virtues.[33]

It is in Plato's doctrine of love that Weil finds Plato's
strongest affinity to Christian spirituality. She does not find
this affinity, however, simply because both Plato and Christianity
use the term 'love' to denote the supreme religious activity;
she also finds this affinity because of a similarity in the content of love wherein love is God's means of acting in human
life, and therefore, it is a mediator of God's own goodness which
bridges the gap between human misery and the divine perfection.
Here Weil's discussion of love in Plato not only is making a
point about Plato but is also important for further seeing what
Weil herself means by God's mediating love.

The notion that Plato's doctrine of love bears strong af-
finities to Christianity is, of course, not novel. The resemblance between the two, however, has not always been universally
recognized, and for this reason it will help to set the discussion in the context of one of the strongest attacks against this
view, that of Anders Nygren's *Eros and Agape*. In this work,
Nygren claims to show by a completely objective historical study
that the motif of Eros, found in its purest form in Plato, and
the motif of Agape, found in the New Testament, especially the
Pauline corpus, are fundamentally incompatible views of love,
although they have been perversely mixed throughout the Christian
centuries. Eros, he wrote, is characterized by three marks: it
is acquisitive or the love of desire; it is man's way to the
divine; and because of the first two marks, it is egocentric.

Agape, on the other side, he claims, has four marks which
strongly contrast with those of Eros: agape is spontaneous and
unmotivated; it is indifferent to value; it is creative of value
where there was none before; finally, it comes from God alone
and is the initiator of fellowship with Him.

The contrast between Nygren's Eros and Agape shows itself
most sharply in religious practice. In Nygren's eyes, Agape
is a love of which God is irreducibly the subject and thus Agape
is always a creative self-giving act which originates in God.
In the case of Eros, though, the situation is reversed. For
Eros, God is the object of a love that originates in human willing. The Eros that desires God's good and wills it is therefore
always willing to be the subject of that good. In this sense,
Eros is always attempting to control what it loves to its own
ends. It is thus always egocentric for no matter how high the
motives for willing, as long as it is an individual will which
wills the objective good, the *summum bonum* must reside in the
will's willing. In short, the will always aspires to be God itself. This sort of love is entirely antithetical to Christian
agape. Furthermore, Nygren, contends, there is not any third
alternative; either love originates in man or it originates in
God, and the forms of love which originate in man are entirely
inappropriate to express a relationship to the divine. He
writes:

> Love towards God is neither *amor concupiscentiae* nor
> *amor amicitiae*, neither "acquisitive love" nor the
> "love of friendship"--to use the common scholastic
> distinction; for both of these take their rise and
> direction from man himself. If love towards God were
> "acquisitive love", then God, though He were described
> as the *highest* good, would in the last resort be the
> means for the satisfaction of man's desires. Nor is there
> any room for the "love of friendship" in a theocentric
> relationship to God, for that love presupposes an
> equality between the Divine and human love which does
> not exist.[34]

To Nygren, nobody embodies this sort of Eros more than
Plato and, in consequence, he regards Platonic love as an antithesis to Christian Agape. But is this, in fact, true of Plato
(and, in turn Weil)? Weil did not think so. We have already
seen in the image of the 'Just Man' that the idea of reward is

subtracted from the argument, and, therefore, in that case there
is no question of Plato making justice or any other virtue the
means of satisfying man's desires. Second, we have seen how
virtue and knowledge in Plato is a life lived on a supernatural
pattern, and this is a pattern which is inaccessible to man except by a divine dispensation. Assimilation to God is only possible in Plato by the agency of the divinity.

The most telling argument against Nygren's exegesis of
Plato, however, can be seen in Nygren's failure to mark certain
proper distinctions in the logic of good and goods. Even if
Nygren is correct in assuming that 'acquisitive love' and the
'love of friendship' are the only possibilities for love which
arises first in the human heart, neither is what Plato is concerned with. As Weil points out, the Socratic dictum, "All desire the good," is at the root of Platonic love. Here what
Plato is saying then is that men ultimately desire *the* good and
not just goods. In this sense, God insofar as he is equated
with the Good, is not a good; not even the highest good among
others. It is, therefore, not even logically possible in Plato
to make God, "in the last resort, the means for the satisfaction
of man's desires."

This notion of Plato's, of course, led him into certain
difficulties when he came to consider what it is that men are
doing when they act badly. His answer, however, is clear;
namely, that all men do desire the good, but that either from
the competing influence of goods or from a lack of knowledge
they give their love to things less than the ultimate good they
desire. In Weil's hands this answer is developed to claim that
real egoism is impossible for human beings. It is Weil's contention that men do feel a need for an ultimate good external to
themselves and that they act on this need in many ways. In the
case of those who truly love God their attention is directed
solely towards him. Those who do not love God, however, still
place love and desire in something external to their essential
soul and make the goods of Necessity into a sort of false god.
What parades by the name of egoism is, in fact, for Weil simply
putting one's heart in the treasure of that which touches him
most closely, such as his empirical personality.

> What is generally named egoism is not love of self, it
> is a defect of perspective. People give the name of
> disaster to that altertion of a certain arrangement
> of things which they see from the point where they are;
> from that point, things at a little distance are invis-
> ible . . . This is not love of self, it is that men,
> being finite creatures, only apply the idea of legitimate
> order to the immediate neighbourhood of their hearts.[35]

But even if Nygren fails to understand the central and
crucial distinction in Plato between loving the Good and loving
goods, two things must, nevertheless, be shown in order to make
strong Weil's claim about the 'Christian' character of Platonic
love. The first is that love is the fundamental means of putting
man in contact with the Good in Plato. Second, it must be shown
that this love is not in Plato something that arises from purely
human capacity.

These claims can be established first through an examination
of Socrates' discourse in the *Symposium*. In this discourse,
Socrates begins by making a point the eulogists of love who have
spoken before him have missed. This point which is basically
grammatical is that love and desire (the two being closely related in the common sense of ἔρως) is always desire *for* something. Furthermore, this desire is always for something one
does not already have--otherwise why should one desire it? Because of this, Socrates continues, Love is not really the fine
and self-sufficient God others have thought it to be; instead,
Love is always lacking in something. Socrates explains this
fact by the myth of the birth of love. The parents of Love are
Need and Resource and thus Love is always lacking in his desired
goal but also always manages to find a way to reach it.

When the grammatical point about desire is made, however,
the question naturally arises as to whether love ceases or continues always. Socrates says it continues. This affirmation,
unfortunately, leads to a dilemma.[36] If one accepts that the
desired goal is attained, one is impaled on the horn of saying
that continued love means something like "fearing the loss of
what one has." This does not seem to be an appropriate thing
to say about love. The second horn is little better. If one
grabs it, it forces him to say that if love does not cease or
is not fearful then the goal of love is, in fact, an impossibility. The consequence of facing this dilemma is inevitable whenever love and desire are closely linked.

The dialogue, though, does not explicitly recognize the dilemma at this point. Instead, it takes up the specification of what love is for. Up to this point, the object of love has been left ambiguously defined as whatever is desired. But, Socrates goes on, there is something common to all that we love and that is goodness. Using the words of his teacher, Diotima,[37] he says: "Love never longs for the half or the whole of anything except the good . . . for what we love is the good and nothing but the good."[38] Thus men always desire the good in things and desire them "to be their own and forever."[39] This, however, still does not escape the dilemma.

In view of this consequence the line of argument is shifted. Rather than continuing to discuss the implications which arise from taking love as desire, Diotima asks what the *activity* of love is. When Socrates cannot answer, she says it is "to bring forth upon the beautiful, both in body and soul . . . So you see that Love is not exactly a longing for the beautiful . . . (It is) a longing not for the beautiful itself, but for the conception and generation that the beautiful effects."[40] Love goes beyond what is suggested by desire as desire of possession; it is desire to propagate the good forever in human life. Among men whose thoughts are chained to this world, this desire takes the form of begetting children and doing great deeds which will live forever in the minds of men. Among those whose thoughts are directed to something higher, the works of love will be found in making the soul as like as possible to the divine patterns of beauty and goodness. "And when he has brought forth and reared this perfect virtue, he shall be called the friend of God, and if ever it is given to man to put on immortality, it shall be given to him."[41]

It is at this point that we can see that the conclusion of the *Symposium* actually accepts the second horn of the dilemma. The object of love, the good, is unobtainable, at least in the sense of possessing it. But this is the way it should be for a Platonic ideal. A Platonic idea, in its most general sense, involves at least four things: 1) it is independent of the mind which thinks it (at least a finite mind); 2) it is absolute and transcendent, in that it is something that is always true in

all systems and yet it does not involve a necessary relation to
mind or depend in any way for its truth on the possibilities of
being verified either concretely or in principle; 3) it is something which is in its totality incomprehensible to the finite
mind in the sense that its operations cannot be exhausted by the
finite mind. This is because any conception of it, because it
is a conception, necessarily bears a relation to mind, which
conception the idea will transcend. The ideal itself, also involves an infinity of factors independent of the mind which thinks
it.[42] 4) For at least moral ideals, a Platonic ideal is a perfection. As such it is a perfection which is infinite and absolute and which can never be completely realized in the finite and
conditioned world, although it does have specific determinations
in such things as human justice. In regard to the ideal and
love, then, the lover in Plato addresses himself to perfection,
which for Weil is always God, the ideas being for her the attributes of God. In so addressing himself, however, the lover
always has to realize that he is never that perfection himself,
for in the very fact that he loves he must understand himself
to be lacking in perfection. And this is why he loves in the
first place.

The fact that one never possesses the ideal is no cause for
disappointment. George Santayana put it well when he said that
Platonic love "would not in respect to that perfect world, be
harassed by remorse, as it must be in an imperfect world when it
counts the cost of existence and considers the dreadful sufferings which plagued it like a nightmare, before something beautiful and good could appear even for a moment."[43] Love in Plato,
and Weil, is not as Nygren says, the way of natural man to the
divine for it is not subject to the purely contingent and human
criteria of satisfaction and disappointment.

What love is in Plato can be seen in the dialectic of good
which it embodies.[44] On the one hand, love, because it is directed towards the good is always subject to ethical criteria
for its assessment. In this sense, whether or not humans really
do love the good, what they do love must always be judged in
comparison to the good which they should love. On the other
hand, love of the good provides the criteria for assessment and
is the actual activity of moral judgment. This is the point of

Plato's making love the activity of conceiving and begetting the
good and not the desire for possession of the good *per se*. The
genius of Platonic love is, as Weil says, putting man *in contact*
with God and His perfection. It is through love that man reaches
for perfection with the effect of that reaching being the introduction of goodness in human life. It is by loving that a man
becomes good and participates in the divine goodness which is
otherwise inaccessible to him. Love in both Plato and Weil is
divine goodness in this world.

     This point can be further seen in a reconsideration of the
myth of the birth of love. This myth is first used to make the
point that love always loves what it does not have since it is
partially made of Need. There is a second correlated sense to
this myth, however, which becomes evident after seeing how Plato
develops his doctrine of love. Love is, he says, a mediator between God and man because he is a *daimon*, that is, something
between the mortal and the immortal (μεταξὺ θνητοῦ καὶ ἀθανάτου).
This is ostensibly to give his material nature. Unfortunately,
this tends to make him neither divine nor human and yet a little
bit of both. He seems a third makeshift entity invented to fill
a gap. But what is important in the intermediate nature of Love
is its *function* as a mediator who "flies upward with our worship
and our prayers and descends with the heavenly answers and com-
mandments."[45] In one sense love is the way *for* man to reach the
divine, but it is also the way of the divine to man. What becomes of critical significance is that Love is born of the divine.
The implication of this is that love is the activity of the divine in the human soul for Love is born when the divine meets the
need of the human soul. In this sense, love is not a human
capacity at all but is what happens when the soul comes into
contact with the divine. Here the effect of the divine on men
is to beget love in them. This love is at once assessed by its
divine form, that is the good it does, and also when predicated
of a human soul is that which gives the soul the means and
criteria of goodness.[46]

     It is not only the *Symposium* which speaks this way. In the
Phaedrus love is also described as a relation between the divine
and the human. It is described as a 'divine madness' which is

sent by the gods. Also, in the *Phaedrus*, and to a more explicit
degree than in the *Symposium*, the activities of love are seen to
be those which do shed abroad the beautiful and good in human
life. Surely the point of the description of the lover's relation to the beloved in the *Phaedrus* is that the lover who seeks
to ascend the 'mount of truth' does so only by helping the beloved become more and more like the ideal. It is only in this
good activity of caring for the beloved that the lover can truly
be said to be a lover and to be becoming like the ideal which
makes him good.

Four things are claimed to have been shown by the foregoing
argument: 1) that through the mediation of love man is put in
contact with the divine; 2) that love is always subject to
ethical criteria for assessment; 3) that love as a mediator is
itself a mediation of the Good; 4) that love, because it is a
mediation of the Good, provides ethical criteria and performs
the activity of assessment. Both #1 and #2 are, I believe, in-
contestable as being Plato's plain and apparent thought. #3
and #4, however, are not quite as evident yet, since #3 has so
far only been established on the basis of a myth which by its
nature does not tell all, and because of this, #4 seems weak
insofar as it depends on #3. Both claims can be strengthened
by an examination of Plato's 'metaphysics of good' set forth in
the simile of the Sun in the *Republic*, a passage on which Weil
draws heavily.

In this well-known and extraordinary passage Socrates is
asked by Glaucon to explain exactly what the Good is. Begging
off this request, Socrates says that he will instead provide
an image of the Good. This is the Sun. Likening clear vision
to the knowledge which the 'possessor' of the Good is supposed
to have, he notes that in order to see at least two things are
required--an object of perception and a seeing object. But,
moreover, he adds, a third thing is required for vision and that
is the medium of light. Without light there is no vision, and
it is the sun which "is the divinity in heaven that is the
author of this, whose light makes our vision see best and visible
things to be seen."[47] Yet, he adds, "the sun itself is not vision, yet as being the cause thereof is also beheld by vision
itself."[48] If we then transfer the analogy of the sun and the

eye to the Good and the soul we find that the soul or an act of
the soul is not sufficient to discern goodness in things or for
an act to be good. References must always be made to the Good
which allows the soul to perceive (νοεῖν) an object as good
and which also allows the act of perception to be good. Thought
is intermediary between the thinker and the object, but it is a
true intermediary only through the medium of the light of the
transcendent good. This understanding can also be applied to
any perception of the Good itself, although in this case the
object provides its own medium. It is this medium which we see
of the Good and that by which we see the Good. Here the Good
always transcends the intermediary perception (νόημα) of itself,
but nevertheless determines that perception and makes it good.
Here it is best to quote Plato's words at length.

> Of that which for the objects of knowledge, is the
> source of truth, and, for the knower, the source of power
> to know, we must say that it is the cause (αἴτιον)
> both of knowledge and of truth insofar as it is an object
> of knowledge. Both knowledge and truth are beautiful
> things, but, rightly speaking, the idea of the good is
> something more beautiful still. One may rightly regard
> light and vision in this world as being sun-like things,
> but not as the sun itself; and in the same way one may
> rightly regard knowledge and truth as being like the
> good, but not as the good itself. That which constitutes
> the good should be even more highly honored. To consider
> still further the likeness of the good. The Sun not only
> makes it possible for visible objects to be seen, it also
> gives them their becoming, their growth and their nurture,
> although it is not itself a becoming. In the same way
> for objects of knowledge, the good not only makes it
> possible for them to be known, but it also gives them
> reality and being (Τὸ εἶναι καὶ τὴν οὐσίαν) although
> it is not itself a being but something higher in dig-
> nity and worth.[49]

Three things can be seen in this passage which support the
claims that love as a mediator is a mediation of the Good and
that love's activity, because it is a mediation of the Good,
provides prime ethical criteria in human life and is the means
of goodness. 1) The relation of any object to the Good is
engendered by the Good itself. In this case, the relation of
any object to the Good, which is that object's being and reality,
is a mediation of the Good insofar as it is a particular determination of the Good by the Good. This mediation has two senses:

a) There is the relation between two finites which is an indirect
determination of the Good. In this case, the Good enters when
there is the real thought of one object to another, that is,
through the medium of the idea of the Good; b) There is a more
direct relation where the thought of a mind is directed towards
the Good itself. In this case that thought which is the relation between the mind and God is determined by the Good. This
relation if applied to Plato's doctrine of love can allow love
which is a very definite relation of man to God to be a mediation of the Good itself in human life. 2) Since any relation to
the Good is a determination or mediation of the Good, that mediation itself is a good by virtue of the fact that it partakes
of the Good. For this reason, love can provide the prime ethical
criteria of human life and be the activity of assessing and doing
good because love, as an activity of the human soul engendered
by the Good, is actually the Good itself making determinations
of goodness in human thoughts, words and deeds. In this sense,
love is the possession of the soul by God. 3) The relation to
the Good actually makes each thing what it is and gives it its
'reality and being.' It is the activity of each thing, performed
in relation to the Good, which gives it its essence and makes
it capable of being known and loved. In the case of intelligent
creation, this activity makes it capable of knowing and loving.
It is in this sense that Weil understands that the love God
bears us at any moment is the sum total of our being.

On the account given above it can now be seen that, in the
final analysis, Nygren's criticism of Eros as a thing fundamentally incompatible with Christian Agape really fails to be a
criticism of Plato's doctrine of love. While it may very well
be the case that there was a type of Eros in the ancient world
such as Nygren describes, a strong enough case has been made to
show that Platonic love was not of this type. Nygren says that
Eros is egocentric, acquisitive and man's way to the divine;
none of these things is truly predicable of Plato's doctrine.
Platonic love is not egocentric because it is not at all a love
for one's own being or the goods thought to be beneficial to
him; rather, it is an unconditional love for the absolute Good.
The man who truly loves the Good in Plato does so regardless
of his own personal advantage. Second, it is not even really

trying to possess the Good; instead, it seeks to be possessed
and the value of this possession is in its making good and being
made good. Finally, Platonic love is not man's way to the divine. Platonic love is, instead, a contact between man and God
which is maintained and initiated by God alone. If this is a
way of man to the divine, it is so only in the sense that this
love makes men more like the divine and this only occurs through
divine causality. It is God's own activity of enlightening the
souls of those who come into the world and leading them to the
goal which is proper to them; that is, to his own love which in
the human soul directs His Good to the world and back to Himself.

Once the argument against the claimed dissimilarity between
Platonic love and Christian Agape has been shown not to work,
some of the positive similarities which Weil claims to hold between the two can be brought to light. These similarities can
be summarized in the following fashion. In both Plato and
Christianity there is a *summum bonum* which is not the product of
any or all finite factors but which does by its own determinations bear specific relations to the world. When related to
the human soul, it manifests itself in wisdom and morality.
Yet, while this wisdom and morality are things to be predicated
of human beings and are goals for them they are not things that
humans naturally have or can naturally attain. In fact, the
natural condition of man is such that he is normally subject to
the pseudo-wisdom and morality of a necessity which is incommensurate with spirit. But not only does man when left to himself follow an illusory wisdom and morality, he tends to unite
his soul with these things and commits an act of denying the
good and thus is further separated from it. Then, in both
Christianity and Plato, Weil sees a grace descending from God
which turns man's head from his natural affections. This act is
accomplished solely through the agency of the divine. In turn,
it effects a conversion in the human soul which makes the soul
look towards the true source of goodness. This turning, however, cannot be partial in either Christianity or Plato; in both
cases the soul must give its undivided attention to God, and
this conversion, Weil says, is a form of death to the world.[50]
When this conversion is complete, then God himself possesses
the soul and the soul is made like him.

The major similarity which Weil sees between Plato and
Christianity, however, lies in the fact that both finally and
irreducibly rely on love being the prime relation between man
and God and therefore the prime means of reconciling the imper-
fections and evils of human life with the divine perfection.
Commenting on Plato in a manner which indicates the absolute
nature of this idea for her, she says:

> 1) THERE IS NOT AND THERE CANNOT BE ANY OTHER RELATION
> OF MAN TO GOD EXCEPT LOVE. WHAT IS NOT LOVE IS NOT A
> RELATION TO GOD.
> 2) The appropriate object for love is God, and *every
> man who loves something other than God is deceived,
> mistaken; as though he ran up to a stranger in the
> street, having mistaken him for a friend.*[51]

For Weil, love is the prime means in both Plato and Christianity for reconciling the divine nature with human imperfection. This similarity, however, is more than semantic for it
involves a real similarity in the content of the terms 'love'
and 'God.' Any number of religions have made claims that God
is love, but in many of them God is quickly defined by what fits
the believer's preconceptions of love. In this sense, love
when taken in its cruder forms quickly becomes divinized and,
to use deRougement's phrase, just as quickly becomes demonic.
In Christianity, however, man learns what love is by first looking at God's own actions and that is looking at the Crucifixion
of the Son. It is on the basis of that looking that a man can
order all the rest of his loves and understand them in the light
of God's own love. Weil sees much this same sort of thing
occurring in Plato. In Plato we see what love is, that is the
activity of begetting the good, by turning and looking at the
Good and seeing its benificent character. Good in Plato is not
defined by whatever we might happen to desire; rather desire is
defined and assessed by the way in which God is present in it.
Although Plato might not say that God loves, what God does do
in Plato is extremely similar for in his mediating activity he
performs the same sort of action as one who loves. Weil says:
"Mediation is exactly the same thing as Love."[52] In both
Christianity and Plato, then, love is the means of deliverance
from sin and error and is the means by which human imperfection
can be related to divine perfection. In both these cases,
according to Weil, this love comes from God alone.[53]

2. *The Pythagorean Doctrine*

Simone Weil saw in Plato a high degree of spirituality that she felt could only have come from divine inspiration. What she saw of equal importance in him, though, was that his conception of spirituality consciously realized and proposed the idea of mediation as the means by which to conceive and discuss the divine love in its manifest areas. But even though mediation does have this crucial theological use in Plato it also has extended uses in other areas of philosophy and mathematics. Weil did not see this double usage as accidental. She felt that it was through an application of the concept of mediation, which essentially deals with relations and proportions, that a harmony can be discerned in all areas of life, beginning with the life of God Himself and extending to the quantitative relations of matter. It is through the mathematical conception of mediated proportions that a way can be given to describe the divine operation of mediation. She says: "Man cannot understand this divine operation of mediation; he can only love it. But in a perfectly clear manner his intelligence conceives a degraded image of it, which is the relationship."[54]

It was in the ancients' comprehensive use of mediation that Weil found a wealth of material on which to draw to form an overall view of the world, a view that is held together by mediation. The two chief essays which present this view are *The Pythagorean Doctrine* and *Divine Love in Creation*. These essays, above all others, are crucial for reaching an understanding of the various ways in which Weil uses mediation and how they cohere in a single doctrine.

One of the marvels of Pythagorean thought was that it embraced all forms of life--religion, music, architecture, sculpture, science and even politics. Weil says of it: "There was then, between the different parts of secular life, and between the secular life as a whole and the supernatural world, as much unity as today there is separation."[55] Because of this ability of Pythagorean thought to embrace so much of life, Weil felt that it is something which demands rediscovery and new application today. Unfortunately, many of the Pythagorean writings

are lost and so in order to find their thought Weil proposes to
reconstruct a doctrine that is Pythagorean in its essence using
an intuition that can only be gained "from inside; that is to
say, only if one has truly drawn spiritual life from the texts
studied."[56]

In order to make this reconstruction Weil cites a number of
texts which are helpful to her case and then draws upon them for
her doctrine. These texts are a number of fragments from
Philolaos, five passages from Plato, a catena of verses from the
Gospel of St. John, and a fragment of Anaximander's which although
not Pythagorean bears a certain resemblance to the others.[57] In
addition to these texts, she also cites two Pythagorean formulae,
"Justice is a number to the second power," and "Friendship is an
equality made of harmony," which are quoted by Aristotle and
Diogenes Laertius respectively. All of these passages embody
various mathematical formulations, yet at the same time also
speak of divinity. It is the connection between these two seemingly incomparable aspects of mathematics and divinity which
Weil felt constitutes the real key for understanding the Pythagoreans. She writes: "the key . . . is the idea of a mean proportional and of mediation in the theological sense, the first
being the image of the second."[58] This claim is central to
Weil's case and in order to understand what she means by it, two
things about it need to be discussed: first, that the idea of
mediation and numbers belongs primarily to theology, and second,
why mathematics is appropriate for theological discussion.

It is a historically confirmed fact that mathematical and
religious contemplation did go hand in hand for the Pythagoreans;
the question which needs to be raised is how and why this was
so? The first thing which needs to be considered is the Pythagorean claim that all created things are number and that one,
which is not number, i.e. plurality, symbolizes God.[59] Weil, in
coming to grips with this claim, lays particular emphasis on the
fact that when the Pythagoreans spoke of number they were first
and foremost concerned with *things* and, therefore, when they were
working with numbers they were primarily interested in working
out the relations between entities. Now, she says, among the
natural numbers, some of them have a particular bond with unity.

These numbers are those which are squares of natural numbers, and
between these numbers and unity there is a mediation which binds
the two by an equality of relations such as 1/3=3/9.

When this mediation is seen to be primarily between God (one)
and creatures (numbers) we can see that the justice which "is a
number to the second power" bears a natural bond to God. In
this sense, the perfectly just man bears a mediated relationship
to the divinity, and in Plato's terms is assimilated to God.
Weil says: "Similarity, in the geometrical sense, means proportion. The mysterious equation of the Pythagoreans, and that of
Plato which seems clear, have the same meaning. Whoever is just
becomes to the Son of God as the Son is to His Father."[60] If
stress is thus laid upon numbers being things, any mediation between one and a square number must first refer to a mediation
between God and a just man.

Further evidence can be given for this interpretation which
makes mathematical mediation in the Pythagoreans refer primarily
to divine mediation. There is a fragment from Philolaos which
is quite unequivocal in making this assertion. It runs: "One
can see what powerful effect nature and the virtue of number has
not only in religious and divine things but everywhere in human
acts and reasonings both in the working of various techniques
and in music."[61] The same idea of mathematics' relation to the
divine also occurs in Proclus' comment on Plato's use of mathematics, when he says, "Plato teaches us many marvelous doctrines
concerning the divinity by means of mathematical ideas."[62] Finally, Weil notes a passage in the *Timaeus* (31c) which ostensibly
deals primarily with proportion, that the condition which Plato
sets for this proportion as "the most beautiful of bonds is that
which, to the highest degree, renders itself one with the terms
which are bound"[63] is only truly realized in the case of unity,
which is to say, God. This interpretation, she notes, does not
appear as self-evident but does gain force when one sees that
"Plato uses the same linking word in the *Symposium* to define the
mediatory function of Love between the divinity and man."[64]
On this account, Weil concludes:

> If the passage from the *Timaeus* on proportion has, besides
> its obvious sense, a theological sense, this meaning
> can be none other than that of Christ's words cited by

St. John, which are so very similar. The allusion is
evident. Just as the Christ recognized Himself as
Isaiah's man of sorrow, and the Messiah of all the prophets
of Israel, He recognized Himself as being that mean proportional of which the Greeks had for centuries been
thinking so intensely.[65]

Whole numbers, however, are of two sorts. There are, on the
one hand, the square numbers which are naturally linked to unity
by a mean proportional, and on the other hand, all the rest.
"If the first are an image of perfect justice, as the Pythagoreans
say, we resemble the others, we who are in sin."[66] The problem
then arises of how these wretched, sinful numbers can be assimilated to God. This is also the problem Weil sees in the essay
God in Plato, which, she says, is the search to relate human
imperfection to divine perfection.

It was because of the theological search for a mediation
of the wretched numbers and divinity, Weil says, that the Greeks
discovered geometry. This claim at first sounds strange until
one realizes that for many of the Greeks (perhaps fewer than
Weil thought, but certainly true of the Pythagoreans and Plato)
the study of geometrical figures was in actuality the study of
number for the λόγος or proportion of geometrical figures is
number.[67] This study of number, undertaken through a search for
proportion, then allows for mediation of non-similar numbers.
This can be seen in a quote from Plato's *Epinomis:*

> What one ridiculously calls geometry (i.e. land measuring)
> is the assimilation of numbers not naturally similar
> among themselves. Their assimilation becomes manifest
> when applied to the properties of plane figures, and
> this, to whoever is capable of thought, is a marvel
> which comes from God and not from men.[68]

If it is then understood that geometry is a search for
proportion, that proportion is a function of numbers and that
numbers refer to a theological problem of mediation, Weil's
claim then becomes that Greek mathematics is, in fact, a theological exercise of purifying the soul, allowing it to be assimilated to God. Weil writes in a letter to her brother:

> I think therefore that from a fairly remote antiquity
> the idea of proportion had been a theme of meditation
> which was one of the chief methods, and perhaps the
> chief method of purifying the soul. There can be no
> doubt that this idea was at the centre of Greek aesthetics

> and geometry and philosophy. . . Purity of soul was their
> one concern; to "imitate" God was the secret of it; the
> imitation of God was assisted by the study of mathematics,
> in so far as one conceived the universe to be subject
> to mathematical laws, which made the geometer an imita-
> tion of the supreme law giver.[69]

It is on the basis of the claim of geometry being found to
offer the marvel of mediation to numbers naturally deprived of
it, that we may begin to see why mathematics was not only a
vehicle for expressing divine truth but an appropriate one as
well. Two basic reasons can be given for this. First, when the
discovery of surd numbers (ἄλογοι) occurred and it was found
that these numbers, which mediated between the sinful numbers
and unity, are unrepresentable as to their exact determination,
it appeared that number was a sort of contradictory thing, for
"this mediation between unity and number is in appearnace something inferior to number, something indeterminate. A *logos
alogos* is a scandal, an absurdity, a thing contrary to nature."[70]
Yet, this inconceivable relationship which mediates between one
and non-square numbers was found in experienced nature to be a
mark of supreme verity. Weil cites Pythagorean musical theory
as an example. Although the geometrical mean is not contained
in the musical scale, the entire scale is disposed symmetrically
around it, and this mean gives it beauty and harmony.

The second reason that mathematics is appropriate to express
divinity, at least the way that the Greeks practiced it, rests
in its requirement of rigorous demonstration. Mathematics above
all other areas of human thought expresses certainty. Weil
therefore says: "The Greeks had such a need of certainty of
divine verities that even in the simple image of these verities
they had to have the maximum of certainty."[71] It was never the
technological application of mathematics with which the Greeks
were concerned for there approximations work very well, but
rather, they were most concerned with the rigor of the demonstrations. This marks a profound difference between them and us,
for whereas modern man tends to regard the empirical as most
certain and the areas of divinity as always being unclear, the
Greeks thought that certainty rested only in the divine and that
the earthly is, at best, a muddied image of it. It was for this
reason that the practice of mathematics, that is, the carrying

out of rigorous demonstrations, could be a purification of the
soul, for by applying oneself to the non-material requirement
of certainty, one could be made more and more like the divinity
by gaining further clarity in mathematics. It is by God's mercy,
Weil says, that this requirement of certainty keeps mathematics
"from being drowned in mere technique."[72] Mathematics she therefore felt can be "one of the openings through which the breath
and the light of God may penetrate."[73]

If both of these reasons can be brought together in a single
human activity, it can then further be seen how the practice
of mathematics is itself a mediation of God which allows the
soul to be assimilated to Him. When the mind is first dealing
with natural numbers a certain degree of clarity about the world
is obtained. When, however, mediation of non-square numbers is
brought into the picture, this certainty would seem to disappear.
Yet, if the mind keeps the requirement of rigorous demonstration
before itself, it must then deal rigorously with that which is
incomprehensible to the material imagination.

> This notion forces the mind to deal in exact terms with
> those relationships which it is incapable of representing
> to itself. Here is an admirable introduction to the
> mysteries of faith. By this one can conceive an order
> of certainty, starting from uncertain and easily grasped
> thought about the sensible world, proceeding to thoughts
> of God which are absolutely certain and absolutely incom-
> prehensible. Mathematics is doubly a mediation between
> these two kinds of thought. It has the intermediate
> degree of certainty, the intermediate degree of incon-
> ceivability. It includes the précis of the necessity
> which governs sensible things and the images of the
> divine truths. Finally, it has for its core the very
> idea of mediation.[74]

After explaining her claim that mathematical mediation is a deliberate Pythagorean image for theological mediation and showing
why mathematics is an appropriate expression for divinity, Weil
begins her presentation of her "Pythagorean doctrine." She does
this by applying the above cited formula, "Friendship is an
equality made of harmony," to the various divine and created
relationships. It is by this application that Weil demonstrates
harmony and mediation in regard to God, God and Creation, God
and man, man and man, and finally, in an extended sense, to the
relations of created matter. In each of these cases there

appears two contraries in the relationship which are harmonized
and mediated into a unity.

In order to apply the formula first to God, Weil says it
must first be juxtaposed with Philolaos' definition of harmony,
namely, "the common thought of separate thinkers" (Diels
10[B61]). This juxtaposition she claims "leads to the best
method of enlightening the intelligence about the dogma of the
Trinity."[75]

When we think only of God as one, Weil contends, we must
either think of Him as pure object or as pure subject. In the
first case we cannot then think of him as act and in the second
case, He needs an object, "else creation would be necessity and
not love. God would not be exclusively love and good."[76] Already a pair of contraries appears, at least in human concep-
tuality, for our own subject arises through contact with an object and if, therefore, we can establish an analogy for God's
perfection we must do so by conceiving the one God as being both
pure subject and object. The contraries arise from the need to
think of God as one, yet two things. But how is this possible
if God is an ever active subject as Weil says He is?

It is possible if we represent God to ourselves as a harmony which is the common thought of separate thinkers. God *is*
essentially subject and He is therefore also essentially thinking
and not thought. Yet this need not preclude the object of God's
thinking from itself being subject. In fact, if God is thinking
this is demanded. Weil writes: "His name is 'I am'. That is
His name as subject, it is also His name as object, it is also
his name as contact with the subject and object."[77]

Thought implies three terms--a thinking subject, an object
thought and the thought which is the contact between the two.
In human thought each of these terms is distinct with there
being a particular disjunction between the subject and the object. In God, however, who is ever active thinking, while each
one of these terms can be represented in the divine thinking,
the divine dignity "exacts that these three be each one a Person, although there be a single God."[78] When any one of these
terms is applied to God it can never be taken in a passive
sense. That which thinks, that which is thought and the thought

itself are all active thinkers. "What God thinks is still a
Being who thinks. This is why we say this is the Son or Image,
or the Wisdom of God."[79]

It is in this way that God can be a single ever active subject for the object of act in the Godhead is itself also a subject willing the same act. When the Father begets the Son, He
begets a Being who Himself actively wills to be the Father's
Son. In the same way, the Spirit which is the thought between
the Father and the Son also wills to be that thought. Here
Plato's "most beautiful of bonds" applies for it is the ideal
unity of three terms, namely 1/1=1/1. Plato says this bond obtains when

> The intermediary is to the last as the first is to the
> last, and reciprocally, the last to the intermediary, as
> the intermediary is to the first, then the intermediary
> becomes first and last. Further, the last and the
> first become both intermediaries; thus it is necessary
> that all achieve identity; and being identified mutually,
> they shall be one.[80]

It may ring strange upon modern ears to hear of actual
identity being spoken of as a relationship between separates,
but Weil's point is clear. God is essentially act and He is
essentially one. Because acting, however, requires more than
one term, God's eternal and infinite action, which cannot be
defined in reference to a temporal and finite entity, is therefore trinitarian. Two things must be kept straight. God's
unity is not a fourth thing which is the *result* of the harmony
of the separate Persons and neither are the Persons the out-
workings of the unity. What Weil is saying quite unequivocally
is that unity of God is strictly identical to the thought of
the separate thinkers *and* vice versa. In short, one is equal
to three and three is equal to one.

The Trinity is thus an equality made of harmony when harmony is defined as the common thought of separate thinkers.
There is already mediation in God Himself which is marked by
His being as a union of contraries, that is, the contraries of
one and number. "The equality is the equality between one and
many, between one and two."[81] But, furthermore this harmony is
also a friendship *par excellence*. It is this friendship in
harmony which is the basis of all other harmonies and friendships.

Weil says, implying the comparison of divine perfection and
finite human participation in that perfection: "The Trinity is
the supreme harmony and the supreme friendship."[82]

Harmony is the union of contraries. As we have seen the
first pair of contraries is that of one and many which is harmonized in the Trinity. The second pair of contraries is the
opposition between the Creator and the Creation. "This opposition expresses itself as a correlation between that which limits
and that which is limitless; in other words, that which receives
its limitation from outside."[83] A Pythagorean creation is similar to that of *Genesis* for it is the imposing of limits on a
formless and limitless Chaos or void. At first, God the One of
all being and the one who limits and the void or unlimited are
contraries. Strictly speaking only one of these two contraries
has any reality and the other is, as it were, a principle of
nothingness. But in creating God goes outside Himself and imposes limits on the limitless, giving it number and thus form and
substance and being. When he does so, the limits or number he
imposes, form, in Plato's words, "the number which is intermediary (μεταξύ) between the one and the limitless."[84]

The passage from the *Philebus* from which this last formulation is taken is perhaps the most fertile of all the Platonic
texts which Weil uses for her doctrine of mediation.[85] For this
reason an explanation of Weil's interpretation of this difficult
passage is needed because in Weil's eyes this text is centrally
concerned with giving a general method of mediation and of the
philosopher's understanding of this method. This she feels, is
evident from the very fact that it is introduced as having been
given to man by "some Prometheus"[86] who is already a mediator.
What is more important, however, is the method itself.

In Weil's interpretation this passage first shows a hierarchy of contraries and then second shows the mediation of the
various contraries. Here the one and the many are the first
pair of contraries and the limit and unlimited the second. The
first pair she understands to be the Trinity, "the first origin."[87] Here "number appears in the Trinity as the second term
of opposition."[88] The contraries of limit and unlimited she
then takes to be the contraries of Creator and created, or God

and the void. This latter set of contraries, however, can be
mediated, for if the number in the Trinity "is identified with
limit, it appears in the principle of creation as the first term.
It is then indeed something like a mean proportional."[89] In
this regard, the Creation, that which is created out of the indefinite, is created by having limits imposed on the indefinite.
The Creation as a single thing then is the union of the contraries of limit and unlimited and is a mediator between God and
his contrary, the void.

A general doctrine of mediation can be evolved out of this
which is applicable to any ontological level through the second
term of opposition of any mediated relationship becoming the
intermediary term for a new relationship between the contraries
of the old mediated relationship regarded as one thing and some
new opposition to it. Just as the primal set of contraries of
one and many are mediated in the Godhead, and the many becomes
the mediating term for a second set of contraries and thus itself regarded as a unit, so too can it be further divided. In
a similar fashion, the secondary numbers arrived at by this
process of division can also be regarded as units and further
subdivided until the entire range of beings is exhausted and
ordered in the whole through a series of intermediate relationships. Two results obtain from this method. On the one hand,
anything that exists, i.e. which has a limit, can be harmonized
in God by participating in the primal mediation of the Creation
as a whole through a series of mediations. On the other hand,
each thing "should reproduce, each one at its own level, the
order of the primordial hierarchy."[90] All things insofar as
they correspond to their limits are therefore microcosms of the
whole.

This method is, as said, general and therefore applicable
to and descriptive of any ontological level. In this place,
however, Weil is only concerned with the mediation of God and
creation and it is here that certain theological problems need
to be raised, the answers to which should help further to clarify
the relationship. Weil has already been seen to have handled
the contraries of one and many in her understanding of the
Trinity, but the second pair of contraries pose certain problems,
for when Weil takes the unlimited to be inert matter, it appears

that she is forced into an irreducible dualism which opposes her own monistic conception of mediation. The problem, however, can be solved in two steps.

The first step is in the recognition that for Weil, as it was for Plato, the unlimited is basically an abstraction. It cannot really be said ever to exist in its own right, for unlike number a formless void cannot be thought. This does not make the unlimited insignificant in *what* is created, however, for in the act of creation God thinks that which does not exist, and in so thinking it, thinks it through the Son. Weil's own symbolic language of the withdrawal or abdication of God at creation helps clarify this point. In His withdrawal God allows what does not exist outside of Himself to exist and thus it does exist. But in this very act of withdrawal, the Son is coincidentally 'crucified' upon the whole of time and space and thus mediates between God and the formless non-existent, giving the latter form and establishing in Himself a relation between it and God.

The first step which shows that this pair of contraries is in God then leads to the problem which needs to be answered by the second step. If, indeed, these contraries are in God and are mediated in Him, then, "not only the principle of limitation but also the inert matter and the union between the two, must be divine Persons, just as the bond which links them must be a Person. But inert matter does not think, it cannot be a Person."[91] This difficulty, Weil says, can be resolved by passing the limit. An intersection can be gained between a person and inert matter if we recall affliction, for in that phenomenon there is a person who is reduced to matter. Affliction would, however, threaten dualism unless it could be shown that a person afflicted, while reduced to matter, still continued to exercise the function of a person, that is, continuing to love. This Christ has done and it is for this reason that He is the Mediator of the contraries. Thus there is a maximum distance between God and matter which is also the distance between the Father and the Son. At the same time, however, there is also a maximum unity between the two in the love which they bear for each other even while separated.

In understanding Weil's view of creation it is necessary to note that when she speaks of Creation as a whole, that is, as a

single ordered entity, she is speaking of Christ in His function
as the Logos, who is the orderer and thus the beauty and truth
of the world. It is for this reason that in *Divine Love in
Creation* she adopts Plato's phrase, "Soul of the World," to
designate Christ as the mediator between the unlimited and God.
This phrase, however, is open to serious misunderstanding. What
she intends by it, though, is that the unlimited is essentially
lifeless and that it is the "Soul of the World" who gives it
life. In this sense, the "Soul of the World" is not something
which comes into being with a created world but is that which,
although eternally a blessed Person in the Trinity, gives his
life to that which had none before. He does this out of loving
obedience to the Father and thus he establishes within the Godhead a mediated unity with the Creation as a whole.

The point of this becomes clearer when it is understood
that Weil is attempting to duplicate an artistic theory of
creation (particularly in *Divine Love in Creation*) which she
finds in the *Timaeus*. What Weil is saying is that the motivating
reason and purpose of creation (the Father's goodness), that
which is the life, beauty and the truth of the creation (the
Son) and the model or inspiration of creation which is the link
between the artist and his work (the Spirit) all exist in God
in unity and actuality before a world ever comes into being.
Said otherwise, God creates out of his own being and life. In
this case, what is good in this world, even if that good is
limited and finite, can be seen as really good and to have proceeded from that which is absolutely good. Thus the joys of
finite goods, when given loving attention, can be seen to be
images of God's own life. As Weil says of the central idea of
the *Philebus*, there is "a sovereign good which incorporates all
forms of good."[92]

There is a double significance to this artistic theory of
creation linked to this view of God. In regard to God Himself,
the creation through the Son is no longer simply an ordering
function, for the Son becomes the mediator between the creature
and God. The creation comes into existence when the Son gives
it His own life and when He as Soul of the World is crucified
on time and space and "placed in its centers and spread out

across the whole."[93] The creation is a work of art in which the
artist, who through his own goodness and who through being inspired by the model of perfection, has created a being of perfect goodness equal to himself. But this view of artistic creation then turns upon the very human activity from which it has
taken its analogical departure. The good artist, that is, the
person who practices a good τεχνή well imitates on his level
the activity of God. He is a good artist when he ceases to reproduce his own self-centered perspective, choosing instead to
produce the perfection of reality with which he has been inspired and giving that production the fullness of life equal to
his own. In this way, the good artist gives his love to the
world's beauty and imitates it in his own microcosmic life. When
he thus embodies and incarnates the Beauty of the World, through
his actions he bears a mediated bond with God. This sort of
activity, Weil says, should be the goal of science and of all
knowledge and labor.

> Thus the Word is a model for man to imitate. Not in
> this case the Word incarnate in a human being, but the
> Word as the orderer of the world, so far as incarnate
> in the universe as a whole . . . We share in the rectitude
> of proportions in which there is nothing arbitrary,
> therefore no field open to the play of the imagination.
> But doubtless this idea of proportion also evokes the
> Incarnation.[94]

This idea of proportions does evoke the human Incarnation
of Christ and His Crucifixion, which is the third form of harmony, when the formula "Friendship is an equality made of harmony" is applied to the friendship between spiritual human beings and God. Weil says: "If one takes harmony in the sense of
geometric mean, if one conceives that the only mediation between
God and man is a being at once God and man, one passes directly
from this Pythagorean equation to the marvelous precepts of the
Gospel of St. John."[95]

Weil employs a definite and deliberate distinction between
the mediation of the creator-creation contraries and the particular mediation of human souls in the Incarnation and Crucifixion of Christ. The first mediation speaks of the creation
as a whole and here the human creature can have a mediated relationship to God by his proportional and harmonious participation

in the creation. This participation through knowledge and craft
is one of the openings through which the breath and light of
God may penetrate. The second mediation is assumed, however,
when there is a realization that, although a creature among
others, man is a spiritual being who bears a unique relationship
to God through God's especial love. But what is this relationship and what distinguishes it from the common creature relationship?

In part, the distinction is seen in the threat affliction
poses to the human ability to imitate consistently the creator's
own act for affliction makes us turn to falsehood in order to
save our lives. Man is an intelligent creature and he can therefore escape into illusion unlike the vast majority of creatures
who obey their limits almost mechanically. Here a special mediation allows men not to be ever separated from God, even in
the face of the worst evil. But Weil's point goes deeper than
this, for in Christ's Incarnation and Crucifixion God shows His
purpose of wanting to give His Son many brothers. The Son is
therefore Incarnated as a human being and crucified to the purpose of creating a unique being who not only obeys God through
operating within the proportional limits of his proper existence
but who also freely loves God. It is through this love that man
becomes a spiritual being who is assimilated to Christ and then
to the Father. In this regard, Weil's point has to be taken
very seriously that there is not a direct relationship between
man and God, just as there is not a direct relationship between
matter and the Father; rather, the bond of equality consists in
two relationships--our relationship to Christ and His to the
Father. This Weil takes to be the basis of the Johannine sayings, that "none comes to Father except by me," and "as thou,
Father, art in me, and I in thee, that they also may be one in
us."

This mediation, however, does not occur simply in the abstract fact of Christ's becoming man and thus making man like
God, for once again mediation occurs through activity. One is
only assimilated to Christ through the active love which the Son
bore for the Father on the Cross and which he continues to bear
in those who love Him. In this sense, the spiritual τεκνή is

not only knowledge but also production and doing. The spiritual
truth of mediation is that the assimilation to God consists in
the spiritual activity of love. One is bound into a friendship
of harmonic equality with God by God's own mediating love. "The
Pythagorean definition of friendship, applied to God and to man,
makes mediation appear as essentially love, and love as being
essentially the mediator. It is this also which Plato expresses
in the *Symposium*."[96]

It is on the basis of the mediating love between Christ and
men that Weil finds another form of harmony and friendship which
is the friendship between men. At first, however, there appears
to be a difficulty in applying the formula to men because there
is not a set of two contrary things needing to be harmonized.
Men *qua* men are of a kind. It is for this reason, Weil notes,
that Philolaos said, "Things of the same species, of the same
root, and of the same station, have no need of harmony." Nevertheless, she claims, "The Pythagorean definition applies to men,
because although they are in fact of the same species, of the
same root, of the same rank they are not so in their thought."[97]

The explanation of this difference between men in their
thought is given by Weil in reference to the fact that each human
being has an ego, which is to say, that to himself, his 'I'
which is the center of his perspective, tends to see other per-
spectives and portions of the universe as important only to the
degree to which they are close to the 'I' and affect it. Although occasionally one may transfer this central portion of the
universe into another human being or thing, the effect is basically the same insofar as everything else is disposed of according
to a limited perspective. This leads to a situation where "excepting the case whereone human being is brutally subjected to
another, who deprives him for a time of the power of thinking in
the first person, everyone disposes of others as he disposes of
inert things, either in fact, if he has the power, or in
thought."[98] The contraries among men are thus established by
the fact that men do not think and act as harmonious equals.
Given then that these contraries exist in human life, harmonization is needed for there to be friendship. This occurs in three
ways.

The first form of friendship and harmony occurs as a natural
phenomenon when it is recognized that an equilibrium of forces
obtains in a relationship between two or more human beings and
where each equally needs the consent of the other in order to
carry out his particular designs. In this case, nobody has
ceased to think in the first person, but the dictates of necessity being what they are, each is obliged to recognize the freely
disposed of existence of another. Each then must allow the
other his free consent to the relationship. This forms a sort
of natural justice among humans.

There are also, however, supernatural forms of harmony in
human relationships and these can obtain when there is a spiritual activity which consists in imitation of God's own harmo-
nizing activity. This activity is renunciation of the perspective of the 'I' out of respect and love for another. "One must
renounce in favor of God, through love for Him and for the truth,
this illusory power which He has accorded us, to think in the
first person."[99] God alone has the right to say "I am"; yet
even He does not exercise this right, for he renounces it in
order to think the existence of other beings. In the same way,
by renouncing our egos, out of love, we see that others are our
fellows.

Weil asserts that this self-renouncing activity is in the
very first place "the love of God whether or not the name of God
be present in the mind."[100] Harmony and friendship is initially
defined by the love of the Persons in the Trinity from which
springs the bond between man and God. But it is also applied
to the relationships between human beings. This can be seen in
a two-fold significance of Christ's mediation. On the one hand,
from the side of God, Christ's mediation harmonizes the contraries of man and God. Through His Incarnation and Crucifixion He
makes spiritual beings who are capable of freely loving the
Father just as He has done. On the other hand, from a human
point of view, Christ is a man who is capable of saying "I" and
disposing of us as we dispose of each other. Yet, He renounces
this 'I' and forms a bond of friendship between Him and us wherein the contraries of 'I' and 'others' are harmonized. His mediation then forms a bond between man and God and a bond between

man and man. Although the love we bear for God always has a
priority over other relationships this love must operate through
a relationship to Christ which is, in turn, a relationship to
our fellows.

> This is why the two commandments make but one. In law,
> the love of God is first. But in fact, as among men all
> concrete thought has a real object, this renunciation
> operates while thought is applied either to things or
> men.[101]

There are then two forms of friendship which can be considered supernatural. The first is the friendship we bear for certain natural equals in which, although we are brought together
by the accidents and bonds of necessity, we nevertheless love
and respect the other's spiritual being of free consent, regardless of the natural bond. The second occurs in our love for
the afflicted where we give up the natural right to dispose of
them as things and instead see them as persons, understanding
that they, too, can love. Both of these friendships are friendships made possible by Christ's love for His friends and for the
afflicted.

In each one of these friendships, God and God, God and the
Creation, God and man, and man and man there is a spiritual
activity of mediation and a proportional participation in God's
own love.

> In each one of the three relationships indicated by
> the word friendship, God is always mediator. He is me-
> diator between Himself and Himself. He is mediator
> between Himself and man. He is mediator between one
> man and another. God is essentially mediation. This
> is why song is appropriate for His praise.[102]

3. *The Pythagorean Doctrine Continued*

There is finally, Weil says, a fifth form of harmony and
this is the harmony of created things. This form of harmony,
unlike the others, though, is not a friendship for it is not
directly concerned with persons. It is important, however, for
man because man, besides being a spiritual being, is also a
created thing and almost entirely so, excepting his faculty of
free consent. This form of harmony then is one which "surrounds
man insofar as a man is a thing . . . (and it) proceeds to
englobe what each one calls himself."[103]

There is again a set of contraries here which need to be
harmonized and these contraries are *related* to the primal contraries of limit and unlimited. A careful distinction needs to
be made here to understand what exactly Weil's point is. Previously she had spoken of a mediation of the limit-unlimited contraries as the contraries of God and the void. There her concern
was with the relation of God to a creation and this relationship
was discovered to be a harmony and friendship because of the
Son's role as the Soul of the World. The spiritual friendship
of Persons obtained because the Son, although not the material
world, is its soul and life. Here, however, she is not so much
concerned with that relationship as she is with the relation of
the natural created being, man, to other created things and finally his relationship to the whole insofar as it is the natural
order of Necessity and he is a being who exists within it.

There is, of course, a bridge between the two discussions
and this can be discerned through the general *Philebus* schema.
Whereas the previous discussion dealt with the mediated equation
of one:number::number: unlimited, where Christ mediated between
the Father and the unlimited, here the emphasis has changed so
that the previous intermediary now becomes the first term of the
equation. In making this change, however, there is also a coincidental qualitative change in which this first term is to be
taken, for it is here only concerned with the ordering function
of the *Logos* and hence Necessity. This qualitative change occurs because Weil is not speaking of the relationship between
Persons, including the supernatural aspect of man, but rather
the relation of non-spiritual things to each other and to the
order of necessity. The equation then becomes with these changes,
necessity:intelligence (man's proper natural activity)::intelli-
gence:matter.

The discussion of this fifth form of harmony is important
in a number of ways, treating as it does several previously un-
answered questions. As said before, man does not bear a direct
relationship to God but only a mediated one and this is just as
true of his natural activities as it is of his supernatural ones.
In this case we need to deal with two basic questions: 1) the
relation of the activity of the human being, insofar as he is

not a spiritual being, to the created world and Necessity; 2) the
relation of the non-spiritual part of man to the spiritual such
that his activity, although having two diverse aspects, can yet
be seen as one activity. Beyond answering these two questions
the discussion of this form of harmony also has a further importance of clarifying Weil's distinction between Necessity and
Goodness in such a way that Necessity while distinct from Good
nevertheless can be seen to be obedient to it.

It is worthwhile before analyzing this last form of harmony
to point out an aspect of the discussion which has to do with
Weil's own intellectual biography and which helps to harmonize
its two periods. As we have seen, Weil's early view of mediation
primarily concerned itself with the relations of mind, matter and
necessity. There she came to a position in which she held that
mind is able to be mediated in the world through thought by considering the necessary inter-relationships of things and of
things to itself. This, she thought, was the highest ideal for
man and was his means of participating in goodness, beauty and
truth. Although she seems to have understood some sort of
transcendent good she did not really bring much attention to bear
on it *qua* transcendent. In the later works, however, after
having had contact with God, her main concern centered on supernatural mediation. While I have claimed that her religious experience and consequent emphasis did not negate her previous
views, putting them into a larger perspective, the actual relations between what is a natural view of mediation and a supernatural one have not been worked out. The fifth form of harmony
is able to do this. In it the issue under discussion is that of
the relations of man to things and necessity through intellectual
activity. But what is also at issue in this discussion is the
relation of natural intelligence to supernatural love and in this
regard a resolution is obtained for the otherwise disjunctive
aspects of mediation in Weil. In a very real sense, therefore,
not only is the general metaphysics of mediation completed here
for all relations but also Weil's own work is synthesized into
a single coherent whole.[104]

The contraries of limit and unlimited as they pertain to
our relation to natural things appear when the Pythagorean dictum, "Everything is number," is applied to the way in which we

know things. It was one of the greatest Pythagorean insights
into human knowledge that it is through the application of number to otherwise undifferentiated sense perception that we can
distinguish one thing from another and are able to mark out the
quantity and function of everything that appears. Without number
our epistemic lives would only be a mass of undifferentiated
sense experience in which we would have difficulty knowing the
crucial difference between ourselves, what is experienced and
the experience itself.[105] One fragment of Philolaos claims this
value of number:

> The essence of number is productive of understanding,
> a guide and a master for whoever is in perplexity or
> ignorance about anything. For there would be no clarity
> in things, either in themselves or in their mutual rela-
> tions, if there were not number and its essence. There-
> fore number, fitting all things into the soul through
> sense perception, renders them comprehensible and mu-
> tually in accord, and gives them a body and separates by
> force each relationship of unlimited and limiting things.[106]

Philolaos' claim is that it is number which gives things a
body and it is therefore through our understanding of number that
we come to know the world in which we live. In order to compre-
hend fully this claim it is necessary to see the way in which
'number' is used. Number for the Pythagoreans, Weil says, is
not just the enumeration of quantity, for this clearly would not
tive us an understanding of all relationships; number for the
Pythagoreans also included the notion of function which is a
quantitative law of variation. "Function is what the Greeks
called number or relationship, *arithmos* or *logos*, and it is also
this which constitutes limit."[107] The gnomon of Pythagorean
mathematics shows this notion of function. A gnomon originally
was the vertical stem of a sundial which remains immobile while
its shadow varies. A relationship then obtains between the invariant stem and its variable shadow which is the function. This
same idea of function can be applied to anything, active or inert, in the natural world and a rigorous formula of function
which defines the object can then be obtained.

Weil says that it is somewhat surprising to hear that it is
number which gives things a body. Yet, she adds, it is literally
true and "the quantitive relationships which play the part of

the gnomon do indeed constitute the body of the object."[108] Although in perception we never see, for example, all the sides
and angles of a cubic box and their inter-relations, nevertheless we understand "that the cubic form is what determines the
variation of the apparent form."[109] It is this unperceived, yet
understood, form which is indeed the body of the object for us.
It is this understanding then which differentiates perception of
the real world from hallucinations and illusions. It is also
a contact with necessity, for

> Necessity always appears to us as an ensemble of laws
> of variation, determined by fixed relationships and
> invariants. Reality for the human mind is contact with
> necessity. There is a contradiction (sic) here for neces-
> sity is intelligible, not tangible. Thus the feeling
> of reality constitutes a harmony and mystery.[110]

The reality of the universe is therefore the necessity constituted by the gnomic laws of variation. But this is not the
entire story as if the physical universe were only a Berkleian
system of ideas. The necessity with which Weil is concerned is
itself conditional and needs to stand on a base. But what is
this base? Weil says that we really cannot have a conception
of it for if intelligibility is determined by number then the
base which is not number cannot be known. Nevertheless, the
Greeks did have a word for this basis (ἄπειρον) which means indeterminate and unlimited. This indeterminate is what Plato in
the *Timaeus* calls the receptable and matrix of all becoming. It
is itself without limits and thus has no quantities or qualities,
yet it admits what does have limits.[111] It is in this way that
our physical world is composed of both limit and unlimited.

In our dealings with things these dealings are always with
matter and hence with that which is subjected to necessity and
its quantitative laws of variation in the appearances. This
necessity is all that we can know about matter. But although we
can know necessity our relations to it can be manifold, constituting an enmity or harmony which depends on whether or not one
thinks in the first person. One can have a least three relations
with necessity in which there is an enmity, or at least a truce
in lieu of an enmity. Man can be related to necessity by fantasy or by the exercise of power. In this case necessity appears

to be man's slave. He can be related to necessity through suffering and affliction in which case necessity seems to be his
master. Finally, he can establish a sort of equilibrium of
forces between himself and the natural world through methodical
action. Here necessity "by its conditional character, presents
man with obstacles and with means in relation to the partial ends
he pursues and wherein there is a sort of equality between man's
will and necessity."[112] If this sort of equilibrium can be established certain goals of natural happiness can be met and certain forms of evil can be abolished.

But, Weil says, this equilibrium which is established between the human will and necessity through methodical action is
at best only an image for "effectually, the human will, although
a certain amount of sentiment of choice be irreducibly attached
to it, is simply a phenomenon among all those which are subject
to necessity."[113] The will itself is a natural thing and has
its own proper functions and limits. When fatigue or affliction
beset man the limits of his will are reached and he seeks refuge
in illusion quite naturally. At that moment his methodical action is destroyed. On this level man experiences necessity only
as an object of necessity when he experiences it through his
will and "henceforth the experience of necessity is never entirely free of illusions connected with the exercise of will."[114]

But there is one area in which man's activity is not subject
to the forces of necessity and where he can pass beyond the limits of will. This area is found in the act of mind by which man
thinks necessity under its conditional (i.e. purely mathematical)
aspect for here the thinker "is not present under any heading,
he has no part in it outside the very process by which he thinks
it."[115] This is to say, the mind itself is not forced when
dealing with conditional necessity to think it in any particular
way determined by necessity; rather mind *comprehends* conditional
necessity and necessity is only present to mind in the mind's
act of thinking of things according to necessity. For the mind
"the purely conditional progression of necessity is the progression of demonstration itself."[116] At this level "necessity is
for man no longer either an enemy or a master"[117] for necessity
does not stand above the mind, like the it does over the will,
determining its function. But neither is man the master of

necessity at this level for in thinking necessity he does not
change it. He simply sees and knows things as they are as natural things.

    This mathematical necessity which exists in the mind's dem-
onstrations is, Weil says, "an intermediary between the whole
natural part of man and the infinitely small portion of himself
which does not belong to this world."[118] The relationship of
man as a natural being to necessity is always the relation of
one force to another. The relationship of the intelligence to
necessity, however, is not a relationship of this sort for it is
not a master-slave relationship. But neither is it the supernatural relationship of friendship between two persons; instead
it "is the relationship of the object contemplated to the contemplation."[119] Furthermore, it is not the supernatural faculty
of consent for even when man has conceived necessity he still
remains free to consent to it or not. In both these ways the
contemplation of mathematical necessity is intermediary between
the natural and supernatural aspects of man for it is "at the
intersection of the two worlds."[120] It is a faculty which thinks
this world but is also one which is not of this world.

    Once mathematical necessity is seen as intermediary between
the two worlds, however, it can also be seen as a sort of mediator between the two, and two reasons exist for this. On the one
hand, the thought of mathematical necessity is an image of consent and renunciation because it does not view the world from
the empirical perspective of the self. In this case, the self
has, as in supernatural consent, already been suspended as the
determining value in human life. On the other hand, it is a mediator because supernatural consent cannot be given until necessity is actually contemplated and freely given as an object of
consent. It can only be given freely without the constraint
that belongs solely to the level of force and natural objects.
Weil writes:

        This liberty is not actual in him except when he con-
        ceives of force as necessity, that is to say, when he
        contemplates it. He is not free to consent to force as
        such. The slave who sees the lash lifted above him
        does not consent, nor refuse his consent, he trembles.
        And yet under the name of necessity it is indeed to
        brute force that man consents, and when he consents it is
        indeed to a lash. No mover, no motive can be suffi-
        cient for such a consent.[121]

The supernatural consent to necessity is pure love. But it
is also a madness: "man's own particular madness, the madness
that belongs to men, like Creation, like the Incarnation, together with the Passion, constitutes God's own madness."[122] Two
things need to be noted of this madness. Initially, it needs to
be discerned that Weil calls it a madness because of its free
and unmotivated character. In fact, she says, almost all kind
considerations would seem to dictate against this consent for
in giving our love to necessity we give our love to that which
can destroy us and our fellows. This leads to a second aspect
of the madness. When we give our consent to necessity the love
which is this consent goes beyond necessity as the object of
love and "the visible world of which it is the stuff."[123] When
man loves he does not love matter but a person. When necessity
is then formed as an object for our consent it actually becomes
like a work of art which is a living memento of its maker and
it is to this Person that our love is given. Mathematical necessity by itself does not possess any motivating reason which can
enjoin our love. It is what it is and we have no way of seeing
behind it to grasp its reasons and purposes, and it, certainly,
does not give any answer as to its purpose. "But when love,
from which the consent to necessity proceeds, exists in us, we
possess experimental proof that there is an answer. For it is
not out of love for other men that we consent to necessity . . .
It is for the love of something which is not a human person, and
who is yet something like a person . . . This consent constitutes participation in the Cross of Christ."[124]

It can now be seen that man can through the mediation of
his intellectual activity pass beyond the limits of his crea-
turely relations to a friendship of persons in God. Moreover,
it can also be seen that in his consent to necessity man reproduces in his life the original consent of God to necessity when
He created the world by causing His son to be subject to necessity, the only difference being between God's consent and man's
is that God's consent to necessity is His Will for He consents
to necessity by thinking it. This leads Weil to conclude, "Just
as the Christ is, on one hand, the mediator between God and
man, and on the other the mediator between man and his neighbour,

so mathematical necessity is on one hand the mediation between
God and things, and on the other between each thing and every
other thing."[125]

These conclusions, however, raise some important questions
about the harmony of things under necessity and about the relation of necessity to goodness, the two of which Weil has maintained to be distinct from each other. In order to answer these
questions it is necessary to clarify what Weil means by the necessity which is the order of the world and then to discern its
relation to God.

Order means, Weil notes, equilibrium and immobility. The
universe, however, being subject to time is a perpetual becoming
which stands opposed to equilibrium since the becoming of any
one thing must rupture the equilibrium. Nevertheless, Weil says,
the becoming as a whole can be an equilibrium "because the rup-
tures of equilibrium compensate each other. This becoming is
equilibrium refracted in time."[126] Each little thing, each little gnomon of activity, includes a principle of destruction of
a previously existing order, and on the natural level, its relation to other things ia a relation of one force trying to overcome another. But each gnomon also has a relation to things
through the order of the world. Each thing, by the fact that it
is a gnomon, is a limited entity, but it is also this entity and
not another. This limit then "puts it in relation to an equal
and inverse rupture of equilibrium."[127] No thing is ever an unlimited quantity that can ceaselessly expand for it is constantly
being acted upon as it acts and this prescribes a certain limit
to its activity. The actual limit of each thing's activity,
which is in a sense its definition, however, comes from and is
incorporated into an invariant union which is the network of all
limits. This network, or order, is what Weil calls the order of
the world. This order, though, is not to be confused with its
particular determinations since it is the invariant determinate
of all variations. In this sense, each thing as a force has its
own proper existence as it seeks to expand itself, but it also
has another aspect in which it is confined and obeys the overall
order through remaining within its assigned limits. The fact
that each thing is, is because it acts as a force, but the fact

that it is this force and not another, nor can become another,
is because of the world order.

This gives us two distinct aspects to the world. Weil makes
this point quite clearly in *Divine Love in Creation* when she says:

> God does no violence to secondary causes in the accom-
> plishment of his ends. He accomplishes them all through
> the inflexible mechanism of necessity without warping a
> single wheel. . . Each phenomenon has two causes, of
> which one is its cause according to the mechanism of
> nature, that is natural law, the second cause is in the
> providential ordering of the world, and it is never per-
> missible to make use of the one as an explanation upon
> the plane to which the other belongs.[128]

But since there are two distinct aspects to the world, there are
also two distinct relations of necessity, for "we (must) conceive
of God's will with regard to necessity, and with regard to matter, as being two different relationships."[129] The two relationships, nevertheless, are connected. God's will with respect to
matter is that it should be governed and ordered by necessity.
In this regard, insofar as things keep within their assigned limits with regard to other things, they are obeying necessity. Indeed, as natural things they literally have no choice but to obey
necessity and this includes man in his natural relations. On
this level there is no question of divine goodness for things are
what necessity makes them. But there is a second relationship
which is God's will with respect to the governing necessity and
this is that it should reflect perfectly the divine goodness.
On this level, necessity as the overarching order of the world
is the Soul of the World and the only begotten Son.

The two relations cannot be confused and this accounts for
the difference of necessity and goodness. If things obey necessity, they do so because it is their nature. While it is true
that in obeying necessity things are indirectly obeying God, this
does not alter the sense that they are doing so blindly and that
on the level of obedience to necessity there is no communion with
God. Divine goodness implies communion, and in this sense, no
one can claim divine goodness simply because he acts within the
world order. The order as a whole may be good because it directly
obeys God but it does so because of its particular relation to
God.

Man is in a peculiar position since he can participate in
the two separate relationships at once. As a natural created
thing he is bound in all his empirical relationships to obey
necessity. At the same time he is also a spiritual creature who
is meant to participate in communion with God. These two relationships are not without connection, however, for through the
intermediary of intellect they can be united and harmonized in
one being. Man by an act of mind stands above necessity when
he contemplates it. When he does so he is no longer simply the
object of necessity, but neither is a communion established with
God. What does happen, however, is that by no longer obeying
necessity as a thing he has the opportunity, through grace, to
consent to necessity freely, something which what is purely matter cannot do, and thus participate in the relation of necessity
to God as well as participating in the obedience of matter to
necessity.

When mathematical necessity is understood to be a mediator,
it can be seen how there is a correlation of the natural and
supernatural aspects of one being, man. This correlation obtains
when it is realized that "necessity is relationship--that is to
say, thought in action."[130] Mathematical necessity does not exist for man unless he uses attentive intelligence to carry out
the connections. Weil says: "The necessary connections which
constitute the very reality of the world have no reality in
themselves except as the object of intellectual attention in action."[131] There is, therefore, here a correlation between necessity and the free act of attention. When necessity and act are
correlated in the act of mind, intellectual attention becomes
an image of God's own creative act of thinking a world that had
not previously existed, for by bringing intellectual attention
upon the world, reality is given birth in us.

Intellectual attention, however, needs to be distinguished
from supernatural attention. Intellectual attention, because it
sees only the mathematical relations and neither the unlimited
or the final purpose of necessity, only produces half of reality.
But this is a half which man had not seen before. With intellectual attention the soul ceases to be subject to the distortions
of perspective, and has, by thinking it, accepted the principle

of co-existence in which each thing is seen as existing in its
own right. Here man shares in a certain natural justice for he
freely sees his own limits and the relationships he has with
other existing things. He begins to see them as real things.

But there is a further step. Once man has freely given his
intellectual attention to necessity, it yet remains for him to
give his consent to it and therefore to accept in full reality
the entire range of necessity as it touches his mind on the intermediate level and finally as it is God's own love and will.
His consent at last is a full consent to the will of God and a
handing over of all his life to God's own action.

Yet, even if through intellectual attention a harmony of
things can be recognized and this mathematical necessity be correlated with God's goodness, there remains a problem of why man
should ever be inclined to renounce his determined perspective
in the first place. An answer to this problem, however, can be
obtained through a final correlation of beauty and the order of
the world and its harmony.

Weil says in many places that beauty is the snare that God
sets to trap the human soul. In *The Pythagorean Doctrine* she
clarifies this when she says: "It is the beauty of the world
which permits us to contemplate and to love necessity."[132] Intellectual attention is a free act and one which renounces the
perspective of the self. It is, as we have seen, an image of
supernatural renunciation. As free it cannot be forced but this
does not preclude its being inspired, and this inspiration, according to Weil, can come from the beauty which is found in the
order of the world. Man when he gives his attention to the world
reproduces in his thought its reality. But he does not do this
idly. He reproduces reality in thought because he finds reality
beautiful and worth reproducing. His first initiation into beauty
may come in any number of ways when for one moment his perspective is unguarded and he sees the beauty of a song, of a paint-
ing, a poem or a figure. This beauty does not force him to reproduce reality; in fact, enough people shun doing so. What it
does do, though, is lure him, and if he is willing to be lured
he will reproduce reality. At first, the lure of beauty on his
intelligence leads him to produce only the half of reality of

conditional necessity, but in time it will serve as a memento
of its maker and man will give, unconditionally, his love to
Him. In this regard, even in the seemingly quite natural act of
thinking mathematical necessity, grace is already really present,
for the order of the world--its necessity--is this order by design and purpose and constitutes God's own means of leading the
soul to Himself while still respecting human consent and love.

"At the end of such meditations," Weil says, "one reaches an
extremely simple view of the universe."[133] At the end of these
meditations, Weil's own general doctrine of mediation is also
completed. Beginning with the mediation which is the binding
of the Persons in the Trinity and proceeding to the forms of mediation which constitute the order of the world and man's communion with God, all things can be found to be bound in an unity
in God through their various direct and indirect relationships.
It is a view of God in which no distinction is lost and yet one
in which nothing escapes the binding goodness and love of God.

> The supreme mediation is that of the Holy Spirit uniting
> through infinite distance the divine Father to the
> equally divine Son, but emptied of His divinity and
> nailed to a point in space and time. This infinite
> distance is made of the totality of space and of time.
> The portion of space around us, bounded by the circle
> of the horizon, the portion of time between our birth
> and our death, which we live second after second, which
> is the stuff of our life, is a fragment of this infinite
> distance entirely pierced by divine love. The being
> and life of each one of us are together a tiny segment
> of this line whose extremeties are two Persons and a
> single God, this line where Love circulates is also that
> same God. We are a point through which God's divine
> Love for self passes. In no case are we anything else.
> But if we know this, and if we consent to it, all our
> being, all that in us appears to be ourselves, becomes
> infinitely more foreign, more indifferent, and more
> distant, than this uninterrupted passage of God's love.[134]

This doctrine of mediation is perhaps best seen as it relates to man and the unity of his life in God. At first man is
a created being who must blindly obey the dictates of necessity.
At this level, his only relation to the rest of the world is by
force within the strict limits of necessity. Yet, he also becomes something more than matter when he transforms his activity
by renouncing his determined perspective and seeing necessity
as it is. Finally, he reaches a highest level on which he

consents with every part of his soul to have no other life than
that which comes from God. Here he participates in Christ's
Cross.

Mediation in human life, however, does not mean that man
escapes his material world with all its messiness, for "in those
who love God, even in those who are perfect, the natural part of
the soul is always entirely subject to mechanical necessity."[135]
Although man has in one sense risen above being the object of
necessity, he still remains one being composed of both the matter
which is subject to necessity as well as spirit. But his love,
thought and actions are different for "the presence of supernatural love in the soul constitutes a new factor of the mechanism and transforms it."[136] Whereas he once tried to find all
goodness in the things of necessity and ordered his life by
force, or more accurately was ordered by force, he now orders
his life as God orders His world. Each aspect of his being is
given its own proper object which is limited and ordered according to its proper function. The supernatural, Weil says,
does not descend into the domain of nature, nor can it be reproduced *qua* supernatural in the natural. But the presence of
the supernatural can change the natural order, or as Plato said,
it can persuade necessity towards goodness. Just as divine
causality orders a world so too can love in a soul order a life,
and the latter can be an experimental confirmation of the former
both to ourselves and to our neighbors.

> The consent to obey is mediator between blind obedience
> and God. The perfect consent is that of the Christ.
> Our consent can only be a reflection of that of the
> Christ. The Christ is mediator between God and our-
> selves on one side, and on the other between God and the
> universe. Likewise we, insofar as it is granted us to
> imitate Christ, have this extraordinary privilege of
> being, to a certain degree, mediators between God and
> His own creation.[137]

CHAPTER IV

MEDIATION IN DAILY LIFE

It is in Simone Weil's fifth form of Pythagorean harmony
that we can begin to see a definitely worked out relationship
between her early theory of mediation of mind in the world and
her later doctrine of religious mediation. When this relationship is recognized a link can be forged which joins together her
dual concerns of labor and social relations and of religious
life. This is apparent in what has been called Weil's 'mysticism
of labor' in which she makes labor into a consent to necessity
and therein a spiritual microcosm of Christ's consent to necessity. It would be easy simply to trace the lines of her thought
in this area and show the overall applicability of her doctrine
of mediation were it not for the fact that the theme of mysticism
of labor does not exhaust her later writings on labor and social
relationships. At the same time that she is engaged in seeking
a spiritual solution to the problems of labor she is also engaged in working out concrete and rational solutions for the
daily problems of labor and society, answers which seem to have
no apparent religious base. Gilbert Kahn writes of one of the
essays concerned with this latter concern, *Experience de la
vie d'usine:*

> This study, written in 1941, only after the (factory)
> experience of 1934-35, shows that Simone Weil continued
> to probe for a solution, let us say, a rational solution,
> to the problem of labor parallel to her efforts to find
> a mystical solution by recourse to symbolism.[1]

The two concerns, of course, do not need to be mutually ex-
clusive and it is not surprising to find a philosopher such as
Weil writing on practical issues. The question which her attempt
to seek out concrete and rational solutions to the problems of
labor and social relations raises, however, is whether this is
an independent but parallel project or whether there is some essential philosophical connection between it and the religious
concerns. If it is the former, then although we might not say
there are two Simone Weils, there would nevertheless be a serious

195

lacuna in her work which sought so earnestly to unify life in
spirit, thought and action since there would be no apparent link
between quotidian solutions and those according to grace. If it
is the latter it is then incumbent on us to show how Weil conceived the relationship between the two.

It is my claim that the link can be supplied in Weil's
theory of the μεταξύ,[2] or intermediaries. It is these μεταξύ
which are Weil's means of showing a spiritual basis to work and
social relations as well as a means by which we are obliged to
see conduct in these areas, even at mundane levels, as crucial
to spiritual life and vice versa. This theory I argue in the
first section is directly dependent upon the metaphysics of mediation described in *The Pythagorean Doctrine*, particularly in
the fifth form of harmony. In order to demonstrate this I shall
first describe the general features of what I take Weil to understand a μεταξύ to be, and shall then relate this description to
her Platonic metaphysics of mediation.

The theory of the μεταξύ bridges the gap between the 'rational' solutions and the 'mystical' solutions. But it also has
another important feature which is that it allows for a synthesis
of Weil's major concerns into a unified view of mediation in
which Christ is the primordial mediator of all relations with
God and in which all good earthly relations with God are ultimately derived from His mediation and direct the acting subject
in the direction of His Cross. Here the metaphysical structure
of mediation and the fact of Christ's crucifixion are connected
in such a way that the chain of interlocking and mediated relationships which extends from the fullness of love in the Trinity
to the void in affliction can be seen to be the love which unites
the Father and Son "both in the eternal unity of the one God and
also across the separating distance of space and time and the
Cross."[3] It is in the light of this connection that the theory
of the μεταξύ not only bridges the gap between levels of solution, but also, and what is more important, gives the means by
which we are pointed to the Mediator and are then led towards
Him. It is there that we are joined to God. In order to show
this in Weil I shall then in the last sections apply the theory
of the μεταξύ to Weil's major opus, *The Need for Roots* in such

a way that the μεταξύ of social life can be seen to lead to an
appreciation of participation in an activity that deliberately
imitates and participates in Christ's redeeming act, namely work.
Here it can be seen that the very structure of the universe,
which is founded in Christ's submission to necessity and described
in terms of mediation, leads those who regard it with attention
and love to the Mediator.

1. *The Theory of the* μεταξύ

Weil's theory of the μεταξύ has been perhaps one of the
least analyzed of all her theories, although the term μεταξύ has
been always cited in treatments of Weil's thought. Richard Rees'
treatment of it is confined to the following statement: "(μεταξύ
are) things which, without being of absolute value in themselves,
can serve as intermediaries between man and the absolute beauty
which is the real object of his love.[4] Jacques Cabaud's treatment hardly goes further when he defines a μεταξύ as "a bridge
towards transcendence"[5] and as: "Upon the mystical path man meets
with certain types of help. These are the metaxu, the intermediaries; they at once eliminate sensory differences and signify
God."[6] This lack of treatment seems to be due to two factors.
In the first place, the definition of a μεταξύ as something
which serves as a bridge towards transcendence does, in fact,
cover an essential aspect of the term's usage and thus it may not
easily be seen that there are other equally crucial aspects to
it. Second, it often seems to be assumed that there is no real
theory behind the term μεταξύ, other than its application as a
bridge to transcendence. Here, the term is thought to be applied
to those things which Weil already takes to be bridges, however
varied they might be, rather than signifying any sort of theory
which provides criteria for determining whether or not something
is, indeed, a bridge.[7] It is for this latter reason, I believe,
that Cabaud cuts off his discussion by saying: "The plasticity
of the term mataxu, the variety of its application, and the lack
of any definitive formulation limits its further consideration."[8]

Weil scholars have indeed recognized the first essential
aspect of the μεταξύ as being bridges to the transcendent. It
is absolutely crucial for man's spiritual progress that these

bridges exist since his present state is one of separation from
God and not one of being filled with spiritual light. Because,
for Weil, no one can turn towards God or take one step upwards
towards the heavens on his own a certain amount of aid is needed.
This aid is found in the μεταξύ. Weil writes, commenting on
Plato's analogy of the cave:

> For the transition from darkness to the contemplation
> of the sun there is a need of intermediaries, or μεταξύ.
> The ways differ according to the chosen intermediary . .
> The role of the intermediary is, first, to be at a point
> half way between ignorance and the plentitude of wisdom,
> between temporal becoming and the plentitude of being
> (it is 'between' in the manner of a geometric mean, be-
> cause the process is that of the assimilation of the
> soul to God). And then it also has *to attract the soul*
> *upwards towards being, to evoke the faculty of thought.*[9]

"The μεταξύ," Weil says, "form the region of good and
evil."[10] They are things, states, or activities within this
world which are subject to the correlates of good and evil.[11]
But, as μεταξύ, they are not equivocally either for good or for
evil; instead, because they are essentially bridges towards the
Good, they are things which can in a limited way be used to bring
the soul into contact with God. They do this in a manifold way.

In the first place, they can act as an object of attention
since "the directing of the attention towards God needs to be
sustained by intermediaries."[12] Without these intermediaries
the soul would have to orient and then direct its attention towards God in the void. For a soul that is unprepared, having to
love in the void is at best a dangerous thing, for just when it
needs to grasp onto something it has nothing. The slightest
shock could be sufficient to plunge it into affliction. It is
for this reason that Weil says: "No man should be deprived of a
single one of his μεταξύ."[13] If one were to be deprived of his
μεταξύ, harm would be done to his soul, not because some finite
good has been taken away from him which he should ultimately be
able to do without, but because his consent would have been violated and because while desiring good he received only evil.
Until he consents to give up these finite goods by which he is
supported he runs the risk of losing all when these props are
taken from him.

Something is not a μεταξύ, however, simply because it supports one in the void since imagination and falsehood also serve

this purpose. In order to sustain *attention* and be a μεταξύ,
the object of attention must also be capable of drawing the soul
upwards. In order to understand how this is possible, though,
it is necessary to note Weil's insistence that nothing is present
to human consciousness as a pure object; instead, every object
present to consciousness is, as present, a representation made
up of the object's influence on the subject and the medium of the
knowing subject's own modes of thought. An object is therefore
only efficacious as a μεταξύ for the subject when it is related
to the subject's own attention. For this reason nothing is capable of serving as a μεταξύ simply by physical possession or
proximity. But through attention the object, whether it is a
thing, state or act, can serve as a μεταξύ when it causes one to
direct the soul beyond the represented finite good towards the
unrepresentable transcendent God. Weil writes: "μεταξύ. Every
representation which draws us toward the non-representable. Need
for μεταξύ in order to prevent us from seizing hold of nothingness instead of full being."[14]

When related to the attention, however, the object in a
μεταξύ can draw the soul towards the non-representable Good
through a finite representation in a two-fold manner. On the
one hand, it does so by being a "mirror of the light"[15] which
reflects supernatural light into the soul and onto all that surrounds it. If a μεταξύ is incapable of providing the infinite
Good of the soul's desire, it at least awakens love and provides
a nourishment which keeps the soul from denying love. According
to Weil, it is by desire alone that we are saved and this desire
needs to be continually awakened. The μεταξύ then perform the
function of lifting the soul by awakening a desire for the Good.
Their sustaining function is further confirmed in this. On the
other hand, a μεταξύ can draw the soul towards the non-representable Good by virtue of the fact that it is a finite representation. Whenever some finite good suggests the infinite Good
it presents us with a dilemma for we become attached to it for
something it cannot provide by itself, but of which it constantly
makes us aware. For this reason Weil says, "An attachment which
contains an impossibility is a μεταξύ."[16]

Because a μεταξύ for the subject is an attachment to some
good through which he loves a transcendent Good, its paradoxical

nature invites a wrenching away[17] from the less spiritual and a
transition towards the more spiritual. In giving one's love to
the Good through a finite good one reaches the limits of that
finite good; if he were to continue to be attached to it, at
least in the same way, he could do so only by the idolatry of
making that good the ultimate object of his desire and consequently denying the real Good. One must therefore pass beyond
the original limits of attachment and re-establish new μεταξύ.
These new μεταξύ may indeed be new objects of attachment, but
just as often as not they are a reformation of the previous attachment on a higher level with new limits. Here one is not engaged in using and discarding objects as stepping stones towards
the transcendent but rather finding new significance in them.
Weil thus envisaged the possibility of an indefinite series of
such ascending μεταξύ on the way towards God.

Since any μεταξύ implies something which can and should be
transcended, there is an ultimate point at which one can love
God without intermediary. This is evidenced when Weil says:
"True earthly goods are μεταξύ. We can only respect those of
others . . . if we regard those we possess ourselves only as
μεταξύ--which implies that one is on the way towards the point
where one will be able to do without them."[18] This final point
is one where we directly and explicitly love God without external
aid, similar to the way Christ loved the Father from the depths
of affliction. Although Weil understood this point to be the
goal of love, she also understood that it is a condition which in
this life belongs perfectly only to the Son and in a participatory
way to those rare individuals who are manifestly His saints.
For most individuals, therefore, she saw the μεταξύ as critical
to their spiritual well-being for sustenance and improvement.
Furthermore, she also saw it as necessary for man to understand
that he lives in the realm of the μεταξύ where his actions and
satisfactions do not enjoy the automatic goodness which belongs
to those whose souls are united with God. It was in this context that she often quoted Plato's words from the *Philebus* that
we must be careful not to make the One too quickly, forgetting
all the intermediaries. Because the μεταξύ are so important for
the spiritual well-being of the soul and because it is necessary
that one understand that they are only intermediates and not the

goal of desire, Weil felt it was imperative that they be made
evident in every area of life. It was this that led her in later
works to speak of the spiritualization of labor.

> We should turn everything into an intermediary leading
> toward God (everything--occupations, events, public
> functions, etc.). This does not mean adding God on to
> everything (it is then the imaginary form of God). But
> each thing must be wrought upon to bring about a change
> so that it may be made apparent to the light.[19]

There is a certain similarity between Weil's early theory
of intermediaries and the μεταξύ. Weil held in the early theory
that for one to attain a desired goal an entire series of intermediate actions are required. The goal, properly understood,
was the ideal of the realization of mind in the world. In order
to be realized in a physical world, however, mind had to mediate
itself through its conception of a necessary order for action
which established the intermediate actions. In much the same
way the μεταξύ as bridges to transcendence play the same role of
intermediates which have to be gone through in order to reach
the desired goal. The analogy, however, breaks down when the
goal is not an immanent possibility, for whereas the exercise
of human reason is possible for man without any apparent grace,
the full and explicit love of God is not. This breakdown, though,
can lead to seeing a second aspect of the μεταξύ which has
rarely been recognized--that they are not only bridges to transcendence but are also bridges from transcendence. In fact,
for them to be the former they must first be the latter.

There are three senses in which the μεταξύ are bridges from
transcendence. There is, of course, the sense in which once the
conjugal union between the soul and God has taken place, the soul
itself becomes an intermediary between the rest of the world and
God. This is an ideal Weil unequivocally points to when she
says: "May my soul be for the body and God only what this pen-
holder is for my hand and the paper--an intermediary."[20] And
further: " . . . by means (of the conjugal union) a man's person will become simply an intermediary between his flesh and
God."[21]

But one does not need to have reference to this highest
level, however, to show the second sense in which the μεταξύ

or intermediaries are bridges from transcendence since it can be
made plain even at lower levels before spiritual union has taken
place. Although attention needs to be sustained by intermediaries this can only happen when the intermediate objects of attention truly reflect light and are capable of drawing the soul
upwards. They could not have this capability of allowing gravity
to be overcome, however, unless by some means they were conveyors
or assistants of grace. It is for this reason that Weil refuses
the notion that they are either arbitrary or manufactured by the
subject. She says: "These intermediaries must not be manufactured; they must be found inscribed in the nature of things, for
they exist there providentially."[22] In this sense, although
man lives in a world of things and is therfore subject to a
necessity which separates him from the goodness of God, nevertheless, that which separates him from God can also be the very
means of communication[23] through the mediation of a world order.
This is only possible, though, when there is a descending grace
which provides for this order. An ordered necessity which mediates between the unlimited and God can allow for μεταξύ to be
discovered in the world and if we apply ourselves to Necessity
we can begin to discover its maker.

Third, a μεταξύ is a bridge from God to man because, in
regard to the subject, the attention of the soul which is manifest in love is an operation of grace. This obtains in two ways
which can both be seen in the essay *The Implicit Forms of the
Love of God*. The first is that these intermediate implicit loves
are loves in which God is really, though secretly, present in
the soul of the lover. It is only by His presence that they have
the virtue of being intermediate and preparatory loves towards
explicit love. Their being intermediate depends upon this presence. Second, these loves are not only God's grace towards the
loving subject into whom He descends and thus bridges from
transcendence in that sense, they are also bridges from transcendence in that sense, they are also bridges from transcendence
in the sense that they are intermediate means through us of God's
goodness for our objects of love such as the afflicted and our
friends. Elsewhere Weil says: "Those minds whose attention and
love are turned towards (the Good) are the sole intermediary

through which good can descend from there and come among men."[24]
While it is only Christ and those saints who have full participation in Him who are mediators in the fuller sense in which
God's love is manifestly present in their thoughts and lives,
all the rest of creation are also intermediaries for God's activity, whether by consent and goodness or as matter by necessity.

> The highest form of stimulant is: if I do not do that,
> that will not exist. For a work of art that is ob-
> vious . . . The same applies to a good action. I am
> only an intermediary, but an indispensable one. And if
> I refuse to play this role? I then form part of the
> matter of the universe through gravity.[25]

Once it is recognized that Weil's μεταξύ have the dual aspects of being bridges both to and from transcendence it can
also be seen how the relationship of the two elements can be
understood.

In order for the soul to overcome gravity certain supports
are needed in the forms and objects of action, just as Kant's
dove needs the resistance of the air in order to fly. These
supports are the objects in the μεταξύ which are given through
God's gracious ordering of the world, and in some cases (such
as the Eucharist) by his implicit presence. But the attention
of the subject which makes one stand present to the object is
also due to grace, and it is through this grace that gravity
can be overcome and the object become an actual support. But it
is important here to recall how grace operates. It operates,
not by ignoring gravity or necessity, but by freely consenting
to it. Whether in the Creation or in the redemptive act of the
Crucifixion grace comes through the self-emptying of God in which
He gives up His own life so that others might live. This understanding of grace also applies to the subject's role in the
μεταξύ for the soul is only led upwards through intermediate
stages by intermediate forms of emptying itself. When one ceases
to use things for his own ends and be attached to them for himself these things can be efficacious, within their proper limits,
in proportional degree for uplifting the soul.

It is when the thing is loved for itself that one sees its
reality and thus gains a foothold on all reality. One is made
good by doing good. Weil says:

We should detach ourselves also from virtue--lose consciousness of it . . .   One loves a husband, a wife etc.
all things *for oneself*.   Fundamental idea: *To restrict
one's love to the pure object is the same thing as to
extend it to the whole universe*.   It is the same notion
as that of the Stoics (I carry away with me every-
hing that I possess).   Precious things are, quite
rightly, μεταξύ.26

The term 'μεταξύ' first appears in the *Notebooks* in a context which helps show this inter-relationship of God's descending
grace and man's ascent in intermediate stages.   There Weil discusses the μεταξύ of the subject in terms of being a sort of
spiritual apprenticeship.   Immediately after the lines quoted
above she writes:

To change the physical relationship between oneself
and the world (is 'physical' the right word?), in the
same way as, through apprenticeship, the workman changes
the physical relationship between himself and the
tool . . .   The relationship between the body and the
tool changes during apprenticeship.   We must change the
relationship between our body and the world.27

Initially, as it were, we are simply creatures of necessity
whose major contact with the world is through the sensations
through conditioning and thought.   Through an apprenticeship,
however, we can deliberately and methodically change the way in
which we are in the world[28] and thus move from behavior motivated
purely by pleasure and pain, or any limited perspective, to a
point where "through and beyond each sensation, we must feel
the universe."[29]   Because this final point does not come automatically it is necessary that one make the effort of an appren-
tice who learns the intermediate steps of the trade in an order
that actually modifies both his physical and psychical behavior
until the final point is reached.   But there is also a second
aspect to an apprenticeship beyond this self-modification.
This aspect is that an apprenticeship is already a practice of
the master's craft, except at lower levels.   One does not become
a master stonecutter by writing advertising copy nor does one
become a scholar by watching television.   Instead, one becomes
a master stonecutter or a scholar by first rough hewing stones
or thinking through a text.   This notion of an apprenticeship
can then be applied to the spiritual μεταξύ.   One's soul is up-
lifted by the practice of renunciation in the face of the

object to which he is attached so that the object may have its
full reality, just as creation as a whole becomes real by God
renouncing His right to be All. Although in the beginning we
are not ready to consent fully to God's love and the beauty of
the universe, whenever we truly and actually consent to the
existence of another outside of ourselves, this consent and the
attention we bring to bear on the object acts as a lever by which
the quality of our attention increases and causes us to see more.
This consent in the act of doing good to another is an image of
God's own consent and an actual means by which His goodness comes
to have an effect in the world, whether it be on the recipient
of the act or on the one who performs it.

Weil gives two major examples of μεταξύ in *God in Plato*
which demonstrate the inter-relationship of man's ascent and
God's descent.[30] The first is the intellectual way of mathematics and science. The operation of this μεταξύ has already
been seen in the appropriateness of mathematics in theological
discussion and in the fifth form of harmony. We saw there that
in mathematics, according to Weil, the mind moves from a certain
representable clarity about the world to greater clarity which
is absolutely certain, yet incapable of finite representation.
It does this by keeping before itself a requirement of rigorous
demonstration, and in Greek mathematics, by dealing essentially
in terms of mediated relationships. But what is most important
is that in mathematics the perspective of the 'I' is excised
from the operations until the Necessity of the world order is
itself presented as an object of attention to which man can give
his consent and thus pass from a natural understanding to a
supernatural one. This consent, even at lower levels, is an
imitation of God's own renunciation in the Creation and the Cross
and is an act which has grace at its roots. Weil writes in the
Notebooks:

> Renunciation. Imitation of God's renunciation in crea-
> tion. God renounces--in a sense being everything. This
> is the origin of evil. We have got to renounce being
> something. Herein lies our only good. Numbers as
> μεταξύ. No "I" in numbers except as a cause of error.[31]

The second example Weil describes is "the non-intellectual
way, the way of love,"[32] which she finds in the *Phaedrus.* "The

Phaedrus indicates a way which is not in the slightest degree
intellectual: it involves nothing resembling study or science or
philosophy, but is salvation through feeling alone--a feeling
which at the beginning is purely human, the love which consists
in falling in love."[33]

When Weil begins her description of love as one of the prime
μεταξύ she does so by first pointing out that grace is the essential means in love by which the soul is raised. In commenting
on the metaphor of the wing which lifts the soul of the lover,
she writes: "It would be impossible to state more clearly that
the wing is a *supernatural organ*, that is *grace*."[34] This is
rarely evident when one first falls in love, though. Instead
this love is first manifest as a sort of madness which is touched
off by the sight of beauty. This first sight of beauty reminds
one of heavenly beauty, and although the first stirrings of
passion excited by beauty are quite far from the love of God,
"the essential point is the grace which flows from the effect
of beauty, and it is applicable to all beauty that is apprehended
by the senses."[35]

It is beauty which forms the connection here between the
physical and the spiritual. While true beauty is a matter for
the soul, its perceived presence in something physical has ini-
tial physical and psychological effects. When Plato then describes (*Phaedrus* 250a-251c) the growth of the soul's wings in
psychological and physical terms, Weil sees him as correctly attempting to give a psycho-physiological theory of the phenomena
accompanying grace. She says:

> There is no reason for not attempting such a theory.
> Grace comes from above, but it falls upon a being who
> possesses a psychological and physical nature, and there
> is no reason against giving an account of the effects
> produced upon nature by the contact of grace.[36]

The effect of beauty is two-fold, "first through the shock produced by the memory of the other world and then as the material
source of energy which can be directly used for spiritual progress."[37] The beauty we first encounter through our senses
serves as a reminder of God to the soul. When it does so it
then also exerts an attractive influence of motivation and becomes a source of energy for the lover insofar as his desire is

enjoined. At first, this energy finds its avenues in purely
material ways. But at the same time, if one keeps the goal of
true beauty before him, he also refrains from consuming the object for fear of damaging its beauty. It is in this way that
one's own ego begins to play less and less of a role in love and
in the respect he pays to the object of beauty his love begins
to constitute an image of God's own love. One can, then, move
from what was originally only a physical love to the love of
God's own beauty through grace. One moves, as Plato says in the
Symposium through the intermediate loves of beautiful bodies,
souls, institutions and sciences to Beauty itself with a corresponding change in the soul appropriate to each form of love.
"This absolute divine beauty by whose contemplation one becomes
God's friend is the beauty of God; it is the attribute of God
under which we see Him."[38]

The love which begins in physical desire can then serve as
a bridge to transcendence by God's descending grace, and this
love insofar as it lifts the soul is a means of goodness from
God for the lover. But it is also one more thing than that; it
is also a means of goodness for the beloved. Weil notes of love
in the *Phaedrus*, "The one who loves tries to make his beloved
resemble as much as possible the god of whom he has recovered
the memory; and when the beloved returns his love there is established between them a friendship based upon a common participation in divine things."[39] The beloved is not simply a stepping
stone to transcendence, something to be used and discarded in
one's "flight from the world" as Nygren put it. Instead, the
beloved is someone to be respected and one for whom the lover
is to do good. Grace only increases in the soul which continues
to keep its attention riveted on the Good *and* also acts for the
benefit of another. Here there is no flight from the world at
all, but rather an increased imitation of and participation in
God. Without this concern for the other, love which begins in
the physical ceases to be a μεταξύ and becomes a lust which constitutes a movement away from God.

We can now see what Weil thought was embodied in a μεταξύ.
A μεταξύ in regard to its objective sense is an intermediate sup-
port and sustainer between nothingness and the fullness of being.
It is also a reflector of light which, when proper attention is

brought to bear on it, helps lift the soul. In regard to the
subject's role, a μεταξύ is defined by the soul's attention intermediate between ignorance and truth and between a total lack
of love and explicit love. But in both the objective and subjective aspects, a μεταξύ is of God's grace. On the one hand,
God's grace gives the object its efficacy as a support, reflector
and lifter either through His presence or by the order of the
world in which the object plays a role. On the other hand, God's
grace is, in the subject, attention. God's grace in the subject,
however, is always presence, no matter how implicit. It is this
grace of presence by which we are lifted, but lifted by descending
to give our love, or rather God's love through us, to the object.

Once the manifold nature of what Weil understands the μεταξύ
to be is made apparent it becomes possible to see them in the
light of her Platonic doctrine of mediation. It is, of course,
not difficult to see that whatever Weil thought about the μεταξύ
has Platonic roots since the term is employed in two of Weil's
favorite texts, the *Symposium* and the *Philebus*. Moreover, it is
in the context of discussing Plato's theology that she gives a
major definition of the μεταξύ[40] and the two prime examples of
μεταξύ cited above. This much is evident, what remains to be
shown is how the μεταξύ can be understood in the context of her
Platonic doctrine of mediation, which understanding should result
in an overall means of setting Weil's thought. The demonstration
is made in two steps: first, by comparing the μεταξύ to the mediation of love, as Weil discusses it vis-a-vis the *Symposium*;
second, by showing how the theory of mediation which Weil develops through the *Philebus* in *The Pythagorean Doctrine* gives a
metaphysical context in which the μεταξύ can be definitively
placed.

One of the major keys to Weil's doctrine of God's mediation,
particularly as she develops it in conjunction with Plato, is
that it provides a bridge between human misery and divine perfection. The doctrine of love which Weil finds in the *Symposium*
provides this bridge, for love which descends from God and is
engendered in human hearts is discussed in that dialogue as being
that which mediates between Need and Plenty. It is therefore a
way, and the only way according to Weil, for man's misery to be

put into relation and contact with God. It is in one sense a way
from man to God, but more important, it is the way of the divine
to man in that as a way for man it is established and determined
by God and in that this love is the activity of God in the human
soul. As we have seen, this love is constituted by being that
which, by God's own descent, puts man into contact with God, is
subject to ethical criteria for assessment, is a mediation of the
Good, and is that which itself provides the ethical criteria,
performing assessment and ethical activity. When Weil then adds
her own contribution to this description of the mediation of
love by centering it in Christ's Cross she then calls this love
Christ's own love for the Father which is stretched out across
all of space and time and instituted in human hearts.

It is Christ's mediating love as a man in affliction--as
one in absolute need--for the Father which provides the primordial means for man to come into contact with God and to participate in His life. It is also this love which underlies any other
positive form of love and is therefore that which makes the
μεταξύ what they are. The μεταξύ embody an intermediate form of
this love which is seen by the similar criteria for both. The
μεταξύ are similar to this mediating love for they exist by
God's descent, are bridges to transcendence which put the soul
in contact with God, and embody an act of renunciation on man's
part which has its standard in God. Once these similarities
have been noted, however, it is necessary to note also the differences between the underlying love and its particular manifestations in the μεταξύ and why these differences are important.

Weil's doctrine of mediation rests in the primal fact of
Christ's Cross wherein she sees Christ taking the entire weight
of sin and necessity on his shoulders while yet continuing to
love the Father. From that she sees Christ as the Mediator between man, necessity and the Father. She also draws on that
understanding to make Christ's Λόγος function a submission to
necessity which provides an order that mediates between Nothingness and the Fullness of Being. In this way she hopes to subsume
all possible relations under the Son's mediation and for this
reason Christ is the standard of mediation as well as the primordial mediator through whom all relations to God must pass.
Christ is, in the terms of the *Symposium*, the mediating love

born of God's Plenty and Man's Need. Distinctions need to be
drawn, however, for while Christ is the mediator between God's
Plenty and Man's absolute Need, man is not always and in every
way in apparently absolute need. There are degrees. It is only
at the furthest limits of human existence in affliction and in
contemplation of the beauty of the world that nothing stands between man and the Mediator who joins him to God. But few men
reach these places and none begin there. Instead, most are spread
out in the intermediate places, in the realm of the μεταξύ.
There is want in these places as well as some degree of fullness
and if man is to reach complete love in God he must move from
his present place through gradual renunciation until he gives his
total consent to the Father's will just as Christ did. In order
to do this, however, intermediate steps are needed and these are
the μεταξύ. The μεταξύ then are intermediate to the Mediator and
not mediators themselves, except in a secondary and derivative
sense. It is through Christ's love that any relation to the
Father is possible and it is this love which underlies all genuine spirituality in man. Owing to man's relative position, however, this underlying love gives rise to important numerous intermediate forms, which are, as it were, mediators of the Mediator.[41] These intermediates, while they do not lead man directly
to God, do lead him to the place where he can be united with Him.

It is through the mediation of love developed in conjunction
with the *Symposium* that Weil can give a basis in mediation for
a general understanding of the μεταξύ and the root for their
criteria. It is the 'Pythagorean' harmonies developed in conjunction with the *Philebus*, however, that allows this understanding to be placed firmly in context and allows for a comprehensive relation of the μεταξύ and the Mediator.

As we have seen, Weil uses the *Philebus* schema first to
reach a mediation between God and Creation in the Soul of the
World and then, by further division according to the schema,
to show how particulars by each receiving a limit can be related
to each other through the order of the world. Further when she
makes Christ's Cross the center of this schema in which the order
of necessity is established by His suffering of necessity, she
then uses this schema to show how man by intermediate steps
which reproduce Christ's renunciation can move from a purely

material relatedness to the world to a spiritual one, either in
affliction or in the joy of contemplating the beauty of the
world. Each one of these levels also has assigned limits. It
is through these limits imposed on all functions in the world by
the Λόγος that there can be a basis for mediations of the one
Mediator for they are all organized within one network both
horizontally and vertically. These limits are what Plato called
the ὁπόσα, or numbers between (μεταξύ) the One and the Indeterminate.[42]

It would seem easy to claim some sort of emanation theory
here for Weil in which she sees an entire range of intermediate
beings stretching from the One towards Nothingness and back up
again. This is not her point, however. She is not concerned
with giving a metaphysics that shows *that* God creates, but a
metaphysics of *what* God has created which shows the relations of
all to his sovereign goodness. Here Weil is not concerned with
levels and relations of Being but with levels and inter-relationships of beings, and with one being in particular, namely, man.

Man, for Weil, lives at numerous levels and embodies a complex set of relationships of these levels within himself and with
the world in which he lives. He is at once a material creature
under the sway of necessity as well as a thinking being who can
conceive Necessity and a soul who can give his consent to it.
At the material level he is one intermediary among the rest of
matter for he is an object and subject of force within mathematical limits. At this level, by operating within his assigned
limits he reproduces the 'consent' to necessity that created the
world, but he does so blindly. There is no spiritual relation
between him and his creator here. At another higher level, that
of intellect, he no longer operates simply as matter under necessity but comprehends Necessity as a mathematical tissue of interlocking relationships. This relation to the world is not that
of master to slave but of object contemplated to contemplation.
Man's relation to the world is here mediated through thought and
it is again a relation which embodies a sort of renunciation.
At the same time he exercises his intelligence, however, man
does not cease being a creature of necessity. He, therefore, has
two separate incommensurate relations to the world; these two
relations, though, can be mediated into a single unified relation

wherein a certain equilibrium is reached between thought and
necessity in action. Even at this level there is still a disjunction and man is not yet in any sort of spiritual relationship with God. This relationship is achieved at the highest
level, that of soul. At this level, man consents in his inner-
most part to Necessity as being the Father's will and actually
participates in the Mediator. But once again, his previous relations with the world do not cease and he is therefore now involved in three separate relationships with the world and God.
These relationships are then mediated into his single activity
which is at once spiritual, intellectual and physical. To use
a mathematical simile, what man is, is the harmony (or dis-har-
mony) of three separate and otherwise incommensurate functions.
This equation bears a distinct resemblance to Weil's definition
of the order of the world as the ensemble of the laws of variation, and in fact, allows a conceptual means by which man is
ordered within the whole.

　　　Lest it be thought that the hierarchy of these three levels
implies a progression through them in man's life *seriatim*, two
points of clarification are needed. The first is that all levels
operate at once, resulting in a single harmonic equation which
may be good, bad or somewhere in between. Because of this,
change in any one of the terms can change the balance of the
whole within the proper limits.[43] The second is that while the
schema allows for various levels of man's life, it also allows
for variations in each level. In this sense, there can be more
or less force applied in earthly relations, greater or less
clarity in thinking Necessity and a greater or lesser degree of
consent. Intermediates, therefore, exist within each level. A
particular genius of the schema, however, is that variations
within a level and the unified formula bear specific relations
to all other possibilities and movement can be effected by increase or decrease in the various terms.

　　　It is through this schema that all possible and actual relations can be theoretically inter-related to each other and
to the Creator. Creation is a composition on several planes at
once and for a creature such as man whose destination is the
full love of God, it is necessary to recognize these levels and

to use them properly in order to move to a love of God. Weil
says in the *Notebooks:*

> Change of level. Not more love, but another kind of
> love; not more knowledge, but another kind of knowl-
> edge, etc. This is because at a given level the human
> being is limited. For example, he is unable to contain
> more than a certain number (as it were) of physical no-
> tions. We only get beyond this limit by raising our-
> selves *or else* by degrading ourselves . . . In the same
> way, everything concerning man, taken at a certain level,
> is subject to a certain limit, and anyone who wants to
> go beyond that limit must either raise himself up--or
> else degrade himself. We degrade ourselves if we have
> regard to quantity. By apprehending with attention both
> the level and the limit we can burst open a ceiling . . .
> The presentation of several forms in the same object
> lifts the spectator (the reader) above form. By that
> means one obtains the without-form which is above form;
> for there is always the danger of falling below form.
> That which is below is like that which is above--in a re-
> verse sense. Each state is a μεταξύ towards a state
> similar to the one below the first, only transposed.[44]

It is now possible by a correlation of Weil's spiritual
μεταξύ with the Platonic ὁπόσα (or μεταξύ) to set the former
firmly within her doctrine of mediation and thereby to clarify
further that Weil means by them. It is with this clarification
that we shall also be able to see a link between her parallel
projects of concrete answers to the problem of social relations
and labor and her 'mystical' solutions.

Weil's concept of the μεταξύ when seen in the light of *The
Pythagorean Doctrine* becomes a theory of the intricately interwoven relations of the various aspects of man's being and of the
relations between subject and object. In order to unravel this
web, it is first necessary to recognize the prime role that the
soul plays in the μεταξύ. It has this role, of course, in the
first place because it is the soul which is raised and because
it is that to which God's grace is most intimately directed. It
also has this role because it is ultimately through the increase
of loving attention, properly directed towards the absolute good
which lies at the root of all man's desires, that the soul rises
through its own intermediate levels and God's grace descends to
earth. But it also has this role because it is the soul that
is primarily responsible for the order of inter-relations within
the person and for the relations he has with the world, and,

consequently, for the intermediary status he has in relation to
God.

At the highest level when God is present to the soul it is
readily apparent that the soul has primary responsibility for
the order of the inter-relationships within the person for there
all parts are given their proper object and kept within their
proper limits by consent. It is when the soul's consent is complete and its desire for God is nourished directly by God that
the intellect has no need to pry unwarranted into the divine
mysteries and simple material existence and the exercise of power
are no longer regarded as an end. Necessity, in short, is no
longer an enemy but the will of God submitted to in every part of
man. It can even be submitted to in the extremes of affliction
because of Christ's acceptance of it, an acceptance which is mediated to our souls by the Spirit. But even at less extreme
levels, soul has this primary responsibility for it is the soul's
consent to something outside of itself, and its consent in a
particular mode, that determines what we are and how we shall
act in the world. Even intellectual attention is already an effect of supernatural love and not its temporal spiritual precur-
sor. Weil says: "But already the fact that the relationship
which makes up the tissue of necessity is dependent upon the act
that enjoins our attention making it a thing belonging to us
which we can love."[45] Just as the first recognition of beauty
in another and attention paid to it (already a function of the
soul) has psycho-physiological effects, so too does a higher form
of attention produce intellectual effects and engage the appropriate faculty. In a very strong sense, it is the soul's consent
to something, and, the attention the soul consequently brings to
bear on the object, which gives us the object. This, in turn,
determines the relations we have to the object. If we completely
refuse the independent existence of something outside ourselves
or put our desire for absolute good in it our relations with it
are that of matter to matter. Similarly, our consent and attention at various levels will correspondingly determine other relations to the world and God. This implies an ordering in the
person in which any aspect is ascendent depending upon our consent to let it be so. In this sense, it is the soul's consent
and attention which makes any object efficacious as a μεταξύ.

'Falling in love' is not a μεταξύ unless one actually consents to the independent existence of another and puts aside his personal advantage in the matter. If he does so, however, the attention he brings to bear on the beloved may be efficacious for one's seeing the beauty of his soul.

Despite the fact that the soul has this prime responsibility it, nevertheless, does not operate unimpeded by the limits of the other aspects of the person or of the world. It does not move in a vacuum: rather, it is always found in material and intellectual occasions which help determine its level. In this sense, although, for example, it is the soul which first recognizes beauty in another human face and is thereby drawn to heavenly beauty, its love for the other is not a heavenly, but a physical love. Its love is physical in a dual sense. On the one hand, the beauty to which the soul is immediately drawn and attached is a physical beauty. On the other hand, its attachment, while to a memory of heavenly beauty, is manifest physically and psychologically. One's care for another in this case is that of preserving and contemplating beauty in a physical form. Here the object is a μεταξύ because of its role in the determination of love.

Two considerations are needed to help specify the relation of subject and object in the μεταξύ. First, whatever it is in the object that becomes an occasion for the subject's consent and attention cannot be arbitrary; it must be something which in some way reproduces in microcosm heavenly goodness and beauty. Second, love in the μεταξύ has certain limits. These limits are in part those of the mode of one's own attention--consent to think the world as a tissue of mathematical relations does not imply consenting to receive its force in one's flesh. But these limits are also inscribed in the object. Because of these latter limits, one cannot legitimately give more attention to something than it can bear without betraying one's own desire for absolute good. For this reason physical beauty as the object in a μεταξύ cannot be the object of anything but a physical sort of love, although what it awakens in the soul may cause the soul to advance to higher loves and although there may be more to the object than simple physical beauty.

There is a period in which the growth of the soul is
divided--partly directed towards the things of this
world and partly towards the other. This is the criterion. All those are worshippers of the true God *who
love conditioned things without exception, only con-
ditionally.*[46]

The role of the object in any μεταξύ is hardly inconsequen-
tial. Beyond helping determine limits, it is also needed to
awaken the soul to its true origins when it naturally clings to
the earthly, hoping to find a good to satisfy it according to
the limits of its own perspective. Through the providence of
the Creator, objects can awaken the soul and bear attention and
direct it upwards.

Thanks to God's wisdom, who has printed on this world
the mark of the good, in the form of beauty, one can
love the Good through the things of this world . . .
Dense matter is attentive to God's persuasion. "This
world consents to thy domination." Through love, matter
receives the imprint of the divine Wisdom and becomes
beautiful.[47]

But these objects do more than simply awaken the soul; they
are also needed to sustain attention. This is seen in a negative fashion when the soul is deprived of them. For a soul that
is at a lower level where physical beauty is important, to be
stripped of it, while not necessarily implying spiritual devas-
tation, may cause the soul to be lost. Although in being attentive to physical beauty one may realize that this love is only
limited and bespeaks a higher good, he may not be able or ready
to conceive and consent to a life without it. There is, Weil
says, a connection between man's sensibility and his desire for
the good and because of this connection to wreak havoc on one's
sensibility can have the unfortunate result of destroying his
aspiration towards the good.[48] There is a connection which is
particularly evident in affliction when all has been stripped
from the person, for there, although one could if prepared, consent to it, all too often he develops a poisoned light of hatred
for his condition which he lets color the whole universe. It
is also a connection that is operative at less extreme levels,
and for this reason the material becomes crucial for the spirit.

When man lives in a material universe, as he does, and his
first contacts with the world are as matter, the order of

material conditions becomes extremely important to the welfare
of the soul. Without beauty his love would never find the most
minimal object outside himself and without regularity in the
conditions of his existence where he can reasonably expect that
the physical laws of the universe are not going to change from
moment to moment, he would never be able to be anything but the
slave of forces. Fortunately, through the providential design
of the universe there is beauty to call him outside himself and
there is an order by which he can take part in the world in every
way open to him. This beauty and order provide the objects for
attention which in connection with his attention become the
μεταξύ to and from God's goodness.

Man, however, does not live alone in the universe and is
not affected only by non-human objects. He also lives in a world
of other men and here the μεταξύ are just as important in his
social relations as they are elsewhere. Man's social relations
are doubly important. On the one hand, these relations are crucial first determinants of one's relations to himself, other
men and the material world through conditioning in such things
as language and economic conditions of existence. On the other
hand, man, in dealing with them, deals with one more form of
physical, intellectual and spiritual relations. Since social
relations play such significant roles in man's life it is important that they also be brought into play in man's life as objects
in μεταξύ. Unfortunately, however, all too often beauty and
good order are not apparent in them and instead of becoming occasions for awakening consent and being sustainers of attention,
they become occasions for the loss of one's soul. It is here
that the μεταξύ provide a link between Weil's practical social
concerns and her religious doctrine of mediation. They are this
link because they embody a way of joining the material and intellectual needs of man with his spiritual goals. They are also
this link practically because unless the social sphere is reformed spirituality will become a matter for hermits alone.

Weil obviously applies the concept of the μεταξύ in man's
quotidian life when she develops what has been called her 'mysticism of labor.' In this she attempts to find in each of man's
labors a symbolic relation to Christ which allows a spiritual
light to surround man's most basic activities. Here man can

consciously reproduce Christ's love in his submission to necessity and in the goods which the products of his labor provide
for others. Ideally, if every aspect of social life could be so
linked to Christ there could be a distinct ordering of social
life which is spiritually rooted in the love of God, and one's
social relations could be bridged to and from the transcendent
Good. Weil writes:

> Christianity will only impregnate society in a general
> manner if each social category has its own specific,
> unique and inimitable link to Christ . . . It is more-
> over necessary, in every measure, without begging the
> texts, to find and to define for each aspect of social
> life its specific link to Christ. This link ought to
> be the inspiration of each grouping of catholic action.
> Thus as the religious life is divided into orders which
> correspond to the various vocations, in the same way,
> social life should appear as an edifice of distinct
> vocations converging in Christ.[49]

For these vocations to be μεταξύ, however, something more
than a symbolic link with Christ is needed since any μεταξύ implies not just a spiritual relation to necessity, although this
is primary, but also physical and intellectual ones as well.
These relations can and do affect the spiritual possibilities of
any vocation. Here the consideration of the material aspect of
the μεταξύ has two-fold value for Weil's concrete and rational
social critiques and solutions. 1) Although the soul cannot be
raised but for grace, a certain 'humanization' of labor and social relations needs to take place in order that the soul not be
coerced into betraying its consent or not be considered at all.
On the one hand, this humanization is a removal of removable
practical obstacles to consent and attention by the corresponding
practical means. It is, for instance, critically analyzing and
effectively removing the oppression that forces the laborer into
the condition where struggling for his daily bread becomes the
goal of his existence. On the other hand, this humanization is
also the logistical organization of social relations so that one
can freely and knowingly participate in them and give them the
devotion they deserve as precious things in human life. In both
these cases, while there is not explicitly a question of the
'mysticism' of labor being raised, unless there is a humanization
of labor the link with Christ becomes so hidden as to be of very

little use. 2) The goal of each vocation should affect the actual practice. If the goal is to participate in Christ then
clearly money or technological progress cannot be final solutions, although they may be introduced as factors in their limited place if they are helpful in some manner. If the goal of
labor is not the abolition of necessity, but free consent to it,
then clearly means must be described which enable one to come
to grips with it. In this case, certain practical solutions are
needed to re-invent tools which can put man into contact with
necessity both physically and intellectually instead of making
him its slave.

Once the theoretical link has been forged between Weil's
social critiques and her religious doctrine of mediation through
the theory of the μεταξύ, it is possible to set these critiques
firmly in the context of mediation and let mediation be an illu-
mining light behind them. With this in mind we shall now turn
to consider Weil's latest writings and see how she, in fact,
intertwines both the concrete and the religious.

2. *Obligations*

In 1943 while working for the Free French in London Weil
wrote a report on the possibilities of bringing about the regen-
eration of France once Hitler had been defeated and a legitimate
government was re-installed. The report which Weil wrote is the
book that has come down to us under the title *The Need for Roots*.
This book is particularly important in the corpus of Weil's
writings since it is the longest and the last piece of work she
did. It is also important because in its body Weil treats in
one place many of the problems which had exercised her mind and
spirit up to that time. In it she brings in elements of the
religious, scientific and of labor and social relations. For
this reason it is a particularly excellent means for us to see
all of these elements of her thought in one context and in interplay. We shall then describe this interplay in *The Need for
Roots*.

Weil opens *The Need for Roots* by first asserting that it
is the notion of obligations and not that of rights that is the
true moral basis on which all human inter-relations should rest.

She says: "The notion of obligations comes before that of rights, which is subordinate and relative to the former."[50] Rights depend upon obligations to be real; if there were no obligations, the notion of rights would be vacuous.

For this reason, Weil contends, it is a mistake of the first order to separate the two notions as if men had certain rights and then, in addition, also happened to have certain obligations. Instead, the two are correlated as subject and object. Obligations are what each person has, as an acting subject; rights are the claims that others have on his obligations. Similarly, the rights one has are simply, the obligations others have towards him as object. "A man left alone in the universe would have no rights whatever, but he would have obligations."[51] Rights, in this sense, are always things of an objective order and are "inseparable from the notions of existence and reality."[52] They are, in effect, obligations that have descended into the world of fact "taking into account actual states and particular situations."[53] Obligations when presented with an object have to consider carefully all the contingencies of the object. These contingencies, however, do not constitute the obligation for it is general. "Obligations alone remain independent of conditions. They belong to a realm situated above all conditions, because it is situated above this world."[54]

Because rights trade in the world of facts by themselves they cannot be the ultimate basis of either individual or social moral action, nor can they in isolation from obligations be any more effective than force makes them. When rights are separated from obligations they are determinants of conduct only by force of habit, wishful thinking or the force of social organization; in short, they themselves become very much determined by necessity and are extremely susceptible to being altered by force. In the essay "Human Personality" Weil notes of rights separated from obligations:

> The notion of rights is linked with the notion of sharing out, of exchange, of measured quantity. It has a commercial flavour, essentially evocative of legal claims and arguments. Rights are always asserted in a tone of contention; and when this tone is adopted, it must rely upon force in the background, or else it will be laughed at.[55]

Rights do in some sense stand above brute force by attempting
to introduce into behavior something that stems the flow of animal passion, but without obligations they give no absolute principles for they are bound up with facts. Among these facts are
the changeable situations of customs and the relative state of
forces, history and jurisprudence; a change in any one of these
is sufficient to throw rights into disarray. But not only are
rights alone such that they can be abrogated by a change in the
equilibrium of forces, by dealing only with *de facto* situations
they quickly descend to the level of the trivial and of perspective limited by the self.

> The notions of rights, by its very mediocrity, leads on
> naturally to that of the person, for rights are related
> to personal things. They are on that level. It is
> much worse still if the word "personal" is added to the
> word rights, thus implying the rights of the personality
> to what is called full expression. In that case the
> tone that colours the cry of the oppressed would be
> even meaner than bargaining. It would be the tone of
> envy. For the full expression of personality depends
> upon its being inflated by social prestige; it is so-
> cial prestige.[56]

If the notion of rights then fails to serve as any sort of
ultimate basis for moral action we must look towards obligations
to see what this basis is. Obligations, Weil says, belong to
another realm than that of facts. They are binding on all human
beings and identical for all, "although these are performed in
different ways according to particular circumstances."[57] Man
has a number of obligations in the world in which he lives but

> . . . the object of any obligation, in the realm of
> human affairs, is always the human being as such. There
> exists an obligation toward every human being for the
> sole reason that he or she *is* a human being, without
> any other condition requiring to be fulfilled, and even
> without any recognition of such obligation on the part
> of the individual concerned.[58]

This obligation towards humans is not conditioned nor based in
any *de facto* situation and cannot therefore be modified. "This
obligation is an eternal one. It is coextensive with the eternal destiny of human beings. Only human beings have an eternal
destiny."[59]

Weil does not fully explain within *The Need for Roots* the
reasoning behind her notion of obligation. Fortunately the text

titled "Profession of Faith"[60] does for it is a sort of précis
of the principles by which Weil came to engage the notion of
obligations. In the beginning of this text Weil sets out two
primary principles: 1) that there is a reality outside this
world and outside any sphere whatsoever that is accessible to
human faculties; 2) corresponding to this reality, there is in
the human heart a longing for an absolute good, a longing that
is always there and is never satisfied by any object in this
world. From there she goes on to say that the outside reality
is the sole foundation of good. "That reality is the unique
source of all the good that can exist in this world; that is to
say, all beauty, all truth, all justice, all legitimacy, all
order, and all human behaviour that is mindful of obligations."[61]
The connection between that outside good and the human realm is,
she says, "those minds and hearts whose attention and love are
turned towards that reality."[62] They are the intermediaries
through which good comes among men. Although this good is beyond
human faculties, man has the power of turning his attention to
it and being enlightened by it. This power is within all men
and whenever it is exercised, a part of the good descends on the
one who has turned his attention toward the good. Then:

> The combination of these two facts--the longing in the
> depth of the heart for absolute good, and the power,
> though only latent, of directing attention and love to
> a reality beyond the world and receiving good from it--
> constitutes a link which attaches every man without ex-
> ception to that other reality. Whoever recognizes that
> reality recognizes also that link. Because of it, he
> holds every human being without exception as something
> sacred to which he is bound to show respect.[63]

The link that attaches all men to the good, Weil contends,
is the only possible motive for universal respect for all human
beings. The world in which we live is composed of variety and
quite inequal objects compete for our attention. If we do not
turn our attention to the good it becomes subject to these in-
equalities and to the forces which make them up. This holds
for our relations with human beings as well as anything else for
"men are inequal in all their relations with the things of this
world, without exception."[64] But there is, nevertheless something equal in all men and whenever we direct our attention to

the good outside this world we make contact with this central and
essential fact of human nature. This contact, however, is not
an inference that there is an identical link in other men, but
is the experimental knowledge that is the result of loving God,
for "only our attention thus directed possesses the faculty, always identical in all cases, of irradiating with light any human
being whatsoever."[65] In effect, the attention which causes us
to recognize the link between God and man is itself a result of
the Good and as we are aware of the Good, by the Good, so also
by that same awareness do we recognize that Good in all human
beings. By Good we recognize that they have souls and therefore
also have an eternal destiny. Our love for the Good enjoins our
respect for them; a respect that we are obliged to give.[66]

But Weil goes on, "The link which attaches the human being
to the reality is, like the reality itself, beyond the reach of
human faculties. The respect that it inspires as soon as it is
recognized cannot be expressed to it."[67] Does this then mean
that the respect for others that we are obliged to give is a
sort of epiphenomenon to the world of fact? Weil did not think
so. The respect we owe to our fellows admittedly can find no
direct expression. There is, however, a possibility of indirect
expression for " . . . it can be expressed to that part of man
which exists in the reality of this world."[68]

The possibility of indirect expression of respect "is offered by man's needs, the needs of the soul and of the body, in
this world."[69] Because there is a connection between man's desire for good and his sensibility there is a need to preserve
and protect those things in man's earthly life which keep him
from affliction and support his aspiration towards the good.
These earthly needs then become a means of fulfilling our obligations to our neighbors.

> The fact that a human being possesses an eternal destiny
> imposes only one obligation: respect. The obligation
> is only performed if the respect is effectively expressed
> in a real, not a fictitious, way; and this can only be
> done through the medium of Men's earthly needs.[70]

This respect paid to man through the medium of his earthly
needs is, Weil says, a point on which human conscience has never
varied. Recalling Christ's parable of the sheep and the goats

she notes that all are liable to hear Christ say "I was hungry
and you gave me no meat." It is simply obvious that no man can
be considered innocent if he has plenty and has, nevertheless,
let his neighbor starve. Food is a prime vital need of the human
being and Weil uses it as a model for the other needs, needs
which if not met can lead to a starvation of the soul. These
needs in the physical realm are plain enough, being such things
as protection against violence, housing, clothing, heating, hy-
giene and medical attention. But Weil adds, there are also moral
needs which have no particular connection with the physical side
of life.

> Like the (physical), however, they are earthly and are
> not directly related, so far as our intelligence is able
> to perceive, to the eternal destiny of Man. They form,
> like our physical needs, a necessary condition of our
> life on this earth. Which means to say that if they
> are not satisfied we fall little by little into a state
> more or less resembling death, more or less akin to a
> purely vegetative existence.[71]

In order then to define the particular obligations it is
enough to list the various needs of the soul for "all (obligations) stem, without exception, from the vital needs of human
beings."[72] This, however, should not be taken to mean that all
our obligations are discharged simply by each individual directly
feeding the needs of others. It also entails obligations towards those things "which with respect to Man, play a role ana-
logous to food. We owe a cornfield respect, not because of if-
self, but because it is food for mankind."[73] One of the most
important of these things is the collectivities in which men
live for they are "food for a certain number of human souls."[74]

It is somewhat surprising to find that Weil insists upon
there being an obligation towards collectivities when elsewhere
a large portion of her remarks on collectivities are negative
and consist of likening them to Plato's Great Beast or the Beast
of the Apocalypse. Yet, at the same time there is something
remarkably sane in her pointing out these obligations. The collectivities within which man lives are extremely important to
him because they are the prime shapers of his life and is something which can provide for certain of man's needs in a way that
nothing else can. In fact, very little comes to us without first

having passed through the filter of the collectivity in some
sense. Moreover, many of man's needs can only be met in a collectivity. Because of this collectivities provide a certain kind
of food for men. The degree of respect then that is owed to
collectivities, Weil says, is very high for at least three reasons. First, each collectivity is unique and once destroyed can
never be replaced. If it is destroyed its members run the risk
of being starved. Second, a collectivity by its continuity moves
towards the future. "It contains food, not only for the souls
of the living, but also for the souls of beings yet unborn
. . ."[75] Third, because of this same continuity, it connects us
with the past and brings the treasures of the dead to the living,
transmitting from generation to generation light received in
ages past.

Two duties are clearly imposed with regard to collectivities.
The first is the obligation and respect that all men owe to
them. This obligation may often come near to entailing a total
sacrifice, as long as it is understood that the sacrifice is
made ultimately for the souls who live in the collectivity. The
second obligation is primarily incumbent on those who have charge
of the collectivity. This obligation is so to order social life
so that is performs the function of nourishing souls instead of
devouring them. For this to be done, however, Weil says, it is
first necessary to define and enumerate the needs of the soul
and then work to organize society in such a way that these needs
can be met.

Before turning to what the needs of the soul are, however,
it is important to note the significance of Weil's intention in
making obligations the basis of goodness in the social sphere and
the connection they have to the μεταξύ and consequently to mediation.

The major import of placing obligations at the very base
of social relations is that in doing so Weil makes the value of
human inter-relationship dependent on God's goodness. Simone
Pétrement has correctly noted this dependency. She writes:

> Simone believes that justice in society depends on this
> faith (i.e. in the transcendent good). If one does not
> understand that the true good is a reality located out-
> side the world which cannot be reached by human faculties

> but toward which all men possess the power to turn, one
> cannot, in her opinion, behave justly with human beings
> . . . The politics of justice cannot be separated from
> religion, or, rather from mysticism.[76]

Weil here is, of course, being completely consistent with
her religious belief by seeing God as the source of all goodness
and making the 'politics of justice' dependent on Him. But there
is also a second consistency between her notion of obligations
and her religious doctrine and this is the converse view that
religion, or mysticism, cannot be separated from the politics
of justice. All throughout her work, one of the chief hallmarks
of Weil's religious thought is that spiritual life cannot be
separated from material and intellectual life; indeed, it must
be incarnated. This is exactly what happens when obligations
are brought into play, for there, whatever fullness of attention
a man might possess must be brought to bear on the needs of his
neighbors and his faith must become effective in action. In
this he imitates the Mediator for his own love for God is acted
out in meeting the needs of others.

The μεταξύ greatly help in understanding the religious
basis of obligations for they play a role here in both their
material and spiritual aspects. Spiritually, obligations are
μεταξύ, both as bridges to and from transcendence. They are
bridges in that by acting on them we do, at various levels, imitate God's love. But they are also bridges to transcendence in
the sense that the performance of obligations can act as a sort
of apprenticeship for the attention.[77] For this reason it is
important in any collectivity that obligations be carefully defined in terms of real human needs and organized so that they
conflict as little as possible. When this happens any citizen
in performing his duty may have an immediate object for his attention to his fellows. Obligations are also μεταξύ in the
sense that they are bridges from transcendence since they are
enjoined in attention through the good we do to others.

It is the obligation to respect others that is at the root
of all other obligations. But since these obligations are defined by the earthly needs of the soul and need to be carried
out in the physical world there is also a material side of obligations that needs to be considered. The needs of the soul

not only imply a particular corresponding obligation but a correlated means of meeting these needs as well. Here the material
aspect of the μεταξύ enters in a two-fold way. On the one hand
that which meets the needs of a human is a μεταξύ in the sense
that it is a support insofar as it keeps one from falling and
also because it may be a purveyor of light. Here a collectivity
is an important μεταξύ[78] because it is a prime human means of
finding security in a world of forces and because it is one of
the original shapers of our goals and a means by which we attain
these goals. A collectivity is, as it were, a launching point
for every soul that lives in it. On the other hand, the means
of meeting the needs of a human also has the material aspect of
a μεταξύ for the acting subject insofar as these means are intermediate objects for fixing his attention. In this sense, while
respect paid to a culture is ultimately respect paid to the
human soul, unless there were a culture or some other precious
thing to be an immediate object of respect, one might cease to
recognize obligations and to act upon them. It is only Christ
who continued to love without any apparent means of love.

Of course, human beings are not separated into two distinct
classes of those who make use of μεταξύ to meet their needs and
those who give their respect to these supports of others. In
fact, the μεταξύ of something like a collectivity plays both
roles for all. It meets one's needs and is a point of take off,
but, for that reason, is also something that deserves everybody's
respect and can, in its limited way support that respect and be
its immediate object of that respect. Nevertheless, it needs to
be recognized that there is not a symmetry between obligations
to a collectivity and the needs it satisfies for him. Often,
the obligations of an individual may extend further than the
needs which the collectivity satisfies for him (he may be asked
to go to war). Furthermore, while one's obligations to the means
of support may require a near total sacrifice, this sacrifice
can never be absolutely total. In part, this is because the
collectivity as a μεταξύ has limits; while it may be a major
means of support for those living in it, it itself has no eternal
destiny and cannot usurp the respect owed to human beings. In
another part, this is also because the earthly needs of the soul

are limited and there is no obligation to provide somebody with
an unlimited supply of bread, or an unlimited variety, when his
need is met in a finite amount. It is, however, an obligation
to see that he gets this amount.

When Weil begins *The Need for Roots* with the notion of obligations she is very plainly doing so in a manner that establishes a religious basis for social relations. This is a basis
that is evident in itself. When the obligations are seen in the
light of the μεταξύ, however, we gain a firmer grasp on all Weil
meant these obligations to be. We gain this grasp because where
obligations and needs are related to the μεταξύ, they are placed
in the context of mediation which allows us to see the full extent of the issues at stake. In the light of the μεταξύ, obligations are seen not only as a means of introducing supernatural
goodness into social relations, although they are certainly
that, but also are seen as things that are crucial for the soul's
destiny. This allows us to place the very particular concerns
of *The Need for Roots* in this ultimate context. The μεταξύ also help us to understand better the relations between obligations
and the needs of the soul for at least two reasons. 1) They allow description of the obligations as a microcosm of Christ's
mediation since obligations undertaken with attention are a
type of fullness meeting the poverty of needs. Although the
needs of the soul in this case are not, strictly speaking, a
spiritual poverty, because of their connection to the spiritual
in the unitary person, they are not unrelated to his spirit and
play a crucial role in his spiritual progress. 2) For Weil, the
good is sovereign and universal and is not bound to have any,
or any particular determinations. It is an unanswerable question
to the finite intelligence of "why these things rather than
others?" and "why anything at all?". But once we do have a
world of particulars the theory of the μεταξύ serves admirably
for seeing the determinations of the Good and their inter-relations. Obligations are such a division of the Good and a sort
of moral and spiritual intermediary between it and nothingness.
But it is necessary to realize that they are this division with
respect to the human creature. There are not obligations *and*
humans; rather, obligations are a form the Good takes in men.

Obligations are, in a sense, a definition of humans, which is to say that they have relations to the Good and are active, consenting and intelligent creatures who live among the same.[79] Otherwise said, obligations, while a determination of the Good, only make conceptual sense when predicated of beings who are capable of having them. In regard to other human beings, then, the prime obligation we have is respect. But once such a prime obligation is predicated of man as a division of the one Good, it can be further subdivided. This does not in any way negate or make abstract our primary obligation for respect. But it does mean that once respect for other men is enjoined, the nature of the object of the obligation has to be taken into consideration. In this sense, the obligation to respect humans divides itself into subordinate and appropriately limited forms that the good may take in regard to creatures (and to those things which serve creatures) who have spiritual, intellectual and physical aspects which they can perform with respect to like creatures. It is not therefore an obligation for a human to save souls since this good is not in his power. It is an obligation, however, for men to discern with the utmost clarity what the needs of the soul are and to feed them in order to keep souls from being impeded from turning to the Good, since this is in man's power. It now remains to be seen what the needs of the soul are for Weil and how she proposes fo fill them. Pétrement has noted that Weil is unique in making such a list. We can now see why it was such an important project for her.

3. *Rootedness in the Universe*

Weil notes two characteristics of the earthly needs of the soul. The first is that these needs are to be distinguished from desires, fancies or vices by that fact that "needs are limited, in exactly the same way as are the foods corresponding to them . . . Food brings satiety. The same applies to the soul's needs."[80] The second characteristic is that, with two exceptions which we shall see, these needs are arranged in antithetical pairs. What is required to satisfy them is not an oscillation between the two, but a balanced mean. Although Weil does not speak of this balance as a mediated unity, we would be

correct in saying that this balance is such a mediated unity of
opposites.

The various pairs of needs then are: liberty and obedience,
responsibility and initiative, equality and hierarchism, honor
and punishment, security and risk, private and collective property, and finally freedom of opinion and truth.[81] Because for
Weil these needs are *donnés* of the human condition which require
insight for discovery and not argument and because many of Weil's
own ways of meeting them are directed specifically to the French
situation, it is really beyond the scope of this essay to do much
more than list them, and refer the reader to *The Need for Roots*
for particulars. There are two needs of the human soul, however,
that have no apparent corresponding antithesis and these are
the need for the soul to be rooted and the need for order. Because the greatest part of *The Need for Roots* is devoted to defining the first of these needs and seeking for its means of
satisfaction, it will be worthwhile briefly noting this need,
although the need for order is that with which we will be primarily concerned since it is that which shows the marks of mediation most clearly and needs mediation for its solution.

The need for roots, Weil claims, is difficult to define, but
it is essential to man because of his multi-faceted participation in the world.

> A human being has roots by virtue of his real, active
> and natural participation in the life of a community
> which preserves in living shape certain particular trea-
> sures of his past and certain particular expectations
> for the future. This participation is a natural one,
> in the sense that it is automatically brought about by
> place, condition of birth, profession and social sur-
> roundings. Every human being needs to have multiple
> roots. It is necessary for him to draw wellnigh the
> whole intellectual and spiritual life by way of the
> environment of which he forms a natural part.[82]

Influences external to one's particular environment are also vital for giving the human soul a food which it desperately
needs but being rooted in one's own environment is a prior condition for being able to appreciate these influences. When one
is rooted, he can receive outside influences, not "as something
additional to itself, but as a stimulant intensifying its own
particular way of life."[83] Unfortunately, the greater part of

Western culture suffers from the malaise of uprootedness which
is a spiritual sickness that renders it insensible to inspiration. The solution to this sickness is one of the most pressing
problems facing humanity for when it infects a culture the people
within it have no sense of belonging, no sense of true loyalty
and no possibility of rejuvenation. But the solution to this
problem is, like human participation in the environment, multi-
faceted and because of the complexity of the inter-relationships
of various levels there is another need which has to be considered and that is order.

Despite the fact that the need for roots does occupy the
greatest portion of the book of that name, Weil herself says
that the first of the soul's earthly needs and the one which
touches most nearly on its eternal destiny, is order: "that is
to say, a texture of social relationships such that no one is
compelled to violate imperative obligations in order to carry
out other ones."[84] Whenever the order of social relationships
is such that obligations become incompatible and such that one
cannot offer any resistance thereto, man "is made to suffer in
his love of the good."[85] He suffers because while obligations
are enjoined for him, he, nevertheless, cannot carry them out
and, in turn, becomes forced to deny them. It is a grave problem
that at present a great deal of confusion and incompatibility
exists between obligations. It is therefore a major duty in
itself to reduce this confusion and incompatibility.

> Unfortunately, we possess no method for diminishing
> this incompatibility. We cannot even be sure that
> the idea of an order in which all obligations would
> be compatible with one another isn't itself a fiction.
> When duty descends to the level of facts, so many inde-
> pendent relationships are brought into play that in-
> compatibility seems far more likely than compatibility.[86]

While a social order in which the conflict between obligations is entirely reduced may seem a fictitious notion, the
notion of an order in which an infinite number of independent
actions are arranged so that in the midst of their variations
there is an unitary order is not. In the universe as a whole
we have before us the very example of such an order; and this is
not just any order, it is an order that we can find beautiful
and love.[87] It is because the universe is beautiful as a whole
and because we can love it as such that we have confidence that
it is ordered. We also have examples of ordered beauty in works

of art. But beyond the order we find in the beauty of the world
and art we have further reason not to abandon the quest for a
decent order in our social relationships. This is the very desire for absolute good which stirs in the depths of our being
which "makes it impossible for us ever to resign ourselves to
situations in which obligations are incompatible with one another."[88] To resign ourselves is to give up on the good. In
regard to the order of social relationships then:

> The contemplation of veritable works of art, and much
> more still that of the beauty of the world, and again
> much more that of the unrealized good to which we aspire,
> can sustain us in our efforts to think continually about
> that human order that should be the subject uppermost in
> our minds.[89]

The sort of politics which Weil here envisages of instituting an order of obligations which takes into account the
various needs of the soul and their levels and relations to
goodness is, as she recognized, of a very complex nature which
demands "that every choice made be preceded by the simultaneous
review of several considerations of a very different nature."[90]
It is something which requires the same high degree of concen-
tration as creative work in arts and sciences, for like them,
politics is "an art governed by composition on a multiple
plane."[91] The art of political action and education needs to
find the good and then make interwoven determinations of it
everywhere in social life. At least as far as presently known
possibilities are concerned, this seems beyond the range of human intelligence. But this does not mean that the task cannot
or should not be undertaken. Nor does it mean that it is impossible to realize it at least partially. As Weil points out,
it is never by striving for a lesser imperfection that progress
in good is made; rather, it only comes by looking for perfection.
Weil therefore insists that we must found our politics in relation to a certain form of perfection.

> When it is a matter of educating a whole people, this
> conception should be that of a civilization. It must not
> be sought in the past, which contains only imperfect
> models; far less still in our dreams of the future,
> which are necessarily as mediocre as we ourselves are,
> and consequently vastly inferior to the past. The in-
> spiration for such an education must be sought, like
> the method itself, among the truths eternally inscribed
> in the nature of things.[92]

It is when politics must find both its inspiration and method "eternally inscribed in the nature of things" that the order of the universe becomes more than an example for us to construct a social order; it also becomes the basis of that order which the social order needs to participate in. In short, the social order is an intermediary of the larger universal order and a μεταξύ by which the individual soul joins itself to the universe. Here we can see that the order of social relations is doubly defined by what it is an order of, that is obligations which meet the needs of the soul, and by the nature of its model-- the order of the universe. When it is so defined by the latter, we are then concerned not just with a schema that orders but also with the *kind* of order it is. For Weil, the kind of order that the universe is, is seen in that it is a cooperation of necessity and goodness, established in God's renunciation, which can lead to our redemption if we submit to it in love. It is here that the metaphysical schema of mediation and the Incarnation of the Word are joined, for not only do we find in the world order a beauty which speak of God but also a necessity that we can submit to, even if affliction should come.

Unfortunately, Weil contends, this structure and basis of the universe is not at all apparent to modern thought. If it were, our science which studies the universe and our religion which tells us about its nature as the will of God would be more closely connected than they are. In order, then, to see where the two have improperly separated and where they need to be rejoined analysis is needed. If we can rejoin the two then it should be possible to see in what the basic order of obligations needs to be centered.

Modern science, Weil says, is particularly responsible for a degradation in our thought and thus our conception of the world in which we live, and it therefore needs close examination, particularly because of the prestige it has in Western culture. In a time when contempt is shown for most everything else, science alone is excepted. "So far as the prestige of science is concerned, there are no such people nowadays as unbelievers."[93] This places an enormous responsibility on savants.

But how have they exercised this responsibility? According to Weil, not well at all, for the conception of the world

contained in our science has led us to believe that force reigns
supreme over all phenomena, and this "at the same time (men believe) that men can and should base their mutual relations upon
justice, recognized as such through the application of reason."[94]
This sets up a contradictory attitude in men's hearts where
"there is only one choice to be made. Either we must perceive
at work in the universe, alongside force, a principle of a different kind, or else we must recognize force as being the unique
and sovereign ruler over human relations also."[95] Despite efforts to the contrary in Marxism, Utilitarianism, etc., force is
not, Weil says, a machine for creating justice. Instead, it is
blind and produces results indifferently which are for men, just
or unjust, but nearly always unjust. This would make justice
unreal; "yet justice cannot be that. We know it experimentally
. . . and if justice is inerasable from the heart of Man, it
must have a reality in this world. It is, science, then, which
is mistaken."[96] Or, rather, Weil adds, to be exact it is modern
science, for ancient science "which was as scientific as our own,
if not more so, had no trace of materialism about it. What is
more, it was not a subject of profane study. The Greeks regarded
it as a religious subject."[97] Modern science, however, effects
a split between itself and any religious conception of the good
which science as a study might pursue. It is a split in which
science has gained the upper hand, and which, Weil says, has
emptied the churches. For those who remain in the churches
their souls are split between science and religion in a state of
uneasiness. Moreover, when people do remain in the churches it
is all too often for the wrong reasons, for they believe in the
truth of science but feel that religion fills an added need some-
how unrelated to a desire for the truth. Thus the spirit of
truth rarely becomes a matter of concern in present day religion
since truth is supposedly under the supervision of science.

Science is thus regarded by the public with the religious
respect owed to truth. But, Weil says, the public is being de-
ceived because modern science is not a fruit of the spirit of
truth. This is apparent when one looks into the motives of
science; that is to say, the love and its object that inspires
scientists to do what they do. Weil argues that

> . . . faith is above all the conviction that the good
> is one. To believe that there are several distinct and
> mutually independent forms of good, like truth, beauty
> and morality, that is what constitutes the sin of poly-
> theism, and not just simply allowing the imagination to
> play with the notions of Apollo and Diana.[98]

It is the one good that causes us to seek knowledge and truth as
a good thing "for the acquisition of knowledge causes us to approach truth when it is a question of knowledge about something
we love, and not in any other case."[99] If it is the good we love
then "we desire truth only in order to love in truth. We desire
to know the truth about what we love."[100] This single love of
good is exactly what is missing in science, Weil says; instead,
it seeks a number of lesser objects which motivate it.

Science since the sixteenth century, Weil argues, has conceived itself to be a branch of study beyond good or evil which
is viewed without any relation to either. In this case since
science does not seek the good it also does not seek truth as
such. But what are its objects of love and the motives inspired
by these objects, then? In great part, she says, they are similar to the stimulants found in games. But more so, they are
directed towards prestige. It is not even a matter of reflecting
on technical applications, rather, "what provides a stimulant is
not that but the actual prestige such applications confer on science."[101] Even the social concerns of science are paltry and
subject to false greatness.

> The primary social consideration for savants is purely and
> simply one of professional duty. Savants are people who
> are paid to manufacture science; they are expected to
> manufacture some; they feel it their duty to manufacture
> some. But that is insufficient for them as a stimu-
> lant. Professional advancement, professorships, rewards
> of all kinds, honors and money, receptions abroad, the
> esteem and admiration of colleagues, reputation, fame,
> titles--all that counts for a great deal.[102]

Yet, if science has come to this, the situation is not
lost. "The remedy is to bring back among us the spirit of truth,
and to start with religion and science; which implies that the
two should become reconciled. The spirit of truth can dwell in
science on the condition that the motive prompting the savant
is the love of the object that forms the stuff of his investiga-
tions." This object, for Weil, can only be the beauty of the

world. This beauty alone can be the object of science and not
matter as such, for human thought has no other object but thought.
This does not mean that science is to become idealism; it does
mean that the mind must be brought into harmony with the universe.

> The savant's true aim is the union of his own mind with
> the mysterious wisdom eternally inscribed in the universe.
> That being so, how shall there be any opposition or even
> separation between the spirit of science and that of
> religion? Scientific investigation is simply a form of
> religious contemplation.[103]

Science once was a form of religious contemplation; why has it
ceased to be such? Here Weil argues the fault is not to be laid
entirely on science since elements within religion have contrib-
uted greatly towards transforming the meaning that should be attached to the object of love and thus the spirit of truth. It
has done this, she claims, by having "no longer admitted any other
conception of divine Providence than that of personal Providence."[104]

   This belief in a personal Providence, she feels, is not
something inherent in Christianity as such, but is a by-product
of the church's attachment to Rome. It is something she also
feels deeply accounts for the split between science and religion
and which degrades the spirit of truth.

> The ridiculous conception of Providence as being a per-
> sonal and particular intervention on the part of God for
> certain particular ends is incompatible with true faith.
> But it is not a manifest incompatibility. It is incom-
> patible with the scientific conception of the world; and
> in this case the incompatibility is manifest. Christians
> who, under the influence of education and surroundings,
> carry within them this conception of Providence, also
> carry within them the scientific conception of the world,
> and that divides their minds into two watertight compart-
> ments, one for the scientific conception of the world,
> the other for the conception of the world as being a
> field in which God's personal providence is exercised.[105]

   Weil sees the problem of a personal Providence as two-fold.
In the first place, it posits that certain physical occurrences
in the world are the result of God's will and not others, or, at
least, some are produced for particular ends and not others.
Yet, she says, "amidst all the events that take place, we have
no right to maintain that certain of them rather than others are
the result of God's will."[106] Second, she sees a moral problem

in the very way that personal Providence is conceived, for when
God alters events to His particular ends, He too often has to be
regarded as a despot whose orders will be carried out, willingly
or not. This latter conception, Weil felt, was due to the Roman
influence on Christianity, for when Christianity was officially
adopted by the Roman Empire, "God was turned into a counterpart
of the Emperor."[107] When this happened God's relationship to
His world was conceived along the lines of an emperor's rights
to his property. This Roman conception of sovereignty, which was
that of master to slave, then became the chief conception of
God's ruling of the world, and Providence became a matter of direct, particular volitional commands. It was as if the world
were an object foreign to God which, if left of itself, would
produce effects contrary to His will.

> The conception of Providence which corresponds to God after
> the Roman style is that of a personal intervention in
> the world on the part of God in order to adjust certain
> means in view of certain particular ends. It is admitted
> that the order of the world, if left to itself, and with-
> out God's special intervention at t particular moment,
> for a particular end, could produce effects contrary to
> the will of God. It is admitted that God should prac-
> tice such special intervention. But it is further admit-
> ted that these interventions, for the purpose of cor-
> recting the play of causality are themselves subject to
> causality. God violates the natural order of the world
> so as to bring about therein, not what he wishes to pro-
> duce by way of result.[108]

This conception, Weil says, is easily imagined in terms of
some Roman patrician who, in order to get something done on his
estate, orders his slaves to do it. It does not matter whether
he takes the slave's welfare into consideration or not, for the
slave must simply obey. It is impossible for him to know the
mind of his master and to consent to his spirit to an order ahead
of time.

If Providence is taken in this way, both science and religious love suffer. On the one hand, science cannot be religious
contemplation because there is nothing to contemplate, which is
to say that there is no order that is not violated. Furthermore,
any order which is violated isn't worth contemplation anyhow
since God obviously does not find it suited to His ends. On the
other hand, when there is nothing to contemplate, it makes

religious life simply a matter of the slave's obedience. It is
true, Weil notes, that the Gospels do speak of slavery, but

> the "slaves" are men who have wanted with all their
> heart to give themselves to God as slaves. . . If we
> were God's property, how should we be able to give our-
> selves to him as slaves? He has emancipated us in
> view of the fact that he has created us. We are out-
> side his kingdom. Our consent alone can, with time,
> bring about an inverse operation and convert us into
> something inert, something analogous to nothingness,
> where God is absolute master.[109]

But if Weil rejects the conception of personal Providence
what does she accept and what is there in it that she believes
will reconcile science and religion in such a way that bring a
spirit of truth back into both? The conception of Providence
which she insists on is that of the order of the world, an order
which in the whole embodies God's intention towards the world.
She says, "Divine Providence is not a disturbing influence, or
anomaly, in the ordering of the world; it is itself the order of
the world; or rather, it is the regulating principle of this
universe. It is eternal wisdom, unique, spread across the whole
universe in a sovereign network of relations."[110] When we so regard Providence we find that brute force is not sovereign but
that it obeys the limits and determinations set for it by the
Eternal Wisdom; brute force "is nothing else in reality but perfect obedience."[111] Order, or Providence, is that to which the
universe submits either blindly, or in the case of man, with
intelligence and love. Here it is only legitimate to speak of
a particular volition on the part of God "when a particular im-
pulsion arises in a man's soul which bears the unmistakeable impress of God's commands. But then it is a question of God considered as a source of inspiration."[112]

A reconciliation between scientific investigation and religion can obtain with this conception of Providence because it is
an object of love in both cases, and is a love of consented obedience to God in both mind and spirit. In spirit, "the order of
the world is to be loved because it is pure obedience to God.
Whatever this universe accords us or inflicts on us, it does so
exclusively out of obedience." When the order of the world thus
becomes an object of consent, love and a means of obedience to
God's will it also becomes an object wonderfully fitted for our
thought.

> Forces in this world are supremely determined by necessity; necessity is made up of relations which are thoughts; consequently the force that is supreme in the world is under the supreme domination of thought. Man is a thinking being; he is therefore on the same side as that which dominates force. He is certainly not lord and master of creation . . . but he is the master's son, the child of the house. Science is the proof of this . . . when he is sitting on his father's knees and identifies himself with him through love, he has a share in it. So long as man submits to having his soul taken up with his own thoughts, his personal thoughts, he remains entirely subjected, even in his most secret thoughts, to the compulsion exercised by needs and to the mechanical play of forces. If he thinks otherwise, he is mistaken. But everything changes as soon as, by virtue of an act of true attention, he empties his soul so as to allow the conceptions of the eternal Wisdom to enter into it. He then carries within himself the very conception to which force subjected.[113]

Once consent and love have given science its true object of contemplation, science becomes a double language, for it expresses in one set of symbols earthly relations and the supernatural relations between God and his creatures. This, Weil reminds us, is exactly what the Greeks did with mediation, for the proportional means became the "image of the divine mediation between God and his creatures."[114] What needs to be understood, Weil insists, is that we never grasp the world directly but through our signs; ". . . the reality of the objects perceived by the senses does not reside in sensible impression as such, but solely in the exigencies of which the impressions constitute the signs."[115] In this regard, our signs need to be well chosen and should not correspond to things that imply the sovereignty of brute force and personal power, but rather should imply the virtue of consented obedience to God and his loving Providence. For Weil, the choice of the value of these signs can only come experimentally, that is, through an act of consent and attention. But once they are given, they also become objects of intelligence which guide intelligence to truth and which, in the language intelligence speaks among men, help to show truth among men. If our language could be so well chosen, it would herald a return to truth in social life.

> If the sciences, which have to do with Man, were founded in this way, according to methods of mathematical precision, and at the same time maintained in close relationship with religious truth; if in the natural and

> mathematical sciences symbolic interpretation were to
> occupy once again the place it occupied formerly--the
> unity of the established order in this universe would
> appear in all its sovereign clarity. The order of the
> world is the same thing as the beauty of the world . . .
> It is one and the same thing, which with respect to
> God is eternal wisdom, with respect to the universe,
> perfect obedience; with respect to our love, beauty;
> with respect to our intelligence, balance of necessary
> relations; with respect to our flesh, brute force.[116]

Thus Weil sees a reconciliation between religion and science
in which the spirit of truth can be re-introduced into both
through conceiving the world as obedient to the Father's will
which we consent to love and contemplate. It is a reconciliation
which, she felt, could have the far reaching result of leading
us to understand the sort of world in which we live, its relation
to Good and how we are consequently to participate in it.

The most far reaching result that the truth of consented
obedience would lead to, though, is that it would make evident
the truth of physical labor, which is our active consent to the
universe. It is here that the metaphysical order of things and
God's redeeming love, historically manifest perfectly in Christ's
Cross, are joined together for the very order of the universe and
the ideal order of social relations converge in such a way that
it becomes possible for the individual soul, through its labor,
to consent and submit to necessity in every part of its being.
It is through science that we can conceive of an order of the
universe, but it is only concommitant with an understanding of
Christ's Incarnation that we can see that necessity is to be submitted to in every part, and that no situation escapes God's love.
Labor is thus a knowing and willing submission to the necessity
from which we would otherwise flee, and constitutes for the individual a consented obedience to God which imitates that of
Christ.

Weil explains the significance of labor through an ingenious
interpretation of the text from *Genesis* in which death and labor
are laid on Adam and his descendants as the punishment for separating themselves from God. This punishment, Weil contends, should
never be understood as an act of vengeance or retribution on
God's part. Instead, it needs to be understood as the means God
has prepared, if man undergoes them willingly, for leading man
back into obedience.

> Man placed himself outside the current of obedience.
> God chose as his punishments labor and death. Conse-
> quently, labor and death, if Man undergoes them in a
> spirit of willingness, constitute a transference back
> into the current of supreme Good, which is obedience
> to God.[117]

To consent to death, to become nothing and to claim no rights of
the self over the universe, is the more perfect form of obedience,
an obedience that Christ undertook on the Cross and in the Creation of the world, and in which we follow Him and for which we
are meant. Labor is next, for it is daily death and obedience.

> To labor is to place one's own being, body and soul, in
> the circuit of inert matter, turn it into an intermediary
> between one state and another of a fragment of matter,
> make of it an instrument . . . Consent to suffer death,
> when death is there and seen in all its nakedness con-
> stitutes a final, sudden wrenching away from what each
> one calls "I," consent to perform labor is of a less
> violent nature. But where it is absolute, it is renewed
> each morning throughout the entire length of a human
> existence, day after day, and each day it lasts until the
> evening, and it starts again on the following day and
> this goes on often until death. Each morning the laborer
> consents to perform his labor for that day, and for the
> rest of his life.[118]

Labor constitutes the root of all other roots, for when the
spirituality of labor is seen as a loving obedience to the
Father's will, and an imitation of the Son's own love, it becomes
the spiritual center of our existence. It is a center which
needs to inform all of our other activities and one on which all
else needs to converge for men to be put into the proper relationship to God. Because it does occupy this place in man's
life, it is necessary that both science and institutional religion be responsible for making labor possible as a spiritual exercise.

> If on the one hand the whole spiritual life of the soul,
> and on the other hand, all the scientific knowledge ac-
> quired concerning the material universe are made to con-
> verge upon the act of work, work occupies the rightful
> place in a man's thoughts. Instead of being a kind of
> prison, it becomes a point of contact between this world
> and the world beyond.[119]

But, also, by concentrating efforts on labor, both science and
institutional religion would also benefit, for by taking labor
as their human starting point, the truth of consented obedience
would continually be in the fore of the activities of both.

For present day labor, according to Weil "the condition of
the workers is such that the hunger for finality which constitutes the very being of all men can only be satisfied by God
himself."[120] This is a privilege that they alone possess, and
she says, nothing separates them from God; all they have to is
lift their heads. But "the difficulty for them is lifting their
heads. They have not, as all other men do, an excess of something of which they need to rid themselves with effort. They
have too little. Intermediaries are lacking for them."[121] Intermediaries are needed to sustain the attention and, unfortunately, the workers have none. What is needed, then, is to give
them these intermediaries so that their labor may become a
μεταξύ. Further, it is necessary that the intermediaries be
given where labor is exercised. "How great is the necessity of
such intermediaries in the workplaces, where one goes only to
gain his life! There hangs all earthly thought."[122]

It is the job of religion and science to make these intermediaries apparent for labor, since labor is one of the prime
means by which we submit to necessity. Examples Weil gives are
such things as portraying the Cross as a balance for those who
carry weights, operate levers or who are fatigued by the weight
of things, and comparing the laws of mechanics to mediation. In
this way, she felt, men's attention could be sustained and up-
lifted in their daily labors. In addition, science and intelligence have another role to play for they must be exercised in
such a way that labor can be undertaken without oppressing the
worker and destroying his attention wherein he freely gives himself to God in his daily activities. In this way labor can become the spiritual core of a society and a μεταξύ for man to love
God. It also lies at the base of all his other activities and
they need to pay heed to it in order to regain their own spiritual truth and participation in God.

There is little explicit reference to mediation in *The Need
for Roots* beyond the occasional use of 'intermediary' and a
reference to the double language of geometry which signifies
both material relations and divine mediation. This, however,
does not need to suggest that mediation has no significance for
that work and for numerous topics treated therein. In fact,

mediation is crucial for completely grasping that work since it
is the illuminating light behind much of it. It is that which
brings *The Need for Roots* into a consistent whole with the rest
of Weil's work. It does this in two ways.

The first is that the major themes of *The Need for Roots*
replay the themes of mediation. These themes are manifold. The
first is that of obligations, which being enjoined in attention,
are a sort of fullness meeting poverty. Second, there is the
notion of labor as daily consented death which "turns one's being into an intermediary between one state and another of a
fragment of matter." This theme obviously recalls Christ's mediatory death on the Cross in which while separated from the
Father, he was joined to him in loving obedience. But the cross
is more than recalled as a theme, it is ultimately the very basis
of labor, and Weil's entire outlook; for without Christ's submission to necessity wherein we are redeemed, we could not give total consent to necessity nor submit to it, nor even see it as
something to which we need to submit in order to be joined to
God. The one major criticism Weil had of Greek spirituality was
that it never comprehended the spiritual value of work. She
does not explain why she thinks this was so in Greece, but at
least in her case we can see why she held to the value of work
while at the same time embracing Greek mediation. Like the
Greeks she was able to see the order of the world as a mediator
to God which embodies all relations, but unlike them, by her consideration of affliction and Christ's endurance of it on the
Cross, she was able to see that spirituality is perfected in
total submission to necessity as God's will, even when this includes affliction. While labor is not affliction, and should not
be, although it may lead to it, when it is consented to freely
it is a submission to necessity. Properly understood, it is at
least a preparation for the Cross for it is a reproduction of
Christ's loving obedience and a participation in the Cross.
That is, it is a μεταξύ. This is particularly evident when Weil
insists that the symbolic nature of labor as linked to Christ's
death be made plain in all fields of work in order that the
worker may bring supernatural attention to bear on his task.
This includes intellectual work as well, for it also needs to

be seen as a consented obedience to renounce self-prespective
and think the world as it is. Third, there is the major theme
of the order of the world, a theme which pervades *The Need for
Roots* as the example we need to follow to be able to bring to
order a myriad of social relations and the object of scientific
contemplation. In *The Need for Roots* this order is once again
defined as the invariant ensemble of varying relations and as
the obedience of creation to the limits prescribed for it by eternal Wisdom. But, in recalling Christ's Λόγος function, we also
understand that this order mediates between the unlimited and
God and that it obtains because of Christ's sacrifice, and that
this is why the Creation as a whole is obedience to the Father's
will. Finally, there is the constant theme of relating everything to the good. This recalls Weil's remark on the *Philebus*
that the sovereign good includes all other forms of good. All
of these themes have their example in Christ's own mediation and
bear some reference to his Cross. In obligations, we are obliged
because in loving God we follow His will in respect to other men;
a will made manifest in Christ's love for His brethren. In labor,
we consent to necessity as Christ did. The order of the world
is because of Christ's mediation, and because of this mediation
through which the world and all therein was created, all bears a
relation, direct or indirect, to God's sovereign goodness.

The second way of construing *The Need for Roots* in the light
of mediation follows from the notions of the order of the world
and the sovereign good incorporating all forms of good. Here
these two notions are not just themes in that work, but the very
organizational principles of it. Many of the particulars in *The
Need for Roots* depend upon insight, and are not systematically
derived from any doctrine, including mediation; but their organization and inner-relations need to depend on a structure. For
Weil, this structure is her Platonic doctrine of mediation wherein she finds a conceptual means to see the one Good mediated in
the order of the world, in supernatural relations with the souls
of men, and in the relations of matter to the order of the world.
Added to this is the basis of mediation in Christ's Cross wherein
the point at which the whole book drives is an imitation of his
consent to necessity as the Father's will. Moreover, this allows
her to relate the various aspects of man's spiritual, intellectual

and material existence in one selfsame being who bears a final
relation to God.

At one point, Weil calls the art of politics an art of composition on several planes at once. The entire *Need for Roots*
is such a composition, for it seeks to organize and inter-relate
obligations and needs, diverse forms of rootedness, and most
important, it seeks to inter-relate them and inspire them in
such a way that they can be seen in relation to the absolute
good. The bare fact of an attempt to inter-relate particulars
is, of course, needed simply to make a written work cohere. But
Weil is doing more than this; she is using a specific organizational principle which is the mediation theory she develops vis-
a-vis Plato's *Philebus*, and which she centers in the Cross.
With it she is able to divide obligations, see the limits of
needs and their inter-relations to each other, their relation to
the eternal destiny of the soul, and finally to God. In short,
mediation is, that which allows her to undertake the project as
she does. It gives her the means by which she can relate concerns of the soul and God which are beyond any final finite representation with the finite concerns of living in a material
world into one mediated whole wherein everything plays its own
distinct and proper role, but also where its relation to God is
brought to light through the order of the world and our consent
to it.

> For us everything is relation.
> In itself, everything is mediation, divine mediation.
> God is mediation. All mediation is God . . .
> To touch God in this way in and through everything.[123]

CONCLUSION

It has been my intent in this book to identify and describe
the doctrine of mediation in the writings of Simone Weil in such
a way that this doctrine can be seen to provide an overall coherence to those writings. Mediation is an important named theme
in Weil's writings, particularly when she is dealing with Christ's
mediation and with spirituality in the thought of the ancient
Greeks. The significance of mediation for Weil, however, goes
beyond a thematic role; what is more important about mediation
is that it is a philosophico-theological doctrine which allows
Weil to develop her thoughts in the way she does. Mediation,
in this sense, is in its most general formulation a harmonization
of incommensurate elements into a unity that does not destroy the
integrity or order of its components. More specifically, mediation is particularly concerned with the harmonization of a transcendent and absolute Good with all else. Because Weil felt this
mediation cannot be accomplished by a progression of necessity
she then contended it must be the result of a descent of absolute
Good wherein the Good joins itself to the world and is thereby
realized in the order of the world and in human thoughts and
actions.

The way in which Weil construed this mediation to take place,
however, differs between the early and later periods of her life;
yet even here a certain consistency obtains if we can see a way
in which her early thoughts on mediation can be incorporated into
the mature form of the doctrine.

In the early years Weil felt that mediation, properly understood, was the descent of mind which has contact with the overarching *toute-puissance* of the world into thought and the methodical action of work. At this time she believed that good could
be realized in the individual if the various aspects of his being could be joined together in a proper order and joined with
the Necessity of the universe as a whole. Further, she felt that
this sort of mediation offered a basis on which to restructure

247

social relations so that the systems of production should no
longer oppress the workers and would, instead, become a means by
which one could bring mind into his actions. When Weil, however,
encountered the phenomenon of affliction she began to see serious
limitations to this view, for affliction threatens to divide
permanently one's body and mind and crush all aspirations to
good. Weil does not say that she was personally afflicted, but
she was nearly so and this along with the contact with the affliction of others marked her to such a degree that all the op-
timism of her early years vanished. In affliction she had found
an absurd and hideous element in the universe which defies reason
and which presents a permanent obstacle that prevents understanding alone from ever grasping total goodness in the universe.
Nevertheless, she persevered in her hope for the good and in time
experienced loving contact with Christ. Here the ultimate sense
of mediation was changed for her. Mediation was no longer
strictly the descent of mind into matter, it was now meant to
refer primarily to the descent of the absolute and transcendent
Good in Christ. In Christ Weil saw God's complete mediation, for
Christ suffered the extremes of affliction, including all the
evil humanity heaped upon him, and yet he continued to love the
Father and to accept affliction as the Father's will. Weil then
saw that in Christ no situation ever need escape goodness, for
even the worst of evils that confronts us is redeemed and even a
means of contact between man and God.

Christ thus became the prime mediator for Weil, for it is
in Him that humanity and God are joined in a harmonious unity
that overcomes the total incommensuration between the two at all
distances. Weil, however, did not stop at considering mediation
as that which happens on the Cross; instead she found in the
Cross the very principle upon which God created the universe
and all its myriad inter-relations. Because of the omnipresent
threat of affliction, she sought out witnesses to the Cross and
its mediation in all times and places. These witnesses, she
felt, were the effect of the sanctifying and redeeming grace of
the Spirit who is the bond of love between the Father and Son
which holds the universe together. The ancient Greeks were the
especial object of this search and in them Weil found an understanding of God's relations with the world that could only have

come from divine inspiration. But her concern with the Greeks
was more than finding in them a witness to the Cross and the effects of divine mediation; it was also to find in their thought
a means of conceiving the transcendent mediation in terms that
would make mediation as representable as is humanly possible
without belying the unrepresentable inspiration. She found this
means in the Platonic and Pythagorean view of mediation which
first and foremost referred to the operation of grace on the human soul and the world. In language this made mediation first
a theological tool and only secondarily a means of treating matter. In the Greeks she found in the description of mediation
something she felt was the effect of divine mediation penetrating
through the soul to the intelligence and which allowed the intelligence to conceive an image of the relation of all things to
God. With this Platonic doctrine of mediation she was then able
to see an order of all relations, including the expression of
the doctrine itself, which is established in Christ's Cross and
which is the love stretching from God to nothingness. This
gives a metaphysics in which, once a relation is understood, one
can move towards an explicit mediated unity with God.

This metaphysics then allows a context in which the early
theory of mediation can be placed. While Weil no longer understood the good for man to exist in mind's descent into matter,
this became at least a necessary first step towards the soul's
consent to the rule of Necessity as the Father's will, even when
this includes affliction. In fact, the mediation of mind is an
intermediate form of this consent.

There is certainly a difference in the ideals presented in
the early and later works, but rather than showing inconsistency
the difference should show an *approfondissement* of the early
views. This is particularly seen in the increasing significance
of work for Weil and the role that intelligence and love play
in it, a significance that is seen in *The Need for Roots*. Work
is there, for Weil, to be the spiritual center of social life.
In part, this is for many of the same reasons and by many of the
same means that work was important in the early writings since
in both it is in work that the intelligence grasps its object
and the body is ordered accordingly. But added to this is the

sense in which work is now to be considered; it is now a submission to necessity even to death wherein we imitate Christ's acceptance of necessity and where, by submitting to necessity, we give back our being to God's own love. Here work is certainly an act of submitting our intelligence and bodies to the order of necessity we find in the world, but it is also an act of love that mediates us to the Mediator wherein God's goodness is fully realized in our love, our thought and our action.

Weil's thought can thus be seen to be a coherent whole and through mediation we have a solid object in that thought which allows Weil to be judged and critiqued without danger of misrepresentation or lack of discernment of the connections of the various elements. In regard to future studies on Weil it is now possible to judge the relative place and importance of certain views. It is possible to see the connection between politics, philosophy and religion, and it is possible wherever there are mistakes, historical errors, anachronisms or other incongruities to see the degree to which they affect the whole, and even what important points there might be hidden in the various incongruities. Weil did not set out to write a system but she did have a doctrine which allowed her to order various insights and it is necessary to take this doctrine seriously so that we may see the order of her ideas. Without it we can only begin with particulars and attempt to move from one to another without ever grasping Weil's whole vision.

Once the overall doctrine is grasped it is then also possible to judge the theological appropriateness of Weil's thought. All too often the theological critique of Weil has centered on particulars such as her dislike of vast portions of the Old Testament and her refusal to join the Church in anything but spirit. While an evaluation of these points is important, it is also important to place them in the perspective of the whole and to see whether or not they are entailed, and if not therefore possibly corrected, or whether there might be overriding reasons for holding them. Here the issue is not so much to determine whether Simone Weil as a person was orthodox or not, but whether her thought is applicable in Christianity. While a complete determination of this remains the subject of future studies, because of the Cross at the center of her thought there is some indication of its appropriateness. I have sought in this essay to show that Weil's doctrine of mediation does depend on the Incarnation and Crucifixion of the Word and that it does not treat Christ only as a symbol that is helpful to explicate other ideas; rather, these other ideas are used to explicate the larger significance of the Cross. Weil's interpretation of Christ's mediation as the acceptance of extreme affliction may be unique, or at least rare in the present theological world, but for that it may be all the more valuable in a time when affliction is a constant threat for which we must be prepared and a constant reality for thousands to whom we must minister. In a time when there abound prophets of a facile hope for an inevitably approaching future of justice--a future that Weil said is made of the same stuff as our uprooted present--it is well to contemplate the truth of Christ's Cross that Truth, Justice and Love are only perfected in death and on its other side. This is a death that may very well come in an affliction which breaks all our hopes, but in which we are nevertheless to continue to love.

It is the subject of future study to determine whether Weil's thought is ultimately applicable. It is worthwhile, however, to note briefly where her thought might have significance if it should be so deemed.

The first place that her thought could have significance is that it could effect recognition of the need she saw for Christian theology to use non-biblical material. She is, of course, her own best example of this sort of effort. It was Weil's view that God's grace which leads to salvation can be present outside historical Christianity and that it can have discernible effects in the thoughts and acts of the people it inspires. Because of this she also felt that inspired material outside the Christian tradition could aid in bringing to light truths that might only be implicit in Christianity. Even though she believed Christianity to contain all the divine truth necessary for salvation, and that it contains the unique truth of Christ's Cross to which other religions may hint, she also believed it would be a sad loss not to recognize truth wherever it can be discerned.

Moreover, she also felt that there is something to be learned
from other religions. She writes:

> The Catholic religion contains explicitly truths which
> other religions contain implicitly. But, conversely,
> other religions contain explicitly truths which are only
> implicit in Christianity. The most well-informed Chris-
> tian can still learn a great deal concerning divine
> matters from other religious traditions; although in-
> ward spiritual light can also cause him to apprehend
> everything through the medium of his own tradition.
> All the same, were these traditions to disappear from
> the face of the earth, it would be an irreparable loss.[1]

Weil's actual criteria for determining whether or not there
is true divine content in non-biblical religions is at its foundation experimental. She writes:

> One might lay down as a postulate: All conceptions of
> God which are incompatible with a movement of pure
> charity are false. All other conceptions of Him, in
> varying degree, are true.[2]

And elsewhere:

> Belief is aroused by the beauty of the texts and by the
> light one gains upon the human condition through med-
> itating upon them.[3]

These criteria at first appear quite general and unspecific
but the point is that we have to pay genuine attention (in
Weil's sense of attention) to other traditions if we are to discern their genius and we cannot simply pass them by as historical
curiosities. This is quite consistent with Weil's view of religion and of the Gospel, for as she says, "The Gospel contains a
conception of human life, not a theology."[4] God's grace descends upon the human soul and when it touches the soul it transforms it and makes it in the image of the Crucified one. This
act of God, Weil believed is Christianity and not a set of propositions, and it is to this we need to pay attention in both
Christianity and other traditions. Christianity, as well as
other religions, is, to borrow Wittgenstein's phrase, a "form of
life"; a form that is given solely by God's grace delivered
through the mediation of the Son. If, then, the ideas of non-
biblical religions and philosophies can be of assistance in the
increase of the love of God, Weil felt it is desirable to recognize the divine content of these traditions and to use them

wherever their insights are applicable. The prime example of
this sort of usage in Weil herself is her doctrine of mediation.
There she finds in the Greek philosophical usage of mediation an
understanding and conception of God which does assist in a movement of pure charity and which therefore can be helpful in
Christianity, particularly as the Greek conception admitted a
wide range of applications to various aspects of human life.

Protestants in particular have always been slightly suspi-
cious of whatever appears to be syncretism and, given certain
excesses in the history of the Church, perhaps rightly so.
Weil's view, however, is not intended to impugn or relativize
the inspired nature of canonical writings; rather, it means to
see where inspiration may be. Weil was not looking for material
to compete with Christianity or to offer alternatives to it, but
she was looking for materials that had the love of God in them
and which were akin to Christian spirituality. It is this love,
she felt, that made them worthy of consideration and that made
them helpful.

There is a certain unavoidable contact in the modern world
between Christianity and other religions and philosophies which
makes it desirable that Christians appreciate the spiritual inspiration of philosophy and other religions. This appreciation
could enrich Christianity as well as be a means by which Christianity could enrich others without the spiritual imperalism that
has all too often marked its evangelical efforts in the past.
But there is a second reason why it is desirable that Christian
theology make this effort of appreciation and this is that by
doing so it could recover its own roots. Here Weil's attempts
to discern the effects of divine mediation in the Greeks give an
example of a people sufficiently close to us in whom we might
discern the Spirit, but, who also in a very strong sense, are
our spiritual parents. In this case, our ignorance of the
genuine spirituality of these people and the beneficial effect
they have had on our thinking is a sign of our own uprootedness.

Weil may very well have overstressed the notion that the
spirit of Christianity is directly derived from the Greeks when
she says, for example, "The Gospels are the last and most marvelous expression of Greek genius . . ."[5] But her point that

the Greeks did have something to do with Christian spirituality
cannot be ignored. We need to consider seriously and in a positive light the appropriate and genuine contributions that Greek
thought has made in Christian theology.

This appreciation is more than academic, it is also critical
to the life of faith since the Greek genius has been incorporated
into the very structures of Christianity. These structures are
a city that supplies a vital need of the human soul by shaping
its original thoughts. Modern theology too often decries a
foreign and antiquated metaphysics that must be expunged in order
for us to seize truly the Gospel message. While there have been
excellent and well-intended efforts to translate the Gospel to
modern people, in many quarters this effort has been undertaken
without due consideration of the inspiration of the past which
caused those before us to write as they did and which still lives
in the hearts of believers. When this inspiration is ignored
and the metaphysics expunged without saving the inspiration the
effort of translation has the opposite of the desired effect,
for the structures by which we first grasp divine reality are
stripped away and there is nothing left for us to hang on to.
When this happens theological thought becomes uprooted and theology becomes a matter of specialization and technical knowledge
since there is no longer any common object of thought. Here
theologians, willingly or no, become the spiritual equivalent
of Weil's "technicians of management" for the believer must depend upon the theologian's judgment of what is acceptable to the
"modern mentality" and what is authentic.

If there were no inspiration in what Christianity has borrowed from Greece there could, of course, be no objections to an
exclusion of it now, even if we have come to depend on the structures which incorporate a Greek spirit. Weil's point, however,
is that what has been borrowed is of genuine inspiration. She
says of Plato, making it clear why she finds him so important:
"Plato's wisdom is not a philosophy, a research for God by means
of human reason . . . the wisdom of Plato is nothing other than
an orientation towards grace."[6] When we cannot see this, it not
only means that we lose valuable roots, it also means that we
have already lost roots, a loss which makes it difficult to see

the inspiration behind Plato or the inspiration of those Fathers
of the Church who also found him valuable. This loss of roots
indicates a corresponding lack of attention on our part.

Weil did not believe in a wholesale conservation of the
past and she recognized that much of our present theological
thinking may indeed be antiquated. But she was at great pains
to point out that in order to make any sort of genuine translation we must be inspired and that much of the needed inspiration
is a continuance of the same inspiration of thoughts and words
of the past. Once this inspiration can no longer be seen and
we have been uprooted, the past no longer speaks to us, not because it is insufficient to the task but because we can no longer
hear what it says. Any further attempt to translate under these
circumstances can then only have the effect of continued uprooting.

This rooting also applies to secular life as well and to the
relation it has to spiritual life. Even if we did recover our
theological roots, Christianity must always face secular life
and the inherited vestiges of pre-Christian culture. Here the
two need to be joined if we are to incarnate completely the love
of God in all of our life. This, however, is exceedingly difficult if the given areas of "profane life" are always seen as
creations independent of God's grace. Weil puts the problem this
way:

> For since all the profane life of our countries (in the
> West) is directly derived from "pagan" civilizations,
> as long as the illusion subsists of a break between so-
> called "paganism" and Christianity, the latter will not
> be incarnate, will not impregnate the whole of profane
> life as it ought to do, will remain separated from it
> and consequently non-active.[7]

Here, Weil's considerations of the Greeks has significance
once more since a major area of our profane culture, namely,
science, is derived from their so-called pagan civilization.
But, she quickly adds, this civilization was not all that 'pagan'; it was, instead, inspired by a love of God. With this inspiration at its center this civilization was able to incorporate
the sacred and profane into one life wherein the sacred thoroughly informed the profane. A positivist history of philosophy
has tended to see this incorporation as part of a movement from

a 'mythological' world view to a purely scientific one, but Weil
saw it as a carefully struck balance that, if recovered today,
would be of considerable value to us who should be its inheri-
tors. The Greeks are here at least a wonderful example of a
balance, but what is more important to recognize in them, Weil
says, is that their spirituality and science came from one central inspiration. For this reason she says we need to see that
the sacred and profane areas of our lives do not have two roots,
but one which is a genuine love of God that both lifts souls and
incarnates itself in thought. If we could recover this inspiration we could be led to order our own profane lives under our
spirituality and let our intellects, within their proper limits,
be an expression of our spiritual lives.

It was not, of course, Weil's belief that if we simply recognize that our derived profane life comes from a supernatural
inspiration that our problems with secular culture will be
solved. Nor did she believe that we could, or should, return to
the more idyllic times of ancient Greece. She fully recognized
that much has happened in our culture that is new and different
and which is unheralded in our cultural Greek ancestors. Even
if many of our philosophical problems are formed by the Greeks,
argument has progressed and the answers which they gave are not
completely sufficient for contemporary versions of the problems.
But what she did recognize to be of supreme value in them was a
spirit that impregnated men such as the Pythagoreans and Plato
who were able to balance secular life around a divine point. It
is this spirit which she felt needs to be recovered today in
those forms of life we have inherited from them. In this sense,
Weil's considerations of the ancient Greeks is more than an
example of how God's love is present in other times and places;
it is also a bridge to her own ideas about the love of God in
quotidian life. The doctrine of mediation plays a crucial role
here. Not only is mediation in the Greeks a location of the
transcendent mediation, its expression is a μεταξύ by which they
were able to incorporate all of life into a harmony in God. It
was by borrowing this concept from them that Weil was also able
to harmonize what crucial problems she saw in life in God.

Weil's doctrine of transcendent mediation could have particular value in rejoining sacred and profane life, not just in

its recognition of the common root of both in Greek civilization, but also by giving us a way to effect a reconciliation between science and religion. It could do this by causing us to see science and religion as different, but hierarchically related, forms of one life. Since the downfall of a positivist view of the total empiricism of science we are in a particularly advantageous situation to make this reconciliation because we are now obliged to see even the most firmly founded of our scientific theories as creations of the human spirit. W. V. O. Quine writes of this in his essay "Two Dogmas of Empiricism":

> The totality of our so-called knowledge or beliefs,
> from the most casual matters of geography and history to
> the profoundest laws of atomic physics or even of pure
> mathematics and logic is a man-made fabric which impinges
> on experience only along the edges . . . But the total
> field is so undetermined by its boundary conditions,
> experience, that there is much latitude of choice as to
> what statements to reevaluate in the light of any single
> contrary experience. No particular experiences are
> linked with any particular statements in the interior of
> the field, except indirectly through consideration of
> equilibrium affecting the field as a whole.[8]

Weil saw this man-made fabric knowledge and beliefs as a two-fold effect of the relation of experience and the way that we understand the world. On the one hand, this fabric is a filter of reality which leads us to experience the world in certain ways, and once we have experienced it in these ways we are led to similar experiences and expectations of experience. As she notes in *The Lectures on Philosophy*, our language gives us an objective structure of the world and we plan our lives according to it. On the other hand, the fabric can be changed by an experience of reality which it cannot accommodate within present categories. In this case, however, the fabric is never changed and reordered completely; instead, when the experience is worked into the fabric, it is accomplished either by the addition of something new to the fabric or, what is more likely, by a change in the understanding of the inter-relations within the field. But here we have a great deal of choice as to which of the inter-relations we will change. We can change the inter-relations within very narrow bounds and fields without changing the basic nature of the object of contemplation or we can change the object and thus the relation between entire fields. The way in which

we change then determines future results. For example, in atomic
physics, experimentally discovered aberrations in certain commonly received laws of the behavior of atoms can lead us to posit
particles of matter smaller than atoms, which we will undoubtedly
'find' since matter is indefinitely divisible. Or, we could
change the object of contemplation to the order of the universe
and stop seeking to find basic matter as such. In this case we
would see that our relation to matter is a relation of our
thought to its order, and what is needed is a clarification of
thought and not discovery of smaller and more elusive particles
of matter. In the same way we also have a choice of reordering
the relations our thought has to the rest of our being.

Here Weil's points about the intermediary role science plays
in our lives and the order of the universe as the proper object
of science can be helpful. Much of Weil's critique of modern
science in *The Need for Roots* inveighs against the motives behind
science which she feels are incompatible with truth and thus she
feels that modern science is not a fruit of the spirit of truth.
As such her argument appears purely *ad hominem*. Yet, if there
is a connection between our thoughts and our spirit, as she contends there is, we cannot divorce the motives or objects of contemplation in the two spheres. The attention we bear in either
case can be critical for determining our relation to the object
and the quality of our attention in the other sphere. If science
is not motivated by a love of the beauty of the world and does
not have genuine love for its object of contemplation it is exceedingly difficult to see how in the future it will produce
anything but a utilitarian technology. Conversely, if there is
no consent to the beauty of the universe in the inner soul, it
is difficult to see how science could be anything but what it is
now. If we flee from wisdom in one area it is likely that we
will do so in others.

Weil appreciated what are certainly profound and essential
differences between religion and science and felt that as fields
of study neither should intrude on the other's domain. But,
nevertheless, with her doctrine of mediation, she also saw critical inter-relations between the two insofar as they are both
activities of the one human subject. The mediated unity of the

incommensurable aspects of the human creature and of the creature
with God cannot be *established* by thought or language since the
supernatural certainty of this mediation is beyond the finite
mind. But this unity can be experienced, and experienced in very
definite ways which have their basis in the Cross. The experience of mediated unity is not an amorphous feeling of being one
with the transcendent, it is an experience of obedience and self-
renunciation in the face of the Truth which renounces itself,
even to the point of being afflicted on a cross. Once this unity
is experienced and we see the universe to be made of consented
obedience, it can be incarnated and expressed in thought and
language. In turn, this expression is critical for the way in
which we change since we do determine ourselves through it. We
then have a choice of using our thought and language as the
μεταξύ of grace or an anchor of gravity.

NOTES

INTRODUCTION

[1]Simone Weil, *Waiting for God* (New York: Harper and Row, 1973), p. 100.

[2]Quoted in Simone Pétrement, *Simone Weil: A Life* (New York: Pantheon Books, 1976), p. 537.

[3]See Jacques Cabaud, *Simone Weil* (London: Harvill Press, 1964), p. 336.

[4]William James, *The Varieties of Religious Experience* (New York: Collier Books, 1961), p. 34.

[5]Steps are being taken in this direction. The most important effort to date has been M. Veto's *La Metaphysique Religieuse de Simone Weil* (Paris: J. Vrin, 1971), which constructs in orderly fashion the various aspects of Weil's religious thought. Also, with the establishment of l'Association pour l'étude de la pensée de Simone Weil in France and the publication of its quarterly journal, *Cahiers Simone Weil*, a group does now exist which is making strong efforts to undertake the necessary analysis and to publish the results.

[6]A complete bibliography for Simone Weil as well as secondary sources may be found in J. P. Little's *Simone Weil: A Bibliography*, London, Cutler and Grant, 1973, Supplement 1980. In addition, recent research is regularly noted and reviewed in *Cahiers Simone Weil*.

[7]Simone Weil, *Seventy Letters* (London: Oxford, 1965), p. 196.

[8]See Phillippe Dujardin, *Simone Weil: Idéologie et Politique* (Grenoble: Presses Universitaires de Grenoble, 1975). Dujardin makes all of these charges plus a few more.

[9]Quoted in A. Fontaine, "Simone Weil ou la cohérence absolue," *Cahiers Simone Weil*, vol. I, no. 1, 1978, p. 12.

[10]Ibid.

[11]Richard Swinburne, *The Coherence of Theism* (Oxford: Oxford University Press, 1977), p. 49. The understanding given here of what constitutes coherence is drawn from this work.

[12]Ibid.d

[13]Simone Weil, *Intimations of Christianity among the Ancient Greeks* (London: Routledge & Kegan Paul, 1976), p. 110.

NOTES

CHAPTER I

[1]Simone Weil, *Waiting for God* (New York: Harper & Row, 1973), p. 64. [Hereafter cited as WG.]

[2]Ibid.

[3]In French, the term *médiation* has a broader use than in English, insofar as it can cover most of the English sense of means. A *médiation* is therefore not only a 'go-between' but a means of passing from one thing to another. In this sense, when I use the term "mediation of mind" I intend by it the determination of means by mind.

[4]Simone Weil, *Oppression and Liberty* (Amherst: University of Massachusetts Press, 1973), p. 38. [Hereafter cited as OL.]

[5]OL, p. 136.

[6]OL, p. 39.

[7]OL, p. 40.

[8]Ibid.

[9]Quoted in OL, p. 41.

[10]OL, p. 9.

[11]OL, p. 12.

[12]OL, p. 13.

[13]OL, p. 42.

[14]OL, p. 43.

[15]It is true that Marx believed he had derived a good part of his thought from Darwin and therefore dedicated *Capital* to him. But Weil says, he really came closer to Lamarck's theory of evolution, that is, that the function creates the organ, instead of the organ finding a function. Where Marx's evolution is similar to Darwin's is that Marx does see conflict as necessary for evolution, but conflict *per se* and a struggle for a definite goal other than existence are markedly different.

[16]OL, p. 44.

[17]OL, p. 45.

[18] OL, p. 47.

[19] OL, p. 48.

[20] Ibid.

[21] OL, p. 49.

[22] OL, p. 50.

[23] OL, p. 53.

[24] Cf. OL, pp. 133ff.

[25] OL, p. 56.

[26] OL, p. 59.

[27] Cf. OL, p. 55. Weil carefully distinguishes between "oppression and subordination of personal whims to a social order."

[28] OL, p. 62.

[29] OL, p. 63.

[30] Ibid.

[31] OL, p. 142.

[32] OL, p. 64.

[33] Henceforth the term 'power' will refer to the human exercise of force.

[34] OL, p. 67.

[35] This contention of Weil's concerning the *Iliad* is found already in *Reflections Concerning the Causes of Liberty and Social Oppression*, which was written in 1934. Her actual essay on the topic, *The Iliad, or the Poem of Might* was not written until 1940. This essay contains many elements which are inherent to her later religious thought, which we will leave aside here. In what follows in this chapter are illustrations drawn from the 1940 essay, which bear directly on the subject at hand.

[36] Simone Weil, *Intimations of Christianity among the Ancient Greeks* (London: Routledge and Kegan Paul, 1957), p. 24. [Hereafter cited as IC.]

[37] IC, p. 26.

[38] IC, p. 31.

[39] IC, pp. 34-5.

[40] IC, p. 32. Weil's translation.

[41]IC, p. 39.

[42]OL, p. 68.

[43]OL, p. 69.

[44]Ibid.

[45]Ibid.

[46]IC, p. 34.

[47]OL, p. 78.

[48]OL, p. 139. Weil avails herself of two examples here, the Fall of the Roman Empire and the French Revolution:

> The great invasions delivered the Roman Empire into the hands of the barbarians, who had already taken possession of it from within, and that the fall of the Bastille, with what followed in its wake consolidated the modern State--which the kings had set up, by handing the country over to the bourgeoisie, who already did everything in it. If the October Revolution, in Russia, seems to have created something new, this is so only in appearance; all it did was to reinforce those powers which were already the real ones under the Tsars--the bureaucracy, the police, the army" (OL, pp. 139-40).

[49]OL, p. 78.

[50]OL, p. 83.

[51]Ibid.

[52]*Science et Perception dans Descartes* was written by Weil in 1929-30 as her diploma thesis at the École Normale. The *Lectures on Philosophy* were not actually penned by Weil, but are rather, the notes taken by Anne Reynaud, a student of hers, in a course on philosophy which Weil gave during the school year of 1933-34. They do, however, seem to represent accurately Weil's thinking and seem to be a marvel of full and faithful notetaking.

[53]Simone Weil, *Lectures on Philosophy* (Cambridge: Cambridge University Press, 1978), p. 40. [Hereafter cited as LP.]

[54]Ibid.

[55]LP, p. 32.

[56]LP, p. 47.

[57]LP, p. 48.

[58]LP, p. 40.

[59]LP, p. 51.

[60]Simone Weil, *Sur la Science* (Paris: Gallimard, 1966), p. 71. [Hereafter cited as SS.]

[61]SS, p. 72.

[62]LP, p. 52.

[63]LP, p. 65.

[64]Ibid. It is artificial for the individual in that he is not born with a language.

[65]LP, p. 74.

[66]LP, p. 75.

[67]LP, p. 59.

[68]LP, p. 74.

[69]OL, p. 60.

[70]LP, p. 70.

[71]Ibid.

[72]Cf. Simone Weil, *Seventy Letters* (London: Oxford University Press, 1965), p. 3. [Hereafter cited as SL.]

Descartes never found a way to prevent order from becoming as soon as it is conceived, a thing instead of an idea. Order becomes a thing, it seems to me, as soon as one treats a series as a reality distinct from the terms which compose it, by expressing it with a symbol. . . .

[73]LP, p. 72.

[74]LP, p. 73.

[75]Cf. LP, p. 78.

The syllogism is, to put it briefly, nothing but a rule of language to avoid contradiction; at bottom, the principle of non-contradiction is a principle of grammar. In general, all ordinary reasonings, which are immediate and performed without effort, are more or less explicit syllogisms.

[76]There is a certain disjunction between *Science et Perception* and the *Lectures* as Peter Winch notes in his introduction to the latter (pp. 4ff.). *Science et Perception* begins with the question of how the conscious self can order experience, without undertaking the consideration made evident in the *Lectures* that "thought is born into a world already ordered." Because of this, there is much that is not explained in the essay. Where some of Winch's criticisms are off base is in his failure

to note that, if one first takes the arguments in "the materialistic point of view," that the argument in *Science et Perception*
can be still held in terms of how one can discern and create a
necessary order in thoughts that already have a certain primary
order due to their rootedness in socially and organically conditioned action. A major point of the *Lectures* is that materialism
fails as a final answer and that one must have recourse to mind.
Weil's reasons for holding to the existence of mind did not
change significantly on this issue, and thus there is a basic
continuity between the two works.

[77] SS, p. 47.

[78] SS, p. 51.

[79] SS, p. 52.

[80] Ibid.

[81] SS, p. 11.

[82] Cf. SS, p. 54.

> It is hardly that I am admitting that this table, this
> paper, this pen, this cosiness and myself are only things
> that I think; things which I think and which appear,
> exist. I think them; they have need of me to be thoughts.
> What of it? For I do not think what I want. They
> foist illusion upon me by their own power. What there-
> fore do they impress upon me? Belief. It is I who
> thinks these illusory things but whether as sure or il-
> lusory, the influence that they exercise over me re-
> mains, nevertheless, intact.

[83] SS, p. 55.

[84] SS, p. 58.

[85] SS, p. 59.

[86] SS, p. 60.

[87] Ibid.

[88] Weil's premise that "all real power is infinite" may,
at first sight, not appear to be immediately obvious. The reasoning behind it, I believe, is that power in itself which is
dependent or limited would not be an agent's power at all, for
its exercise would be the result of something else. The proof
that I exist as a self-willing agent, demonstrates that as an
agent I am not dependent on another existence, and that thus
there is a possibility of the existence of an actual infinite.

[89] The argument is, at root, Spinozism. From my exercise
of power as an agent I understand all-power over myself; but
all-power exists independently of me and is that which allows
me my power. Weil then gives this definition of 'toute-puissance': "It is defined by this impress on me which deprives me
of domination and leaves me liberty" (SS, p. 61).

[90] LP, p. 87.

[91] SS, pp. 61-2.

[92] Winch argues (LP, p. 17) that there is a confusion here on Weil's part.

> But she also tends sometimes in this work and much more
> so in later writings in which Plato's influence becomes
> more marked to speak of the "whole natural order" as
> subject to a single "necessity". . . . In speaking in
> this way she tended, rather like Spinoza, to confuse
> the senses of "necessity" which apply to the natural
> laws established within science, with the fundamentally
> different sense of necessity connected with ideas like
> "fate."

This is, in fact, not quite true. See e.g. IC, p. 97. "Each phenomenon has two causes, of which one is its cause according to the mechanism of nature, that is, natural law, the second cause is in the providential ordering of the world, and it never is permissible to make use of the one as an explanation upon the plane to which the other belongs." What Weil is contending here, I believe, is that all physical laws are parametrically limited by a single necessity, which we by conceiving can then apply particularly to individual functions. Without this larger sort of necessity there could be no necessity of physical laws. Also see n. 117 below.

[93] LP. p. 89.

[94] Jean-Paul Sartre "Existentialism is a Humanism" in *Existentialism from Dostoevsky to Sartre*, ed. W. Kaufmann (New York: Meridian Books, 1956), pp. 302-3.

[95] Sartre, "Existentialism is a Humanism," pp. 303-4.

[96] See e.g. OL, p. 107; LP, p. 89.

[97] OL, p. 85.

[98] LP, p. 102.

[99] LP, p. 90.

[100] LP, pp. 97-8.

[101] SS, p. 74.

[102] LP, p. 77. Weil felt that since Descartes, the scientific project had come to be stood on its head since instead of providing method for quotidian life, it had become a goal in itself. It was for this reason that she had a strong distrust of algebra for she felt that the manipulation of symbols was the whole of the art. She thought that the symbols should be "relegated back to their rank as mere instruments, the rank which Descartes attempted to assign them in the *Rules*; and their real function would be revealed, which is not to assist the understanding but the imagination" (SL, pp. 3-4).

[103]OL, p. 86.

[104]LP, p. 118.

[105]LP, p. 175.

[106]LP, p. 73.

[107]LP, p. 124.

[108]LP, p. 174.

[109]Ibid.

[110]In these early years Weil's moral theories often approach those of Kant. It is not evident exactly how she understood him since she uses him in *The Lectures on Philosophy*, but does not do a critique of him. Because of the similarity, however, an important difference between her and Kant needs to be noted (one she herself may not have recognized). Iris Murdoch in criticizing Kant in her essay "The Sublime and the Beautiful Revisited" (*The Yale Review* [1959]:247-271) says of Kant:

> Kant's moral philosophy rests on the equation that virtue is freedom is reason. Virtue is not knowledge *of* anything; it is rather an ability to impose rational order. We respect others, not as particular eccentric phenomenal individuals, but as co-equal bearers of universal reason. . . ." (p. 248).

Where Weil differs from Kant, even in these early years, is that for her, virtue is knowledge of the world. We do not impose order on it, but *discover* it, although it is incumbent on us to order our own actions. But even this is in accordance with the *toute-puissance* in which we participate for our being and which orders the whole world. Weil further differs from Kant when she sees it as a peculiarly moral human activity to *see* particulars as particulars and not just examples of general ideas. In regard to others, then, we do indeed regard them as bearers of reason, but it is also our moral duty to see the tribulations that keep them from moral activity and to assist (as is morally possible) to remove these things.

[111]LP, p. 174.

[112]OL, p. 60.

[113]OL, p. 86.

[114]OL, p. 129.

[115]OL, p. 87.

[116]OL, p. 100.

[117]The terminology of 'infinite error' may be slightly misleading if error is taken to mean 'inaccurate,' for in this sense 'error' is predicated with the notion in view that

'correctness' falls within assumed boundaries. Weil, however,
is contending that the problem is, in the first place, not one
of accuracy and hence general practicality, but rather one of
exactness and hence incommensuration between two ideas which we
have by mind attention to the imagination and the world's impression on imagination. It can be stated that it was her belief
that 'accuracy' depends upon a prior notion of exactitude, but
that the levels of the two cannot be confused. It is only by
introduction of a third factor that the two can be mediated.
This is the point which Winch (See n. 92 above) does not bring
out in Weil's argument.

[118] OL, p. 88.

[119] See SS, pp. 82-83.

[120] Quoted in LP, p. 179.

[121] See Ol, p. 89.

All tools are thus, in a more or less perfect way, in the
manner of instruments for defining chance events. Man
could in this way eliminate chance, if not in his surrounds, at any rate within himself; however, even that
is an unattainable ideal. The world is too full of situations whose complexity is beyond us for instinct, routine,
trial and error, improvising ever to be able to cease
playing a role in our labors; all man can do is to restrict this role more and more, thanks to scientific
and technical progress. What matters is that this role
should be subordinate and should not prevent method from
constituting the very soul of work. It is necessary that
it should appear as provisional, and that routine and
trial and error should always be regarded not as a principle of action, but as make-shifts for the purpose of
filling up the gaps in methodical conceptions; in this
scientific hypotheses are a powerful aid by making us
conceive half-understood phenomena as governed by laws
comparable to those which determine the most clearly
understood phenomena.

[122] LP, p. 114.

[123] LP, pp. 179, 181.

[124] Simone Pétrement, *Simone Weil: A Life*, (New York: Pantheon Books, 1976), p. 69. [Hereafter cited as *Simone Weil:
A Life.*]

NOTES

CHAPTER II

[1]WG, p. 62.

[2]See Simone Pétrement, *Simone Weil a Life*, p. 204. Pétrement also claims that this year of factory work is the clearest line of demarcation between the two periods of Weil's life.

[3]Ibid.

[4]Simone Weil, *La Condition Ouvrière* (Paris: Gallimard, 1951), p. 92 [Hereafter cited as CO.]

[5]SL, pp. 21-22.

[6]WG, p. 66.

[7]Ibid.

[8]WG, p. 67.

[9]WG, pp. 67-68.

[10]WG, p. 68.

[11]WG, pp. 68-69.

[12]WG, p. 69.

[13]Simone Weil, *Pensées sans order concernant l'amour de dieu* (Paris: Gallimard, 1962), p. 149. [Hereafter cited as PSO.]

[14]FLN, p. 132.

[15]FLN, p. 291.

[16]Simone Weil, *On Science, Necessity and the Love of God* (London: Oxford University Press, 1968), p. 174. [Hereafter cited as SN.]

[17]SN, p. 193.

[18]SN, p. 170.

[19]SN, p. 171.

[20]SN, pp. 170, 171.

[21]The term 'personality' has a technical sense for Weil as being essentially a social concept and is to be sharply delineated from that which is sacred in a person. She writes in "Human

271

Personality" (Simone Weil, *Selected Essays 1934-1943* [London: Oxford University Press, 1962], [Hereafter cited as SE.]): "For the full expression of personality depends upon its being inflated by social prestige; it is a social privilege" (p. 21).

[22]WG, p. 146.

[23]WG, p. 149.

[24]SN, p. 171.

[25]WG, p. 142.

[26]WG, p. 148.

[27]SN, p. 173.

[28]WG, p. 153. The friends of Job are an excellent example of the transferral of the contempt for crime to the afflicted. Even the Hebrew redactor cannot rise above this feeling when he introduces Elihu, who ostensibly is to vindicate God. Although Job is by hypothesis just, Elihu, nevertheless says:

> God does not spurn the blameless men or let the sinner live on in all his power . . . Once you lived in luxury unbounded with rich food piled high on your table. But you did not execute justice on the wicked, you cheated orphaned children of their rights . . . Avoid any tendency to wrong doing, *for such has been the cause of your trials* (Job 36.5, 16-17,21, emphasis mine).

[29]See SN, p. 149.

> Everyone feels the existence of evil and feels horror at it and wants to get free from it. Evil is neither sin nor suffering; it is both at the same time, it is something common to both. For they are linked together; sin makes us suffer and suffering makes us evil, and this indissoluble complex of suffering and sin is the evil in which we are submerged against our will, and to our horror. A part of the evil that is within us we project back into the objects of our attention and desire; and they reflect it back to us, as if the evil came from them. It is for this reason that any place where we find ourselves submerged in evil inspires us with hatred and contempt.

[30]WG, pp. 153-154.

[31]SN, p. 173.

[32]SN, p. 174.

[33]Ibid.

[34]Ibid.

[35]SN, p. 196.

[36] SN, p. 197.

[37] SN, p. 24.

[38] SN, p. 25.

[39] SN, p. 171.

[40] SN, p. 197.

[41] Simone Weil, *The Notebooks of Simone Weil* (London: Routledge, 1956), p. 504. [Hereafter cited as NB.]

[42] SB, p. 545.

[43] NB, p. 294.

[44] SN, p. 172.

[45] SN, pp. 171-172.

[46] SN, p. 181.

[47] Hereafter the use of the term 'contradiction' will refer to one of the following sense, and should not be equated with the standard logical definition. The usage of the term is unavoidable because of Weil's own use of it in texts that shall be quoted.

[48] NB, p. 410.

[49] Plato, *Republic*, 523b-c. The point which Plato leads up to is that in perception, we see, for example, a man as one thing yet many things such as arms, legs, etc. This 'contradiction' evokes thought of essence, particularly under mathematical forms, to see how both can be true. In later dialogues (e.g. *Parmenides* 132d-133a; *Philebus* 14d) he drops this line of reasoning as being a truism and not paradoxical. Weil's point, however, does not rest on the perceptual problem of how one can be many things.

[50] Simone Weil, *Gravity and Grace* (London: Routledge, 1952), p. 93. [Hereafter cited as GG.]

[51] NB, p. 46.

[52] By this equivalence it becomes plain that the logical form of contradiction as (p & not-p) *cannot* be what Weil means, since this form only considers things that are commensurate. This has great significance for Weil's metaphysics of good and evil, for if 'contradiction' is taken at its face value, it would land Weil in a sort of Manichaean dualism, instead of the monistic position she clearly held in which the Good is supreme. By using incommensuration, however, she can see opposition to Good, but an opposition that is not final and which can exist in a world along side the Good. An evil that is logically contradictory to Good, that is, one that is on the same level as Good, cannot be mediated into any unity.

[53]See Sir T. L. Heath, *The Thirteen Books of Euclid's Elements*, vol. II, pp. 117, 118:

> In its primitive sense λόγος was only used of a ratio between commensurables, i.e. a ratio which could be expressed, and the manner of expressing it is indicated in the proposition, Eucl. x.5, which proves that *commensurable magnitudes have to one another the ratio which a number has to a number*. That this was the primitive meaning of λόγος is proved by the use of the term ἄλογος for the incommensurable which means *irrational* in the sense of *not having a ratio* to something taken as rational (ῥητός). . . . But it may happen that the two magnitudes have no common measure i.e. are incommensurable . . . the magnitudes would then *have no ratio* in the primitive sense. But the word λόγος, ratio, acquires in Euclid, Book V, wider sense covering the *relative magnitude* of incommensurables as well as commensurables; as stated in Euclid's 4th definition 'magnitudes are said to have a *ratio* to one another which can, when multiplied, exceed one another,' and finite incommensurables have this property as much as commensurables."

[54]NB, p. 162.

[55]NB, p. 410.

[56]FLN, p. 109.

[57]FLN, p. 131. The notion of the unity of absolute incommensurates (or contradictories) is not unique to Weil. It was a notion held by the 15th century cardinal and Platonist, Nicholas of Cusa, who argued in his *Of Learned Ignorance* (English translation, London: Routledge and Kegan Paul, 1954) that "God encompasses all things, even contradictories" (Book I sec. 22, p. 49). Weil had read Cusanus with obvious great approval. However, she never discusses him at any length, which is a pity, since she holds a number of ideas that are quite close to his.

[58]NB, p. 147.

[59]NB, p. 386.

[60]SN, p. 157.

[61]Austin Farrer in *Faith and Speculation* (New York: New York University Press, 1967) makes much the same point. He writes of the believer's reasons for believing as he does: "The gospel offers God to me as good, not simply as fact. In embracing the good I am convinced of the fact" (p. 10). Furthermore: "That to know real beings we must exercise our actual relation with them. . . . We can know nothing of God unless we can do something about him" (p. 22). For a full examination of the believer's reasons, see Diogenes Allen, *The Reasonableness of Faith* (Washington: Corpus Books, 1968).

[62]SN, p. 176.

[63]Ibid.

[64]SN, p. 194.

[65]FLN, p. 120.

[66]FLN, p. 103.

[67]See NB, p. 515: "In conditional necessity, no limit is inscribed. The sequence of conditions is without limit. Limit is only inscribed in a relationship between several conditions which compensate each other, in an order."

[68]NB, p. 190.

[69]NB, p. 515.

[70]FLN, p. 88.

[71]In fact, Weil derives this dual causality and the two sense of necessity from Plato's *Timaeus*. Platonic necessity (ἀνάγκη) is not what we have come to mean by necessity, that is, the inexorable ordered laws of thought. Instead, ἀνάγκη is chaotic and arbitrary and opposes rationality as a principle separate from reason. Once God creates the world, however, this ἀνάγκη is ordered (although it occasionally creates a bit of disorder in the attempt to live only as rationalists) and thus takes on a new sense, wherein it is persuaded by Wisdom towards the Good. Thus there are two senses to necessity, as either the abstracted unreasoning principle of creation, or with the order under which it submits to goodness.

[72]FLN, p. 134.

[73]NB, p. 99.

[74]Dante, *The Divine Comedy*, Paridiso, canto I.

[75]WG, p. 161.

[76]See NB, p. 60:

May the whole universe become for me a second body in both senses. But one only attains to this by a methodical transformation of oneself. It is through action—a certain non-immediate of action, requiring an apprenticeship—that the blind man's stick becomes a prolongation of the body.

[77]NB, p. 242.

[78]SN, p. 192.

[79]SN, p. 198.

[80]SN, p. 176.

[81]Ibid.

[82]Ibid.

[83]SN, pp. 176-177.

[84]For further treatment of this point, in which Christ's actual historic crucifixion is needed for mediation, see Diogenes Allen and Eric Springsted, "Le Malheur: une Énigme (Simone Weil et Epictéte)," in *Cahiers Simone Weil*, vol. II, no. 4, pp. 184-196.

[85]SN, p. 179.

[86]SN, p. 177.

[87]NB, p. 235.

[88]Jacques Cabaud, *Simone Weil* (London: Harvill Press, 1964), p. 212. [Hereafter cited as *Simone Weil*.]

[89]NB, p. 414.

[90]SN, p. 197.

[91]SN, p. 194.

[92]SN, p. 197. I assume her to mean the Logos sort of necessity.

[93]NB, p. 331.

[94]See SN, p. 194:

> The Cross of Christ is the only source of light bright enough to illumine affliction. Wherever there is affliction, in any age or any country, the Cross of Christ is the truth of it. Any man, whatever his beliefs may be, has his part in the Cross of Christ if he loves truth to the point of facing affliction rather than escape into depths of falsehood.

[95]SN, p. 195.

[96]NB, p. 413.

[97]NB, p. 414.

[98]Simone Weil, *Quelque réflexions autour de la notion de valeur*, unpublished essay.

[99]Ibid.

[100]See Miklos Veto, *La Métaphysique Religieuse de Simone Weil* (Paris: Vrin, 1971), p. 25:

> The most important of our errors, our fundamental error in the sense that it founds our very existence, is to seek in a perspective. All finite being is under the

law of perspective, which distorts in a double sense.
To be under perspective is not to say simply that there
is an inevitable alteration between the world as it is
in itself and the way it presents itself to us. To have
a perspective signifies having a point of view, which
is to say, to be at the center of a field of vision.
Men who live in space and time cannot avoid finding themselves in such a center of vision; what is a problem is
that they end up considering themselves as centers at the
metaphysical and moral level as well.

[Hereafter this book will be cited as *La Métaphysique Religieuse
de SW.*]

[101]WG, pp. 200-201.

[102]FLN, p. 269.

[103]NB, p. 414.

[104]Ibid.

[105]Ibid.

[106]Ibid.

[107]NB, p. 415.

[108]NB, p. 414.

[109]NB, p. 415.

[110]NB, pp. 414-415.

[111]NB, p. 416.

[112]NB, p. 415.

[113]IC, p. 70.

[114]WG, p. 145.

[115]WG, p. 145.

[116]SN, p. 182.

[117]SN, p. 191.

[118]SN, p. 173.

[119]SN, p. 181.

[120]Ibid.

[121]Ibid.

[122]SE, p. 10.

[123]SE, p. 219. There is a strong difference here between Weil and the process theologians of the twentieth century. In Weil, God is noted first by an absence and a need for his love which is specifically unrepresentable. In the course of actual interaction with his love God becomes defined. In process theology there is a presently defined want or desire which must be satisfied for there to be a God.

[124]There is obviously, something here that is strongly suggestive of Plato's theory of Reminiscence and his doctrine that "like is known by like." These two ideas have not been seriously considered for a long time. For her (and she claims for Plato as well), the issue is not one of bare knowledge, but of love. "Like to like" is appropriate in this context, for if there is to be a loving communion between two beings, it must presuppose an equality, if only a proportional one.

[125]For Weil, there are two parts of the soul which correspond to and are defined by the two aspects of spiritual activity. She illustrates this point by using biblical parables.

> "Who among you, having a servant who labors or tends the flocks, when he returns from the fields would say to him: 'Come quickly and sit down to eat?' Wouldn't he say, 'Prepare my dinner and gird yourself, serve me for eating and drinking, and after that you shall eat and drink?' And would he be grateful to the slave because he executed his orders? So you too, when you have done all that is commanded of you, should say: 'We are slaves without value; we have done what we were obliged to.'" (Luke 17:7)
> The servant who receives love, gratitude and even service from his master is not the one who also plows and harvests. That is another one.
> It isn't a matter of choosing between ways of serving God. These two slaves represent the same soul under two different relations, or, two inseparable parts of the same soul. (PSO, p. 144)

[126]SN, p. 148.

[127]Ibid.

[128]SN, p. 149.

[129]SN, p. 150.

[130]Ibid.

[131]Veto, La Métaphysique Religieuse de SW, p. 47.

[132]SN, p. 150.

[133]The concept of the μετοξύ will be further taken up in the last chapter which will discuss at greater length the Platonic basis of this idea and then what some of the most obvious μετοξύ are.

[134]SN, p. 153.

[135]Ibid.

[136] In an unpublished fragment, Weil describes character as "an invariant common to the possible reactions of one and the same person and which limits his possible reactions." The state of character involves a "regime of attention" and can be changed through an increase or decrease in that attention.

[137] Iris Murdoch has played this theme of attention and duty often and in various ways in her novels. For example, in *The Unicorn* the chief character, a colossal egotist, has an experience of a perfect love which allows him for the first time in his life to recognize the independent existence and goodness of other beings. Unfortunately, he never acts on this and shortly returns to his benighted ways. In *The Nice and the Good*, a somewhat Pharasaic lawyer, who is, nevertheless well intentioned and disciplined, has a similar experience but he does act on it and his continued moral improvement is quite evident. In *The Sea, The Sea* there is another clossal egotist who also has such an experience. Unlike the hero of *The Unicorn*, at the end of the novel we see him begin to advance morally. This theme has also been taken up theologically and vis-a-vis Murdoch by Diogenes Allen in *Finding Our Father* (John Knox Press, Atlanta, 1974).

[138] One of the best example of what Weil understands to be the interplay of divine grace and human activity is to be found at SN, 151, in one of the analogical and symbolic μεταξύ of work. She explains there that the law of gravity is sovereign over the earth and the one thing that can overcome gravity is the solar energy which causes seeds to grow upwards. This she says is an image of grace. She then goes on to say it is not the farmer's job to go in search of solar energy or even to make use of it, but to arrange everything in such a way that the plants capable of using it and transmitting it to us in the form of food will receive it in the best possible conditions. And the effort that the farmer puts into the work does not come from himself but from the energy supplied to him by food, in other words, by the same solar energy contained in plants and the flesh of animals nourished by plants. In the same way the only effort we can make towards the good is so to dispose of our soul that it can receive grace, and it is grace which supplies the energy needed for this effort.

[139] WG, p. 137.

[140] WG, p. 138.

[141] Ibid.

[142] Ibid.

[143] WG, p. 139.

[144] WG, p. 143.

[145] WG, p. 147. The ideas of decreation and affliction on the Cross of Christ as being the means to salvation have often brought charges of nihilism against Weil. From what has been said here, it should be evident that this is not so. Weil is

not arguing that we have to ripped apart by force before God's
goodness can be realized, but that through God's love in us we
can recognize the afflicted and through solidarity with them give
them life in the same manner as by the Son's being afflicted we
have the possibility of life. But this can only be the case if
we are willing to lose our lives for his sake, for if we try to
gain them we shall surely lose them.

[146]WG, p. 158.

[147]Ibid.

[148]WG, p. 159.

[149]WG, p. 176.

[150]WG, p. 169.

[151]WG, pp. 195, 197.

[152]Weil's view of the Eucharist tends towards a strong doctrine of the Real Presence. She did not seem to care much for
the descriptions of transubstantiation, except as they included
this element. To my knowledge, she never considered any other
views, such as consubstantiation or symbolic re-enactment theories.

[153]WG, p. 202.

[154]WG, p. 204.

[155]One of the finest examples of this in terms of a friendship where necessity has triumphed over free consent can be found
in Shakespeare's *Measure for Measure*. There Claudio is condemned
to death. He can be saved, in theory, if his sister Isabella,
a novice nun, will consent to the governor's amorous advances.
Rather than bear his just punishment and respect his sister's
intentions towards God, he insists that she give in. She, however, refuses on the grounds that if he dies he does so at the
hands of justice and retains a possibility of salvation. If she
should give in, it means the violation of her consent to God.
She cannot do what Claudio asks because this would consitute a be-
trayal of God, although she is willing to lay down her life for
Claudio.

[156]WG, p. 204.

[157]WG, p. 205.

[158]WG, p. 203.

[159]WG, p. 209.

[160]Ibid.

[161]SL, pp. 136-137.

[162]SN, p. 111.

[163]Ibid.

[164]FLN, p. 132.

[165]SN, p. 183.

CHAPTER III

[1]Simone Weil, *Letter to a Priest* (New York: Putnam's 1954), p. 24. [Hereafter cited as LR].

[2]LR, p. 24. The claim sounds fantastic and can be argued against on the historical grounds that it was St. John and not Jesus who formed the words in question, particularly because the evangelist seems peculiarly influenced by Greek philosophical ideas which he uses to give the book its form. This may be so, but unless it can be shown that *ergo* this idea cannot be the result of divine inspiration, a demonstration which in the past has relied on an anti-Greek prejudice, there is no reason not to claim that St. John uses mediation because it does reflect so well the divine love.

[3]IC, p. 198.

[4]LR, p. 67.

[5]LR, p. 17.

[6]LR, p. 46.

[7]LR, p. 65.

[8]IC, p. 70.

[9]Ibid.

[10]LR, p. 20.

[11]IC, p. 70.

[12]IC, p. 71.

[13]SN, p. 90.

[14]IC, pp. 51, 52-53.

[15]A notable exception is her treatment of Aeschylus' *Prometheus Bound* in the essays, *Zeus and Prometheus* and *Prometheus* (IC, pp. 56-74). Weil sees Prometheus as a Mediator, but even so this contributes nothing new to the idea of mediation, being an application of it.

[16]SN, p. 92.

[17]*Theaetetus* 176b, Weil's translation. SN, p. 93.

[18] Ibid.

[19] Ibid.

[20] SN, p. 93.

[21] *Republic* Book II, 360ff.

[22] *Gorgias* 523ff.

[23] Ibid, Weil translation. SN, p. 95.

[24] Ibid.

[25] SN, p. 96. Weil is correct on both counts. Plato does not say this explicitly but he does certainly imply it. A particularly relevant text for establishing this claim can be found in the *Meno*. There the cocky Meno comes to debate with Socrates, but in the course of the questioning is reduced to aporetic perplexity, a sort of intellectual death. He then compares Socrates to a sting ray which paralyzes and numbs whomever comes in contact with it. This image is carried forward in the dialogue to the slave boy incident. When the slave boy is attempting to solve the problem of doubling a square reaches confusion, Socrates claims to have numbed him (84b). This numbing, however, Socrates says, is actually good for the boy, because once the boy has reached the state of perplexity wherein he knows that he does not know, he is in a far better position to understand. This numbing, or small death, is a prerequisite for understanding.

[26] *Phaedo*, 64a, 67d, Weil translation. SN, pp. 96-97.

[27] SN, p. 97.

[28] *Republic* Book VI 492-3. The image of the Great Beast is also important in Weil's own work and she uses it often.

[29] *Republic* VI, 493bff. Weil translation, SN, p. 99.

[30] SN, p. 106.

[31] *Republic* Book VI, 492-3, Weil translation, SN, p. 98. Although the passage appears to suggest that the problem of the beast pertains to fifth century Athens, Weil claims that it is meant to be a general problem. She supports this claim by her translation, "there is not, there never has been, and there never will be . . . ." (οὔτε γὰρ γίγνεται οὔτε γέγονεν οὐδὲ οὖν μὴ γένηται ἀλλοῖν ἦθος . . .).

[32] SN, p. 99.

[33] SN, p. 101.

[34] Anders Nygren, *Agape and Eros* New York: Harper & Row, 1953), p. 92.

[35] IC, p. 133. This is not to say that Weil does not recognize the phenomenon of egocentricity. The distinction is that egoism is unbridled love for what is the self; egocentricity is

loving and ordering things which revolve around the self, but which, being products of necessity, are independent of it.

[36]On this dilemma, see R. A. Markus, "The Dialectic of Eros in Plato's Symposium" in *Plato* vol II, ed. G. Vlastos (New York: Doubleday, Anchor Books, 1971). [Hereafter referred to as The Dialectic of Eros.] The argument presented here generally follows that of Markus.

[37]Diotima is a priestess of the mysteries. This fact, which Weil carefully points out, is significant in that the doctrine of love seems to be deliberately associated with a religious love.

[38]*Symposium* 205e-206a.

[39]Ibid., 206 a.

[40]Ibid., 206b,3.

[41]Ibid., 212 a.

[42]Strictly speaking, in Plato's metaphysics, the Good is not a form but stands above the forms and gives them reality. The Good of the *Republic*, at least for Weil, is equated with the One of the later dialogues. Here while the Good is not a form it does embrace all forms and is indeed the one mind which knows all of them as they are. Weil also equates the forms as perfections with God's ideas and attributes, and so while there is a certain difference in Plato between the Good (or One) and the forms, the transcendence of the forms gives an adequate introduction of the Good which knows them and which is their source. One of the best examples of a Platonic form or idea can be found in modern mathematics in Gödel's theorem. The jist of Gödel's theorem is that in a system or language (for him that of the natural numbers) which has been formalized in symtax with definite axioms into a "meta-language" there appear fundamentally true propositions which are undecidable within the confines of the meta-language and which appear contradictory. If, however, the meta-language is expanded to accomodate this proposition as an axiom in a higher meta-language, still another proposition which is undecidable can be constructed in the new meta-language. This process can go on to infinity. When Gödel proved this theorem for the natural number system he concluded that the natural number system is beyond the constructions of the human mind (and thus in some sense independent of it) and that God alone could know the entire system of which we know only part.

[43]George Santayana, *Platonism and the Spiritual Life* (New York: Harper Torchbooks, 1957), p. 269.

[44]See R. A. Markus, The Dialectic of Eros.

[45]*Symposium* 202e.

[46]The relationship between man and God is somewhat asymmetrical. Although love is the mediator between man and God, it is not really possible to say that God loves man using the

word 'love' in the sense which Plato does. This is because love
is the effect of God on the human soul. In this sense, Plato
uses love for what we do and mediation for what God does. The
intent is the same, however, and simply reverses what Nygren
does, for Nygren makes faith replace love for God and reverses
love for God alone, while yet claiming that the spiritual reality
denoted by 'faith' is the same as the old 'love for God.'

[47]*Republic* 508a.

[48]Ibid., 508b.

[49]Ibid., 508-509b, Weil translation. SN, p. 103.

[50]In *Republic* VII, 518c, Plato says:

> It is with the whole soul that we must turn away from be-
> coming until we become able to bear the contemplation of
> *reality* and of what is most luminous in reality, namely the
> good. So what is required here is a *method* of conversions,
> providing the easiest and most effective way of changing the
> soul's direction" (Weil translation, SN, p. 104).

Weil, in commenting on this, says:

> Therefore in order to turn its eyes towards God the entire
> soul has to turn away from the things which are born and
> perish, from temporal things . . . And this is death. And
> this death is what conversion is . . . Thus it is total
> detachment that is the condition for the love of God, and
> when once the soul has performed the motion of totally de-
> taching itself from the world so as to turn entirely towards
> God, it is illumined by the truth which comes down to it
> from God. This is the very same idea that is at the centre
> of Christian mysticism" (SN, p. 106).

[51]SN, p. 104.

[52]IC, p. 197.

[53]There are, of course, major differences between Plato
and Christianity, the most important of which is the historic
Cross. Weil does give credit to Plato, though, for a premonition
of the Cross in the Just Man passage. But even this passage does
not give redemption, but rather the need to suffer to realize
justice. She writes:

> Plato, in going so far as to suppose that the perfectly
> just man is not recognized as just, even by the gods,
> had *premonition* (my emphasis) of the most piercing words
> of the Gospel: "My God, my God, why have you forsaken
> me?" The reason which Plato gives for the suffering
> of the perfectly just man is different from redemption,
> differing from the substitution of punishment which ap-
> pears in Christianity, and even earlier, in the *Prome-
> theus* of Aeschylus. But there is a bond between the two
> ideas. It is because of the regression set working in

human affairs by original sin that there is this incompatibility between the appearance and the reality, and it
is this which obliges perfect justice to appear here below in the form of a condemned criminal. If we were innocent, the appearance would be of the same color as the
real and have no veil to be torn away (IC, p. 143).

   Other differences between Plato and Christianity include
certain forms of love eheld in high esteem in Christianity, such
as love for children, which do not appear in Plato as well as
Christianity's commitment to the fact that no person while alive
is beyond grace. There are occasional indications in Plato that
some may be presently beyond help. Weil does not usually note
these differences. She does, however, criticize the Greeks for
not seeing the spiritual importance of labor which becomes (as
we shall see in the next chapter) for her one of the prime ways
that an individual participates in Christ's Cross. However, not-
withstanding these differences, Weil's major point is that in
Plato there is a genuine spirituality which has at its roots the
mediation of God in the love engendered in our hearts which is
efficacious for moving towards a fuller unity with God. If there
is a tendency in Weil to overlook some of the particular differences, it is because she is concentrating on the general aspects
of God's meditation and how this is accomplished.

[54] IC, p. 197.

[55] IC, p. 151.

[56] IC, p. 153.

[57] These passages found at IC, pp. 153-158 are: Philolaos,
Diels fragments, 2(B47); 3(B49); 4(B58); 8(B150); 7(B91);
11(B139-160); 6(B62); 10(B61); Plato, *Gorgias* 507d; *Philebus*
16bff.; *Epinomis* 990d; *Timaeus* 31c; *Symposium* 202d, 210d; St.
John, 17:11, 21-23.

[58] IC, p. 159.

[59] A note must be added on this relation between number
and created entites in the Pythagoreans. There is a great deal
of confusion on how exactly they construed this relationship.
Aristotle, who is our best source, speaks of this relationship
in three different ways: 1) at *Metaphysics* 987b28 he writes,
"They say that things themselves are numbers"; 2) at 987b11, he
says "The Pythagoreans say that existing things owe their being
to imitation of numbers"; 3) at 987b32 he says that " . . . they
assumed the elements of matter to be the elements of all that
exists, and the whole universe to be a harmony and number."
These three ways of construing the relation between numbers and
the world appear inconsistent, although in general, it has usually been assumed that #1 is what was really meant by the Pythagoreans. W. K. C. Guthrie (*A History of Greek Philosophy*, vol.
1, *The Earlier Presocratics and the Pythagoreans* [Cambridge:
Cambridge University Press, 1952]) explains the difficulty by
noting that one of the great advances of the Pythagoreans was
that they did discover the extremely important quantitative

aspect of things, and that they also began to discover the non-material formal causes of reality. This was a marked improvement over their predecessors who confused, in Aristotelian terms, material and formal causes in favor of the material. Unfortunately, the Pythagoreans because of an inadequate terminology went to the opposite extreme, and it was this for which Aristotle--"by nature a naturalist rather than a mathematician" (Guthrie, p. 238)--criticized them. Whatever mistake the Pythagoreans made, if indeed they did think that numbers are spatially extended, is due to an over-extension of their original insight about the nature of numbers and their general applicability to things. Weil's position in all this is clear. She takes the Pythagorean numbers to be symbols, and not extended things. Furthermore, in the case at hand, as long as the emphasis is on things, it does not make much difference how the relationship is construed, so long as the point can be made that when talking about numbers in the Pythagoreans, we are mainly talking about things.

[60] IC, p. 159.

[61] Philolaos, Diels 11(B139, 160). Weil translation, emphasis mine.

[62] Quoted at IC, p. 160.

[63] Ibid.

[64] IC, p. 160. Cf. *Symposium* 202e6, . . . ἐν μέσω δὲ ὂν αμφοτέρων συμπλήροι, ὥστε τὸ πᾶν αὐτὸ αὐτῶ συνδεδέσθαι and *Timaeus* 31c δεσμὸν γὰρ ἐν μέσω δεῖ τινα ἀμφοῖν συναγωγον γίγνεσθοι. δεσμῶν δὲ κάλλιστος ὃς ἂν αὐτὸν καὶ τὰ συνδούμενα . . . The comparison has a two-fold significance. On the one hand, it gives a deeper philosophic meaning to the mythological explanation of the mediation of Love. On the other hand, it gives a theological meaning, related to Plato's doctrine of love, to what appears to be only a mathematical passage in the *Timaeus*. In this regard, Love has a far greater metaphysical significance than might otherwise be thought, as well as offering a reasonable transition from Plato's view of love to his view of mediation.

[65] IC, pp. 160-161.

[66] IC, p. 161.

[67] There is an unpublished fragment which appears to be a variant of *The Pythagorean Doctrine* in which Weil says:

When the Pythagoreans speak of number, it is necessary to know that they always have geometric relations, as well as arithmetic ones, in mind, as modern mathematicians do when they talk about generalized number. What the Pythagoreans called number is the relationship of quantities, and in a general manner, all relationship. Ἀριθμος and λόγος are synonyms in their language.

[68] *Epinomis* 990d, Weil translation.

[69] SL, pp. 117-118. Weil involves herself in two staggering historical claims: 1) that geometry arose from a 'love of

Christ,' that is as a search for divine mediation; 2) she seems
to ascribe a theory of real numbers to mathematicians living before Eudoxus who would only have known the natural number system.
An explanation for both these views can be given. 1) Weil shows
(*A Sketch of a History of Greek Science*, IC, pp. 202-208, and
SL, pp. 112-127) a historical progression of geometrical problems
in which the question of proportions is primary. While she recognized that the problems of proportion in general are not identical to those of mediation (a proportion of three terms a/b=b/c)
she says that the study of proportion greatly facilitated the
study of mediation. Here she can subscribe to the weaker case
that somebody, like the Pythagoreans, who were searching for mediation, would find proportions helpful. She says: "In any case,
whether or not geometry had since its first origin been a search
for mediation, it offered this marvel of mediation for the numbers which were deprived of it" (IC, p. 126). 2) What Weil is
actually saying here is not that the Pythagoreans had a *theory*
of real numbers, but that "they were capable of *conceiving* the
real numbers" (SL, p. 116). It is for this reason that she says
when the incommensurates were discovered, that while this discovery may have precipitated a crisis in public confidence and
speech, it nevertheless was not calamitous for geometers and
philosophers. It was, in fact, something they expected and which
allowed them to round out their system. See SL, pp. 115-116.

[70] IC, p. 162.

[71] IC, p. 164.

[72] IC, p. 165.

[73] IC, p. 166.

[74] IC, pp. 164-165.

[75] IC, p. 166.

[76] Ibid.

[77] IC, p. 167.

[78] Ibid.

[79] Ibid.

[80] *Timaeus* 31c, Weil translation, IC, p. 157.

[81] IC, p. 167.

[82] IC, p. 168.

[83] Ibid.

[84] *Philebus* 16d.

[85] Because of the importance of this passage, I shall reproduce Weil's translation in full.

No more beautiful way either does, or ever can exist. I
am perpetually in love with it, but often it escapes me
and leaves me abandoned, not knowing what to do . . .
Herein is a gift of the gods to men, that at least is clear
to me. And from whatever habitation of the gods it was
tossed by a Prometheus, there came at the same time an
illuminating fire; and the ancients who were better than
we are, and lived nearer the gods, have transmitted this
tradition to us. Here it is: that the realities called
eternal derive from the one and the many, and carry, implanted within them, the determinate and the indeterminate.
We should, therefore, since this is the eternal order of
things, seek to implant a unity in every kind of domain.
We shall find it, for it is there. Once we have grasped
this unity, we should examine duality, if that is present,
or else trinity, or some other number. Then the same
subdivisions must be made upon each one of the subordinate
unities. Finally, what at the beginning appeared not only
as one, and many, and unlimited at once, appears also with
a definite number. One should not apply the idea of the
indeterminate to the plurality until one has perfectly well
seen the number of that plurality, that number which is
the intermediary between the indeterminate and unity.
Only then should one abandon the specific unity of all
things and lost oneself in the indeterminate (infinite).
The gods then, as I was saying, have transmitted this
method of research for our use in learning, and in
teaching. The educated men of our time fix unity at random, and the plurality more quickly or more slowly than
should be, and pass from the unity to things which are
indeterminate; the intermediary escapes them (IC, pp.
155-156).

[86] Scholarship has taken this Prometheus to be Pythagoras.
Weil herself understood this, but she wanted to make the tradition even older.

[87] IC, p. 168.

[88] Ibid.

[89] Ibid.

[90] IC, p. 169. For at least human beings, the reproduction
of the primordial hierarchy comes through τεχνή. The word τεχνή
is highly loaded, however, for both Plato and Weil. The common
English translation of this word as 'skill' or 'art' really
does not capture its sense. A τεχνή for Plato is something that
involves a heavily underlined theoretical aspect of knowing. In
this sense, τεχνή is knowing something, and although the word is
applied to mundane activities such as cobbling and carpentry,
Plato indicates (*Philebus* 55e, see also *Republic* 522c, *Laws* 818)
that "it is the extent of the use of mathematical techniques that
makes a τεχνή a worthwhile τεχνή (J. C. B. Gosling, *Plato Philebus* [Oxford: Oxford University Press, 1975], p. 154). At the
same time, a τεχνή produces and is a definite activity. In this
sense, the method of the *Philebus* is not only something to be
known and applied; it is also the philosopher's τεχνή, that is,

what he needs to be doing to be a philosopher. Moreover, the
τεκνή of the philosopher which is thinking the method in life
and thought is a microcosmic reproduction of God's own creative
activity which we see in the *Timaeus* where God creates a world
with mathematical knowledge and skill.

[91] IC, p. 169.

[92] FLN, p. 174.

[93] *Timaeus* 34b.

[94] IC, p. 96.

[95] IC, p. 170.

[96] IC, p. 172.

[97] Ibid.

[98] IC, p. 173.

[99] IC, p. 174.

[100] IC, p. 175.

[101] Ibid.

[102] IC, p. 176.

[103] IC, p. 177.

[104] I am not claiming that this was Weil's deliberate intention in giving this fifth form of harmony. What I am claiming
is that once this form of harmony is completed, it gives Weil a
very strong reason for saying that her work was a solid whole.

[105] This, of course, is a point which Weil has already used
in *Science et Perception dans Descartes*.

[106] Philolaos, Diels 11(B139-160), Weil translation.

[107] IC, p. 179.

[108] IC, p. 178.

[109] IC, p. 179. Weil takes this example from the French
philosopher Jules Lagneau, who was the teacher of Alain, who, in
turn, was Weil's teacher.

[110] IC, p. 178.

[111] It should be stressed that the ἄπειρον does *not* constitute what Aristotle called prime matter. Matter for both
Plato and Weil is ultimately knowable through its mathematical
forms and it is not so in Aristotle. It does, however, keep one
from pure idealism.

[112] IC, p. 180.

[113] IC, p. 181.

[114] Ibid.

[115] Ibid.

[116] Ibid.

[117] Ibid.

[118] IC, p. 182.

[119] Ibid.

[120] Ibid.

[121] Ibid.

[122] Ibid.

[123] IC, p. 183.

[124] IC, pp. 183-184.

[125] IC, p. 185.

[126] Ibid.

[127] IC, p. 186.

[128] IC, p. 97.

[129] IC, p. 186.

[130] IC, p. 187.

[131] IC, p. 188.

[132] IC, p. 190.

[133] IC, p. 193.

[134] IC, p. 198.

[135] IC, p. 194.

[136] Ibid.

[137] IC, p. 195.

NOTES

CHAPTER IV

[1]G. Kahn, "Valeur du travail manuel chez Simone Weil," *Cahiers Simone Weil*, vol. I, no. 3, p. 58.

[2]The term μεταξύ is a Greek adverb or preposition meaning 'intermediary' or 'between,' although Weil uses it as a noun, variously singular or plural. It is a term which mainly occurs in the *Notebooks*, and occasionally in parentheses in translations as the Greek word which has just been rendered. It, therefore, appears to be a shorthand term for her technical sense of 'intermediary'; one which is particularly revealing, as we shall see, because of its roots in her understanding of Platonic mediation.

[3]SN, p. 194.

[4]R. Rees, *Simone Weil: A Sketch for a Portrait* (Carbondale, Illinois: Southern Illinois Press, 1966), p. 76.

[5]J. Cabaud, *Simone Weil*, p. 139.

[6]Ibid., p. 227.

[7]J. P. Little in her dissertation, *The Theme of Mediation in the Writings of Simone Weil*, takes this tack. She examines those things (usually symbols) which Weil uses as intermediaries and then asserts that thematically they have their union in Christ. This is in contrast to the method of determing what a μεταξύ ought to be and then using this determination to decide whether anything that presents itself to the mind is in fact a μεταξύ or not.

[8]Cabaud, *Simone Weil*, p. 227.

[9]SN, p. 113.

[10]NB, p. 48.

[11]Before confusion ensues, it needs to be noted that Weil uses the term μεταξύ in both a subjective and objective sense for reasons that shall become clear later. At this point it is necessary to realize this when she moves from one to another.

[12]NB, p. 596.

[13]NB, p. 48.

[14]NB, p. 233.

[15]CO, p. 266.

[16]NB, p. 222.

[17]At NB, p. 22, Weil summarizes a list of possible μεταξύ as "everything that wrenches."

[18]NB, p. 258.

[19]NB, p. 328.

[20]FLN, p. 132.

[21]FLN, p. 244.

[22]NB, p. 596.

[23]See NB, p. 497: "Two prisoners whose cells adjoin communicate with each other by knocking on the wall. The wall is the thing which separates them but it is also their means of communication. It is the same with us and God. Every separation is a link."

[24]SE, p. 219.

[25]NB, pp. 206-207. That Weil clearly intends the μεταξύ also to be bridges from transcendence can be seen in some of the μεταξύ she cites, such as "pure compassion" (NB 282); the Platonic "madness of love" (NB 318); "obligations" (NB 250); and "acceptance of suffering" (NB 103). All of these things she understands to bear the marks of divine grace.

[26]NB, p. 21.

[27]Ibid.

[28]See NB, p. 22. "We do not choose our sensations. But we do choose (subject to an apprenticeship) what we feel through their medium. A good·deal of choice." This notion of apprenticeship is also closely connected with her technical term 'reading.' Of this she says:

> *Reading.* All we are given (in a sense) is sensations, and whatever we may do about it we can never, never think anything else (in a sense) but sensations. But we can never actually think sensations; we read through them, as through a medium. What do we read? Not just anything at all, according to inclination. Nor, of course, something which does not depend in any way whatever on ourselves. The world is a text containing several meanings and we pass from one meaning to another by an effort--an effort in which the body always participates, just as when we are learning the alphabet of a foreign language, this alphabet has got to enter into our hand by dint of forming the characters. Apart from that, any change in the manner of thinking is illusory (NB, p. 23).

On the notion of 'reading' see B.-Cl. Farron-Landry's excellent "Lecture et non-lecture chez Simone Weil", *Cahiers Simone Weil*, vol. III, no. 4, pp. 225-244. Farron-Landry's interpretation is I think independent support for the present interpretation of the μεταξύ.

[29] NB, p. 23.

[30] The implicit loves are, of course, other major examples.

[31] NB, p. 193.

[32] SN, p. 117.

[33] SN, pp. 117-118.

[34] SN, p. 118.

[35] SN, p. 122.

[36] SN, p. 124.

[37] Ibid.

[38] SN, p. 129.

[39] SN, p. 125.

[40] I.e. *God in Plato*, see the quote corresponding to n.8.

[41] The underlying love is the love which binds the Son to the Father, or in other words, the Spirit, which proceeding from the Father and the Son brings grace and love. The intermediate forms of love are then, theologically, the effects of the Spirit. The grace which comes through the Spirit is two-fold. In the first place, it is the means by which the essential goodness of God enters human life. Second, by this love in the Spirit, one can be led through a process of sanctification to full recognition of the Mediator, through whom the Spirit proceeds. It is because the Spirit does proceed through the Son that the love it brings has the marks of Christ and is the reason Weil can say that any genuine love has Christ present in it.

[42] It would be technically more correct for Weil to use the term ὁπόσα rather than μεταξύ, if she does have the *Philebus* in mind. The term μεταξύ, however, has the advantage of bringing out the idea of mediation more clearly. She does introduce, though, her first discussion of the μεταξύ (NB 21-23) by using ὁπόσα and then quickly switching to μεταξύ.

[43] This is to say that the limits of the physical may be such that they can only affect the whole to a certain degree and no more. Because of the Cross, we can see that there is no point at which necessity *need* destroy the soul.

[44] NB, pp. 62-64.

[45] IC, p. 188.

[46]FLN, pp. 138-139.

[47]FLN, p. 139.

[48]See SE, p. 221:

(there is a) connection in human nature between the
desire for good, which is the essence of man, and his
sensibility . . . Because of it, when a man's life is
destroyed or damaged by some wound or privation of soul
or body, which is due to other men's actions or negligence,
it is not only his sensibility that suffers but also his
aspiration towards the good . . . On the other hand,
there are cases when it is only a man's sensibility that
is affected . . ."

Weil makes much the same point in the essay "Human Personality"
(SE, pp. 9-34) when she argues that although things such as
eyes are not essential to a person's spiritual life, one cannot,
nonetheless, go around poking eyes out. She says "What would
stay (the hand) is the knowledge that if someone were to put
out his eyes, his sould would be lacerated by the thought that
harm was being done to him" (SE, p. 10).

[49]PSO, pp. 31, 33.

[50]Simone Weil, *The Need for Roots* (New York: Harper & Row,
1952), p. 3.   [Hereafter cited as NR.]

[51]Ibid.

[52]Ibid.

[53]Ibid.

[54]NR, pp. 3-4.

[55]SE, p. 18.

[56]SE, p. 21. Weil here uses the terms 'person' and 'personality' as the ego based non-essential aspects of man which depend
upon the force of prestige. She contends that these things have
come to be confused with what is truly sacred in a human being.

[57]NR, p. 4.

[58]NR, pp. 4-5.

[59]NR, p. 5.

[60]This text at SE, pp. 219-227, along with another titled
"Statement of Obligations" is under the single title of "Draft
for a Statement of Human Obligations." The "Profession of Faith"
is in a sense a preliminary draft to the opening of *The Need
for Roots* but one which is perhaps more remarkable than the
finished product.

[61]SE, p. 219.

[62] Ibid.

[63] SE, p. 220.

[64] Ibid.

[65] SE, p. 221.

[66] There is an obvious lack of mention of Christ's mediation here. Remembering the third and fourth forms of harmony,
that of God and man, and man and man, we can understand that this
link exists between man and God because Christ became man, and
the respect we owe others is due to the fact that in participating
in the Mediator we act as He did towards our fellows.

[67] SE, p. 222.

[68] SE, p. 221.

[69] Ibid.

[70] NR, p. 6.

[71] NR, p. 7.

[72] Ibid.

[73] Ibid.

[74] Ibid.

[75] NR, p. 8.

[76] S. Pétrement, *Simone Weil: A Life*, p. 500.

[77] See NB, p. 250:

> How does one learn to read obligations? In the same
> way as one learns to read, essentially through the at-
> tention, the latter being helped by exercises in which the
> body takes part. Every time one performs an obligation
> one makes progress in this art, provided this performance
> be accompanied by genuine attention. The attention in
> apprenticeship is directed towards what one does not
> yet know.

[78] At NB pp. 258 and 298, Weil does, in fact, call a city
a μεταξύ. Cabaud points out that Venice in Weil's unfinished
play *Venise Sauvée* plays the role of a μεταξύ (*Simone Weil*,
p. 199) and in the essay "What was the Occitanian Inspiration?"
that Weil considers the Occitanian culture as a μεταξύ (p. 222).

[79] For other creatures, the prime form good may take would
be entirely different. Creatures entirely subject to necessity
have a limited goodness in their blind obedience to necessity,
but it would make no sense to say of turtles, for example, that
they have even limited obligations.

[80] NR, p. 12.

[81] In this list as it appears in *The Need for Roots*, initiative is not given a separate entry. Instead, it is discussed together with responsibility. Also freedom of opinion and truth are separated in the list. In the "Draft for a Statement of Human Obligations," however, Weil does pair them together (SE, p. 225). She also makes initiative and responsibility distinct, linked needs (SE, p. 226). The draft also has one pair that is missing from *The Need for Roots* and that is solitude or privacy and social life.

[82] NR, p. 43.

[83] Ibid.

[84] NR, p. 10.

[85] Ibid.

[86] Ibid.

[87] It should be apparent that for Weil the order of the universe is really more than an example for ordering social relations, for in fact, as we have seen in *The Pythagorean Doctrine*, any true order within the world is a microcosm related to the order of the world. The theory of mediation is particularly helpful for understanding why order is not only a need of the soul, but the first of them.

[88] NR, p. 11.

[89] Ibid.

[90] NR, p. 216.

[91] NR, p. 212. By suggesting that politics is a "composition on a multiple plane" Weil recalls the passage of NB 62-64 where she speaks of the μεταξύ as a "composition on several planes." I believe Weil has mediation in mind in making this statement about politics.

[92] NR, pp. 218-219.

[93] NR, p. 239.

[94] NR, p. 241.

[95] Ibid.

[96] NR, pp. 243, 244.

[97] NR, p. 245.

[98] NR, p. 252.

[99] NR, p. 253.

[100] Ibid.

[101]NR, p. 255.

[102]NR, pp. 256-257.

[103]NR, p. 262. In this union of the mind Weil replays a central theme of her early works, namely, the "original pact between mind and the universe." See, for example, OL, p. 124.

[104]NR, p. 262.

[105]NR, p. 282.

[106]NR, p. 266.

[107]NR, p. 271.

[108]NR, p. 279.

[109]NR, p. 277.

[110]NR, p. 285.

[111]Ibid.

[112]NR, p. 284.

[113]NR, p. 291.

[114]NR, p. 292.

[115]NR, p. 293.

[116]NR, p. 295. This division corresponds plainly to the division in the fifth form of harmony, wherein what is brute force becomes the object for intellectual contemplation of mathematical relations, which in turn, becomes the object of consent by which we participate in God.

[117]NR, p. 300.

[118]NR, pp. 300, 301.

[119]NR, p. 94.

[120]CO, p. 265.

[121]Ibid.

[122]CO, p. 266.

[123]FLN, p. 91.

NOTES

CONCLUSION

[1] LR, p. 33.

[2] LR, pp. 14-15.

[3] FLN, p. 123.

[4] FLN, p. 147.

[5] IC, p. 52.

[6] SN, p. 99.

[7] LR, p. 85.

[8] W. V. O. Quine, "Two Dogmas of Empiricism" in *From a Logical Point of View* (New York: Harper Torchbooks, 1963), pp. 42-43.

BIBLIOGRAPHY

The following is a select bibliography of Weil's works in French and English translation. In cases where there has been more than one edition, I have listed only one, not necessarily the first. English editions often overlap in their contents. For a complete bibliography of primary and secondary works see J. P. Little's *Simone Weil: A Bibliography*, (London, Cutler & Grant, 1973, update 1980). See also my "The Works of Simone Weil" (*Theology Today*, Oct. 1981) for a description of some of the most important essays by Weil. This also includes information about content overlaps in English editions.

I. Weil's Works in French

    A.   L'Attente de Dieu, Fayard, Paris, 1966
          Cahiers I, II, III, Plon, Paris, 1970
          La Condition ouvrière, Gallimard, Paris, 1951
          La Connaissance surnaturelle, Gallimard, Paris, 1950
          Ecrits historiques et politiques, Gallimard, Paris, 1960
          Ecrits de Londres et dernières, Gallimard, Paris, 1957 lettres,
          L'Enracinement, Gallimard, Paris, 1949
          Intuitions pré-chrétiennes, LaColombe, Paris, 1951
          Leçons de philosophie de SW, Plon, Paris, 1959 (presented by Anne Reynaud)
          Lettre à un religieux, Gallimard, Paris, 1951
          Oppression et liberté, Gallimard, Paris, 1955
          Pensées sans ordre concernant l'amour de Dieu, Gallimard, Paris, 1962
          La Pesanteur et la grâce, Plon, Paris, 1947
          Poèmes, suivis de 'Venise Sauvée', Lettre de Paul Valery, Gallimard, Paris, 1968
          La Source grecque, Gallimard, Paris, 1953
          Sur la science, Gallimard, Paris, 1965

    B.   The following are unedited manuscripts and fragments in the collection of Weil's manuscripts in the Bibliotheque Nationale in Paris which have been used in the preparation of this book.
          De la Médiation (Quand las Pythagoriciens . . .) (a variant fragment of "The Pythagorean Doctrine"?)

De la notion de droit (a variant of "Human
    Personality")
Quelques réflexions autour de la notion de valeur
    (essay)
" . . . grâce à Parménide . . ." (fragmentary
    essay)
Charactère (fragmentary sketch for an essay)
Histoire de l'Hérakles égyptien et Zeus (essay)
*Note sur les relations primitives du christianisme
    et des religions non hebraïques* (essay)
Various untitled short fragments and variants

II. Weil's Works in English

First and Last Notebooks, London, Oxford, 1970
Gateway to God, Glasgow, Collins, 1974
Gravity and Grace, London, Routledge and Kegan Paul,
    1972
Intimations of Christianity among the Ancient Greeks,
    London, Routledge and Kegan Paul, 1976
Lectures on Philosophy, Cambridge, Cambridge, 1978
Letter to a Priest, New York, G. P. Putnam's Sons, 1959
The Need for Roots, New York, Harper & Row, 1976
The Notebooks of Simone Weil, London, Routledge and
    Kegan Paul, 1976
Oppression and Liberty, Amherst, Univ. of Mass. Press,
    1973
On Science, Necessity and the Love of God, London,
    Oxford, 1968
Selected Essays, 1934-43, London, Oxford, 1965
Seventy Letters, London, Oxford, 1965
The Simone Weil Reader, New York, David McKay Co., 1977
Waiting for God, New York, Harper & Row, 1973

INDEX OF NAMES

INDEX OF SUBJECTS